Mary McLeod Bethune
& Black Women's Political Activism

Mary McLeod Bethune
& Black Women's Political Activism

| Joyce A. Hanson |

University of Missouri Press
Columbia and London

Library of Congress-in-Publication Data

Hanson, Joyce Ann.
   Mary McLeod Bethune and Black women's political
activism / Joyce A. Hanson.
        p.   cm.
Includes bibliographical references and index.
     ISBN 0-8262-1451-7
   1. Bethune, Mary McLeod, 1875–1955.   2. African
American women political activists—Biography.   3. African
American women educators—Biography—Juvenile literature.
4. African American women social reformers—
Biography—Juvenile literature.   5. African American
women—Political activity—History—20th century.
6. African Americans—Politics and government—20th
century.   7. African Americans—Civil rights—History—20th
century.   I. Title.
E185.97 .B34 H36 2003
370'.92—dc21   2002153613

Designer: Kristie Lee
Typesetter: Bookcomp, Inc.
Printer and binder: Thomson-Shore, Inc.
Typefaces: Adobe Cason and Caslon No 540 SwashD italic

*To all the women who have
brought us to this moment.*

Contents

Acknowledgments

Historical writing is a solitary endeavor. However, doing the research and revising a long-term project is really a group effort. I do owe many people my profound thanks and I am grateful to everyone who encouraged and supported me throughout this project. First, I want to thank Buddy Enck, who reawakened my interest in African American history and encouraged me to pursue a graduate degree. Susan Porter Benson possesses the very best attributes of a graduate adviser. She has been there to reassure me, but more important, she prodded me to think harder and reconceptualize many of my ideas. Donald Spivey has been with me on this project from its inception. He unfailingly promoted my work while subtly persuading me to expand my original range of interest. For that, I am eternally grateful. The dissertation on which this book is based was immeasurably better because of their patience and commitment. I also owe a special thank-you to everyone at the Institute for African-American Studies at the University of Connecticut, especially Rose Lovelace and Ron Taylor, who provided both financial and moral support.

The archivists at the National Archives, Library of Congress, Harvard University, and the Franklin D. Roosevelt Library gave vital assistance on this project. I would particularly like to acknowledge archivist Susan McElrath and the staff at the Bethune Museum and Archives. Their knowledge of archival resources and interest in this project made my trips to Washington, D.C., pleasant and productive experiences.

Thank you to Beverly Jarrett at the University of Missouri Press for seeing the value in this study and for her commitment to the completion of the project. I am also grateful to the anonymous readers who commented on the manuscript. Their comments and suggestions have made this a more valuable study.

Fellowships and research grants defrayed the costs of research trips. I would like to thank the University of Connecticut for providing support through its Doctoral Dissertation Fellowship. The Woodrow Wilson Dissertation Grant in Women's Studies allowed me to complete my research. The College of Social and Behavioral Sciences and the History Department at California State University, San Bernardino provided release time to hasten the transition from dissertation to manuscript.

Three of my colleagues in the History Department deserve special recognition: Kent Schofield for his encouragement, inspirational stories, and unrelenting sense of humor. He is my mentor and became my friend. Ward McAfee, who provided me with evidence of his family connections to Mary McLeod Bethune and who read and commented on the manuscript in its entirety. He is an insightful historian. Last, but not least, Cheryl Riggs, who was there to listen, commiserate, and push me forward when I most needed encouragement. Her commitment to her colleagues, scholarship, activism, and teaching are an inspiration. She is my role model.

I could never have reached this goal without the infinite and unfailing love and encouragement of my family—Jennifer, Michael, Alison, and especially my husband, Jim.

Abbreviations

AW	Aubrey Williams Papers
BCC	Mary McLeod Bethune Papers–Bethune-Cookman College Collection
BFC I	Mary McLeod Bethune Papers–Bethune Foundation Collection, Part I
BFC II	Mary McLeod Bethune Papers–Bethune Foundation Collection, Part II
ER	Eleanor Roosevelt Papers
FDR	Franklin Delano Roosevelt Papers
MCT	Mary Church Terrell Papers
MMB	Mary McLeod Bethune Papers
NAACP	National Association for the Advancement of Colored People Papers
NACW	Papers of the National Association of Colored Women's Clubs, 1895–1992
NCNW	Records of the National Council of Negro Women
NUL	National Urban League Papers–Southern Regional Office
NYA	National Youth Administration Papers–Office of Negro Affairs

Mary McLeod Bethune
& Black Women's Political Activism

Introduction

In many ways, Mary Jane McLeod Bethune's life was representative of the lives of many African American women of her time: she was deeply grounded in religion and family, and intensely committed to racial advancement. Yet, Bethune became one of the most important African American women in American political history. She came to occupy a prominent place among a select group of black men and women designated as "race leaders"—men and women who devoted their lives to advancing African American equality. They became the public voice of the voiceless masses, speaking of the collective identity of people of color and arguing for equal social, economic, and political rights.[1] Bethune was certainly a pivotal member of this group as her efforts advanced equal opportunity for black Americans on all levels for nearly half a century. Yet, Bethune distinguished herself from other race leaders by steadfastly incorporating the struggle for gender equality within her efforts for black equality. By advocating and training black women for visible and increasing *public* leadership roles, she ensured an expanding role for African American women in the formal political realm. She believed this would automatically lead to advancement for the entire race, as black women then were more inclined than black men to use public positions for group advancement. Bethune's exposure to strong, independent female role models allowed her to develop her unwavering belief in the primary responsibility of black women for sustaining the race. Her grandmother, mother, and female teachers demonstrated how black women who embraced "a larger appreciation for good citizenship, cleanliness, beauty, thoughtfulness" could lead

1. For a discussion of the meaning of the terms "race leader," "race man," and "race woman" see Evelyn Brooks Higginbotham, "African-American Women's History and the Metalanguage of Race."

African Americans as "the mothers of the race, the homemakers and spiritual guides." Bethune believed African American women had an obligation to understand these responsibilities and use their status to fight for equality. She publicly endorsed the notion of women's higher moral capacity, recognized the important contribution women could make to racial uplift, and continually worked to expand women's roles toward that end.[2] Bethune was a truly multifaceted and multidimensional race woman. She fought on a variety of levels and used multiple outlets—education, government, and women's associations—in her quest for a more just society. Some black women leaders before her gained more recognition than she achieved in her lifetime, but none before her, and few afterwards, were more effective in developing women's leadership for the cause of racial justice.

Despite her multiple political activities, Bethune has not been recognized as a black political leader. This is attributable in large part to the traditional definition of political activity used by many historians and political scientists: political activity encompasses the actions of individually elected officials and the workings of government. It also rests upon a conventionally accepted and gender-biased idea of a leader as a "spokesman," and of politics as voting, electioneering, and office holding. This traditional research defines women's political participation as atypical, seeing women as inadequately socialized into the political process. It ties women's political activism to their social roles as wives and mothers. Women such as Bethune who entered the public arena and fought for substantive reform while remaining grounded in networks of kin, church, and community were left out of political history. As feminist historians have become more interested in political history, they have worked to redefine politics as any "activity [that] includes all community work which is oriented to change through multifaceted goals including service, support, public education and advocacy. Political orientation [is adapted] to changing the public agenda through planned and implemented actions." Empowerment is an important part of women's politicization and begins when women "change their ideas about the causes of their powerlessness, when they recognize the systematic forces that oppress them, and when they act to change the conditions of their lives."[3] Using this definition, black women who worked

2. Mary McLeod Bethune, "Faith That Moved a Dump Heap," *Who, The Magazine about People:* 34; Mary McLeod Bethune, "A Philosophy of Education for Negro Girls," n.d. in MMB.

3. Bernice McNair Barnett, "Black Women's Collectivist Movement Organizations: Their Struggles during the Doldrums." Milton D. Morris, *The Politics of Black America;* Hanes Wal-

through voluntary associations and community organizations became political leaders because they brought particular issues to the attention of politicians and the public. They fought for equal opportunity for African American men and women at a time when America had neither the will nor the desire to make a commitment to racial or sexual equality. Bethune is one such woman who deserves recognition as a political leader based upon the depth and breadth of her political activities.

However, even the few historians who have given passing attention to Bethune's political accomplishments have misinterpreted the means, techniques, and actions she employed in pursuing equality. When examined individually, the choices she made throughout her lifetime often appear contradictory, unless we understand that Bethune had one foot in the nineteenth century and one in the twentieth. She was a transitional figure. Initially grounded in the nineteenth-century belief that advancement would come through changing individual behavior, Bethune in the twentieth century quickly recognized that inequality was deeply rooted in American institutions. She began to see that the focal point for African Americans should no longer be on changing individual attitudes and behaviors, but rather on changing social, economic, and political institutions that shaped collective opinions. She worked diligently to transform local community groups into political power bases and promoted the formation of a national coalition that would work to alter social, economic, and political institutions. In these efforts, she used two conceptually distinct levels of activism. In some instances, Bethune based her activism on informal political activities that were distinctly nonconfrontational and designed to quietly undermine racial and gender stereotypes. Yet, when dealing with egregious incidents involving institutional inequality, Bethune often engaged in overtly formal political action that publicly challenged the basic principles of the American democratic system. She astutely gauged her activism to fit the particular circumstances. And no

ton, Jr., *Invisible Politics: Black Political Behavior;* Hanes Walton, Jr., *Black Politics: A Theoretical and Structural Analysis.* Martha Ackelsberg and Irene Diamond, "Gender and Political Life," 509; 518–19; Vicky Randall, *Women and Politics;* Sophonisba Preston Breckinridge, *Women in the Twentieth Century: A Study of Their Political, Social and Economic Activities;* Ellen Cantarow, *Moving the Mountain: Women Working for Social Change;* Jean Bethke Elshtain, *Public Man, Private Woman: Women in Social and Political Thought;* Esther Ngan-Chow, Doris Wilkerson, and Maxine Baca Zinn, eds., *Race, Class, and Gender: Common Bonds, Different Voices;* Karen Beckwith, *American Women and Political Participation: The Impacts of Work, Generation, and Feminism.* Linda Christiansen-Ruffman, "Women's Conceptions of the Political: Theoretical Contributions to a Study of Women's Organizations." Ann Bookman and Sandra Morgan, eds., *Women and the Politics of Empowerment,* 3–29.

matter which course Bethune decided to pursue, she sought a peaceful, yet ALWAYS
political, means to achieve social, economic, and political justice.

❦

Mary Jane McLeod Bethune was born on July 10, 1875, in Mayesville, South Carolina, the fifteenth of seventeen children born to Samuel and Patsy McLeod. She was educated at the local missionary school, then received scholarships from a Quaker dressmaker that enabled her to attend Scotia Seminary and Moody Bible Institute. Between 1895 and 1903, she taught at a number of small missionary schools throughout the South, including Haine's Institute in Augusta, Georgia. In 1898, she met and married Albertus Bethune and in 1899 gave birth to her only child, Albert McLeod Bethune. In 1904, she traveled to Daytona Beach, Florida, where she established the Daytona Educational and Industrial Institute for Negro Girls capitalized with her personal savings of $1.50. By 1912, the school offered a liberal arts high school curriculum and employed nine full-time teachers. In 1923, Daytona Institute merged with Cookman Institute, becoming the coeducational Bethune-Cookman College. Bethune-Cookman became the first fully accredited four-year college for blacks in Florida. Bethune served as its president until 1942.

In addition to establishing and operating Daytona Institute, Bethune served in a variety of roles in a diverse array of commissions and organizations. She was recognized as an expert on black education and was an active member of the National Commission for Child Welfare under Presidents Coolidge and Hoover. She was also president of state, regional, and national women's clubs including the Florida State Federation of Colored Women's Clubs, the Southeastern Federation of Colored Women's Clubs, and the National Association of Colored Women's Clubs (NACW). In 1927, she met Eleanor Roosevelt through her position as president of the National Association of Colored Women's Clubs and by 1935 their growing friendship led to her appointment as director of the Office of Minority Affairs in the National Youth Administration, the first federal office created for a black woman. In the same year, Bethune organized the National Council of Negro Women (NCNW), an umbrella organization designed to give black women political visibility and access to political power on the national level. Bethune continued to serve African Americans through a federal appointment in 1942 as special assistant to the Secretary of War for Selection of Candidates for the first Officers Candidate School for WACS. In 1945, President Harry Truman named Bethune to his Civil Rights Commission and as the only African American woman consultant to the San Francisco Conference to draw up the charter for the United Nations.

During her lifetime, Bethune received numerous awards, eight honorary degrees, and held affiliations with at least seventy-five organizations, including the General Conference of the Methodist Church, the Women's Army for National Defense, National Commission on Christian Education, American Women's Volunteer Service, Southern Conference Education Fund, American Mother's Committee, Council of Church Women, Social Service Commission of the Methodist Church, Americans for Democratic Action, National Civil Liberties Union, First Daytona Beach Housing Authority, American Council on African Education, Inc., National Committee on Atomic Information, Good Neighbor Association, Daytona Beach, Florida, the International Longfellow Society, National Council of Women of the United States, vice president of the Southern Conference for Human Welfare, a director of the Afro-American Life Insurance Company, and the vice president of the Central Life Insurance Company. She founded the Mary McLeod Bethune Foundation, and Bethune Beach, Inc. Bethune received honorary degrees from Wilberforce University, South Carolina State College, Lincoln University, Tuskegee University, Howard University, Bennett College, West Virginia State College, and Rollins College. She was rewarded for her service to the race and her commitment to American democracy by receiving the Spingarn Medal, the Thomas Jefferson Award, the First Annual Youth City Award, the Haitian Medal of Honor, and the Star of Africa. In addition to her service work, Bethune made many literary contributions, including one chapter in *What the Negro Wants,* one chapter in *Spiritual Autobiography,* a weekly column in the *Chicago Defender* and the *Pittsburgh Courier,* and numerous articles in magazines and periodicals including editorials for *Afraamerican Woman* and *Women United,* the official publications of the National Council of Negro Women. Journalist Ida Tarbell named her among the fifty women regarded as having done the most for the welfare of the United States. Bethune died on May 18, 1955.[4]

☙

4. "Biographical material on Mary McLeod Bethune," NCNW, Series 5, Box 5, Folder 91; Genevieve Forbes Herrick, "Loved, Feared and Followed," *Bethune Cookman Advocate;* NACW; "Mrs. Bethune Spingarn Medalist," *Crisis,* MMB; untitled biographical interview BFC I.

Throughout this study Bethune's commitment to a multifaceted and multidimensional approach to the struggle for racial and gender equality are highlighted. Chapter 1 examines Bethune's family life and her socialization into community activism. As a woman who was born and came of age in the nineteenth century, Bethune was imbued with what historian Stephanie Shaw has referred to as an "ethic of socially responsible individualism."[5] According to Shaw, the families of young women born in this first generation after slavery sacrificed to educate their daughters, and the "head-heart-hand" philosophy of the missionary education available to them shaped their lives. Missionary education was not synonymous with industrial education. The principle focus of missionary education was teacher training in the classic liberal tradition. Educational experiences centered on literacy and professional education to develop a black leadership class that would fight for political and civil equality.[6] Missionary teachers encouraged individual academic achievement, stressed personal sacrifice, and emphasized racial obligation.

At home, mothers often supplemented their daughters' formal education with additional lessons in responsibility and racial obligation. This orientation was clearly present in Bethune's early years. Patsy McLeod, Mary's mother, was the dominant partner in her marriage and the business manager of the McLeod family. She raised seventeen children while carefully managing the family's assets and negotiating with local whites to acquire a thirty-five-acre family farm. Patsy also watched over an extended family in and around Mayesville.[7] As a community "othermother," she took on the role of nurse and midwife, and conveyed the interchangeability of "family" and "community" obligations to young Mary. Patsy used family and community to develop a female sphere of influence that nurtured a sense of self-worth and self-reliance in her daughter. According to education historian James Anderson, secular and religious mentors stressed the importance of education for leadership training because they realized, "the masses could not achieve political or economic independence or self-determination without becoming organized, and organization was impossible without well-trained intellectuals."[8]

---

5. Stephanie Shaw, *What a Woman Ought to Be and to Do: Black Professional Women Workers in the Jim Crow Era*, 2.

6. James D. Anderson, *The Education of Blacks in the South, 1860–1935*, 67–68; See also W. E. B. Du Bois, *The Souls of Black Folk*; V. P. Franklin, *Black Self-Determination: A Cultural History of African-American Resistance*.

7. Untitled biographical interview with Charles Williams (hereafter referred to as Williams interview) in BFC I, 2.

8. Anderson, *The Education of Blacks in the South*, 28.

Consequently, educated young women came to believe that they had a unique responsibility to develop a better society and advance the entire race through their education. Bethune's formal training at the local missionary school, Scotia Seminary, and Moody Bible Institute between 1886 and 1895 situate her squarely within this generation.

Chapter 2 examines Bethune's educational philosophy within the context of the industrial versus liberal education debate that raged at the turn of the twentieth century. The idea that African American women should use their education for racial uplift and as a political tool to overturn segregation was the organizing principle behind the founding of Daytona Educational and Industrial Institute for Negro Girls. Although Bethune often professed her admiration for Booker T. Washington and his work at Tuskegee Institute, Daytona Institute did not adhere to the Tuskegee model of industrial education. In fact, industrial education was a relatively insignificant part of Daytona Institute's curriculum. Like many educated black women of her time, Bethune developed an educational philosophy based on a balance between industrial and liberal education that combined the educational ideas of Washington and W. E. B. Du Bois. Like Washington, black women saw the need to offer industrial training, since most African American women would need training to support themselves and their families. Because of this basic need, schools taught the essentials of homemaking and several skilled trades. Most schools founded by women also offered programs that included classes in the social graces, homemaking, and religion designed to raise public opinion of black women's morals and values. Du Bois concepts of the importance of the "Talented Tenth" were also in evidence at many of these schools. Most female-run schools did not ignore liberal education. Rather, they included programs focused on preparing teachers and other black professionals. At Daytona Institute, coursework included and encouraged instruction in history, math, economics, and English, as well as other liberal disciplines.

Bethune's objectives for the education of black girls included "economic mobility through job training, leadership preparation for service to the community, and improved standards and conditions of health in the Black community." Industrial education was a practical part of Bethune's educational philosophy. She believed that industrial training should have a place in the school curriculum. However, she did not believe that only blacks should receive industrial education, or that it should replace academic and cultural development. She called for developing a variety of educational programs for African Americans. She argued that developing programs of industrial and agricultural training did not relieve states of their obligation to provide educational opportunities to meet students' higher educational needs. All people, she believed, regardless of "color or condition of life," deserved to develop their abilities. While she believed vocational training was important, she also insisted that all children should be educated to the level of their unique abilities and capabilities. She held that black educators had a responsibility to identify gifted students and give them every opportunity for higher education and the development of individual talents. Bethune dreamed of building an educational institution capable of producing professionals in the sciences, medicine, and law, as well as political leaders.[9]

Chapter 3 follows Bethune's growing public role through her involvement in the black women's club movement. Bethune steadfastly believed that women had a central role to play in the struggle for racial equality. During her tenure as president of various local, regional, and national organizations, Bethune consistently emphasized the need for unity and sisterhood. She called upon black women to harness "the great power of women in a force for constructive action." As president of the National Association of Colored Women, Bethune worked to mold the association into a cohesive body that could speak as the official voice of African American women on public issues. At the same time, she began to reassess the legitimacy of widely held notions of women's proper roles. Eventually, Bethune concluded that commonly accepted boundaries that limited women to church, home, and family were too confining. By the early 1930s, she began to emphasize the need for women to work for systemic change, and she began to focus on ways to put more African American women in decision-making positions in government. Bethune came to believe that black women had a right and a responsibility to participate in mainstream politics and to play a substantive role.

Chapter 4 traces Bethune's development as a formal political leader in the New Deal administration of Franklin D. Roosevelt. Bethune used her government position as director of the Office of Minority Affairs for racial advancement. Bethune was an astute politician who knew she served at President Franklin D. Roosevelt's pleasure. Mounting a public challenge to the racially biased programs instituted under the New Deal was sure to result in her release. Instead, she used a dual dialogue to effect change. Publicly, she did not condemn Roosevelt or New Deal programs. Rather, she worked to publicize programs and celebrate the few benefits that accrued to blacks under them. She quietly altered the procedures of separate National Youth

9. Carol O. Perkins, "The Pragmatic Idealism of Mary McLeod Bethune," 30–35. Mary McLeod Bethune, "What Causes Chiefly Impede Progress in Interracial Cooperation and Can We Hope to Make More Rapid Progress during the Next Ten Years," n.d., MMB.

Administration (NYA) programs and empowered African Americans. She
took full control of state-level programs away from white administrators by
having qualified African Americans appointed to key decision-making positions within them. She worked to ensure that black administrators dispensed
funds to black people and reported directly to her. In this way, Bethune built
an independent black field staff that was free to report on the discriminatory
practices of white administrators. She also created a Special Negro Higher
Education Fund to secure graduate training for African American students
by distributing funds directly through the Office of Minority Affairs. She
organized the "Black Cabinet," an unofficial think tank on African American
issues, and used her position to arrange public conferences between civil rights
activists and key government officials that focused government attention on
economic, political, and social inequality.[10]

Chapter 5 considers the creation of the National Council of Negro Women
(NCNW) in 1935. This most clearly reflects Bethune's transitional place in
African American women's history. Bethune's organization of the NCNW
cultivated a female culture of resistance and fostered female autonomy.
Through its work, the NCNW created a female sphere of influence, authority, and power. Its objectives, however, reflected twentieth-century political
realities. The council worked to make black women astute political activists
and lobbyists; to build women's political strength by gaining appointments to
policy-making boards and committees; and to eliminate discriminatory legislation in housing, health, employment, public accommodations, and political
representation. Bethune believed African American women needed a separate association where they could articulate an independent worldview, build
political strength and solidarity, and prepare to take public office. Bethune
designed the NCNW to link local and regional organizations in the struggle for representation in the national political process. She envisioned the
Council as the hub of a wheel with various educational, business, religious,
fraternal, labor, and welfare organizations as the spokes.[11] Recognizing the
interconnectedness of race, class, and gender inequality, Bethune brought together organizations that had addressed these issues separately to gain collective power. Not all African American women activists shared her vision, and
not every black woman's organization affiliated with the council. Ultimately,
Bethune succeeded in aligning twenty-two women's organizations with the

10. The papers of the Office of Minority Affairs and Bethune's correspondence with New
Deal administrators is held at the Franklin D. Roosevelt Library, Hyde Park, New York.
11. "Minutes of the founding meeting held December 5, 1935," Series 2, Box 1, Folder 1,
NCNW.

council and creating a nonpartisan political lobby to empower African American women. The council created an enduring black women's political network that continued to incorporate new generations of women into its programs. It institutionalized African American women's political gains.

As Bethune's activities illustrate, African American women often brought about substantive reform from outside conventional electoral areas. Politics was not merely elections, voting, and lobbying. Political action served to empower, and women activists built political coalitions on firmly established relationships. The goal was to develop leaders, build leadership for the future, and create lasting networks that had the ability to sustain advances. Bethune's life story also demonstrates that race, class, and gender shape women's political actions and the resistance strategies they employ. In Bethune's case, the ethic of socially responsible individualism and her understanding of the duties and responsibilities of educated black women informed her actions. She believed that highly educated black women must work to attain leadership positions not for individual gain, but to help the race achieve autonomy, self-determination, and self-development. As historian V. P. Franklin has argued, black leaders attained and maintained their legitimacy as political leaders because they articulated and represented the cultural values of the masses—most importantly the desire for education and liberation—while advancing a viable program for racial advancement.[12]

Mary McLeod Bethune worked from both inside and outside the political system. She compromised with political realities when necessary while she worked to develop viable strategies to ameliorate short-term conditions and bring about long-term change. She had the ability to draw women together, captivate them with her ideas, and give them a sense of purpose and a vision of the future. Bethune consistently struggled to make black women's voices heard. She used her insight, determination, and persuasive power to move African American women from the sidelines to the center of American life. The institutions she founded and the work she engaged in nurtured black women's resistance to oppression and their political activism. She told African American women they could make American democracy better—they could save the soul of the nation—by "hammering on the portals of government,"[13] and she gave them the skills and opportunities necessary to do so.

12. Franklin, *Black Self-Determination*, 25.
13. "Which Way America," Radio Broadcast on WWDC, Washington, D.C., Sunday, June 22, 1947, BFC I.

1

The Making of a Race Woman

Mary Jane McLeod Bethune emerged from humble beginnings to become a leader of her race. Born on July 10, 1875, in Mayesville, Sumter County, South Carolina, she was the fifteenth in a family of seventeen children. In terms of wealth and education, the McLeod family was typical of many black families in the post–Civil War period: illiterate and poor. Despite the best efforts of the Freedman's Bureau, northern missionary associations, and the freed people themselves, illiteracy remained widespread among black South Carolinians. In 1880, the illiteracy rate was 78.5 percent for all blacks ages ten and over, compared to 21.9 percent for whites. In raw numbers, four times as many blacks as whites lived below the poverty line, and four and a half times more blacks were imprisoned than whites.

Sumter County was characteristic of many rural counties in the post–Civil War South. In 1870, Sumter County was home to 25,268 residents; slightly more than 40 percent (10,211) of all persons over the age of ten could not read. Of the 7,463 whites living in the county, about 14 percent (1,012) of those over the age of ten could not write and only 9 percent (672) were attending school. The county statistics for African Americans were even worse. Of the 17,805 black residents, about 57 percent (10,110) over the age of ten could not write and only about 6 percent (1,079) were attending school. Economic indicators were equally dismal for blacks. In 1890, 68 percent of black South Carolinians worked in agricultural occupations, a figure that fluctuated little until the end of the 1930s. In 1880, about 80 percent (3,348) of Sumter County's 4,167 farms were smaller than one hundred acres. Only about 38 percent (1,563) of landowners farmed their own land; about 49 percent (2,052) rented their farms for cash payments; about 13 percent (552) were sharecroppers. In 1870, the average farm income in the county was $847 per year, but regular economic cycles and the declining price of cotton dropped income levels to $347 per year by 1879. Ten years later, average income had risen to only $462 per year. In a county where most farmers made their living by raising livestock, Indian corn, and cotton, the small size of farm holdings and the large number of tenant farmers and sharecroppers were barriers to economic advancement. Since African Americans constituted about 70 percent of the county's population, they represented the majority of poor farmers in the area.[1]

In Sumter County, as in many areas of the rural South, a small white minority controlled the social, political, and economic life of the poor, illiterate black majority, who survived on their meager earnings as small landowners, sharecroppers, and tenant farmers. The McLeods were one of these families, but family dynamics, religious convictions, and community standing made them atypical.

Family experience was one important factor in the formation of Mary McLeod Bethune's worldview. However, her distinctive opportunities, her teachers, her mentors, the worsening racial climate in post-Reconstruction America, and the ideology of Victorian womanhood also played significant roles in her developing ideas on race and gender.

Only a few main sources give insight into Bethune's early life: an incomplete, unpublished autobiography, a partial biography, and two oral history interviews. Pieced together between 1927 and her death in 1955, these sources are more an account of how Bethune *remembered* or *reconstructed* her past than of how she *lived* it. Taken together, they are a story of triumph meant to impart her wisdom to others. Bethune makes this clear in personal correspondence when she expresses her reasons for dedicating her home as the Mary McLeod Bethune Foundation: the foundation was to be a "Shrine" where the files about her life would be kept and a "place of research and contact for those who may come after me."[2] These few lines are instrumental in understanding Bethune's assessment of her life and legacy, as the word "shrine" implies. Perhaps she saw herself as a saintly soldier in a war against racial injustice, or a key role model, but it is certain that she saw racial injustice as a long-term

1. Population and Vital Statistics sections of the Ninth, Tenth, Eleventh, Twelfth, and Fifteenth Censuses of the U.S. Bureau of the Census.

2. Mary McLeod Bethune to Charlotte Hawkins Brown, April 14, 1953, Mary McLeod Bethune to Witherspoon Dodge, March 4, 1953, BFC II.

problem and believed others would be interested in studying the ways she fought to undermine all forms of segregation, overcome discrimination, and end racial prejudice. Clearly, Bethune left behind these sources to fashion her identity, highlight her public achievements, and justify her choices. Since we have little corroborating evidence about her early life, what follows is less a biographical account than a collection of recalled incidents that Bethune used to explain her lifelong work for the race.

෨෧

The declining status of African Americans in the post-Reconstruction South had a profound impact on Bethune's views of race relations. During the time she came of age, conservative whites, encouraged by their notions of black racial inferiority, used first custom and then law to force freed people back into positions of social, economic, and political dependence.[3] Historian Guion Griffis Johnson has argued that southern white attitudes toward former slaves could be classified into five paternalistic concepts: modified equalitarianism; benevolent paternalism; separate but equal; separate and permanently unequal; and permanently unequal under paternal supervision. Johnson asserts that the majority of southern whites believed most strongly in categories four and five, which were most unfavorable to blacks. He further contends that most southern whites believed that black progress within the confines of the black race would be limited because of blacks' uncivilized African heritage and accepted the premise of permanent inferiority for African Americans. Johnson maintains that these southern paternalists were politically powerful men who used "the fear of ignorant whites as a weapon of control over the lower classes of both races."[4]

One by one, lawmakers in the states of the old Confederacy altered state constitutions written during Reconstruction to reflect these ideas and institutionalized a barrage of discriminatory laws that *legally* separated the races and assigned an inferior social, economic, and political status to blacks. The legal separation of blacks and whites began on trains in 1887 and rapidly spread to every imaginable place where blacks and whites might come together. By 1900, thoroughgoing legal segregation was commonplace. Economically,

3. Guion Griffis Johnson, "Southern Paternalism toward Negroes after Emancipation," 485–86, 497–98, 501.

4. For a discussion of the development of racist attitudes in the United States see Winthrop Jordan, *White Man's Burden: Historical Origins of Racism in the United States.*

white landowners fostered black dependence by manipulating sharecropping systems, originally conceived as a compromise between white landowners and black agricultural workers, to keep African American farmers landless and dependent. Soon, black tenant farmers and sharecroppers found themselves trapped in a debt-peonage system as prices for cotton crops declined and landowners and merchants conspired to set high prices and interest rates for farm supplies in the cash-poor southern agricultural economy. Political avenues of redress closed for African Americans as literacy tests, "understanding" and grandfather clauses, poll taxes, and white primaries disfranchised the majority of black voters.[5]

In addition to legal constrictions, mobs used organized violence and systematic intimidation as an extralegal means to keep African Americans "in their place." Conservative white southerners reinstated "home rule"—most often through violent means. In the post-Reconstruction South, violence against blacks became common, and lynching became its most visible image. In the last sixteen years of the nineteenth century, about twenty-five hundred lynchings took place. Between 1900 and 1914, approximately eleven hundred more people lost their lives to extralegal violence. Almost 96 percent of all lynchings in the United States occurred in the South, and the vast majority of these acts targeted blacks.[6] Although most of the victims were black men, black women were not immune to the rampant violence as nineteenth-century ideas of gender excluded black women. In 1872, an unnamed black woman testified before the Joint Select Committee to Inquire into the Conditions of Affairs in the Late Insurrectionary States about her experience with the Ku Klux Klan: "They whipped me from the crown of my head to the soles of my feet. I was just raw. The blood oozed through my frock and all around the waist. After I got away from them that night I ran to my house. My house was torn down. I went in and felt where my bed was. I went to the other corner of the house and felt for my little children and I could not see them. Their father lay out to the middle of the night and my children lay out there too."[7] Simple statistics cannot convey the sense of terror blacks lived under in

5. C. Vann Woodward, *The Strange Career of Jim Crow;* Joel Williamson, ed., *The Origins of Segregation;* Joel Williamson, *The Crucible of Race: Black/White Relations in the South since Emancipation;* Joel Williamson, *A Rage for Order: Black/White Relations in the South since Emancipation;* Leon Litwack, *Trouble in Mind: Black Southerners in the Age of Jim Crow;* Eric Foner, *A Short History of Reconstruction,* 79–81.

6. Ronald C. White, Jr., *Liberty and Justice for All: Racial Reform and the Social Gospel,* 11–12; John Hope Franklin and Alfred A. Moss, *From Slavery to Freedom,* 282–86.

7. House, *Reports of the Joint Select Committee to Inquire into the Condition of Affairs in the Late Insurrectionary States,* 42d Cong., 2d sess., H. Rept. 22.

the post-Reconstruction South. Although federal actions worked to force the Klan to disband officially in 1872, white supremacist vigilantes continued to use terrorist tactics against a select group of black men, women, and children.

In 1887, at the age of twelve, Bethune witnessed this type of mob violence firsthand in an experience that influenced her interactions with whites. On a trip into town on market day, Bethune saw a white mob attack "Marse Eli Cooper's Gus" because he refused to blow out a match for a white man and then in his anger knocked the man to the ground. In "bewildered terror," young Mary saw the mob put a rope around Gus's neck and heard her father's command not to look back as he pulled her from the chaotic scene. Despite Samuel's warning, she watched the event unfold. She saw "Marse Eli, the sheriff and other calm men of authority" arrive at the scene. They "stopped the hanging after the rope had been tightened around Gus' neck." Decades later Bethune remembered the "solemnity and fear" among blacks in Mayesville for several days after the incident.[8] The immediate fear this episode invoked was only a short-term consequence of the experience for Bethune, however. The experience became a pivotal event in determining the nature of her interactions with whites. Throughout her lifetime, she remembered those "calm men of authority" and formed alliances with them, trusting that they would work with her to help end legal segregation.

Throughout the South in the post-Reconstruction era, white landowners, merchants, and businessmen often did not condone lynching, but generally did nothing to stop it. At certain times and under certain circumstances, however, upper-class whites interceded, most often because of their dependence on black labor. According to historian Leon Litwack, some whites expressed concern about the migration of black labor out of their state. Others expressed concern because they feared mob violence was a sign their region was descending into "barbarism." Vigilante violence fed a "spirit of anarchy," and was a sign that the "entire social order might be in jeopardy." Many worried about the impact of such actions on the "economic well being of the New South." Landowners and merchants considered blacks a valuable economic asset, and believed "It is not good business to kill them." This was especially true in South Carolina, where African Americans comprised 68 percent of the agricultural workforce. In Sumter County, upper-class whites played the role of protector toward blacks to win their loyalty. Random acts of terror would severely disrupt the social and economic systems by which this small

8. "Autobiography of Mary McLeod Bethune," unpublished manuscript, chapter 4, BFC I.

number of powerful whites profited. An occasional show of upper-class white protection was a part of a wider scheme of white control, and a few selected interventions of this nature reaped a high return for those whites involved. However, these interventions were not common. As historian Allen Trelease has argued, "It has been the accepted view that wealthy, cultured whites, including larger ex-slaveholders, cherished a kindlier feeling toward Negroes and exhibited less race hatred than their lower-class brethren. Close investigation, however, uncovers so many exceptions that the truth or usefulness of the belief is open to question."[9] Yet, this one violent incident witnessed by Bethune firmly planted in her mind the idea that upper-class whites were potential protectors. This lack of introspection had implications for the future. Bethune often relied on men and women of this class for financial and political help in undermining segregation, with few positive effects. Moreover, she then found herself struggling to limit white paternalism. This becomes clear in two events explored further in later chapters: the founding of Daytona Educational and Industrial Training School for Negro Girls in 1904, when she would depend on the financial support of white philanthropists and their wives, and during her government service, when she would look to white racial liberals for political support in her work as director of Minority Affairs in the New Deal administration.

By the turn of the twentieth century, conservative whites had effectively constricted black social space, limited economic opportunities, and undermined black political participation in the South. However, vigilante mobs worked to silence many fair-minded southern whites as well. White supporters of black rights often risked attacks on their homes and families. This was a possibility many racial liberals in the New South sought to avoid. In the post-Reconstruction era, African Americans struggled under the shadow of vigilante violence and without legal protection to maintain family and community ties, and looked to each other for social relationships, to promote economic development, and to address political concerns.

African Americans endured horrific conditions in the South, but anti-black sentiments were not restricted to the region, or to white mobs. Academics and intellectuals nationwide played an important role in fostering anti-black beliefs. White Americans increasingly perceived "race purity" as a national problem as expanding numbers of southern and eastern European immigrants

9. Litwack, *Trouble in Mind*, 311–12; Allen W. Trelease, *White Terror: The Ku Klux Klan Conspiracy and Southern Reconstruction*, xix.

migrated to America after 1880. This quest to maintain "race purity" intensified again as increasing numbers of blacks moved from the rural South to the urban North during the first decades of the twentieth century. Social Darwinism and new pseudo-scientific biological evidence allegedly "proved" that African Americans as well as other ethnic minorities were innately and irreversibly inferior to whites. In 1916 Madison Grant, chairman of the New York Zoological Society, warned in *The Passing of the Great Race* that America had become "an asylum for the oppressed." A new wave of immigration contained "a large and increasing number of the weak, the broken, and the mentally crippled races." According to Grant, these "lower races" were incapable of understanding American ideals; their incorporation into American society would only serve to "mongrelize" the white race.[10] Grant's work reinforced stereotypes and gave proponents of the eugenics movement an academic basis to advocate the sterilization of these "lower races" to ensure the purity and superiority of the white race.

Cultural media also avowed the inferiority of these new immigrants and African Americans. Books such as Henry James's *The American Scene*, Edward Ross's *The Old World in the New*, Charles Carroll's *The Negro a Beast*, Robert W. Shufeldt's *The Negro: A Menace to American Civilization*, and Thomas Dixon's trilogy *As to the Leopard's Spots*, *The Clansman*, and *The Traitor* gained large audiences. Dixon, however, wanted his work to reach a much larger audience. He saw a new medium, the motion picture, as the means to reach and influence millions of people. After several unsuccessful attempts to find a producer, he approached D. W. Griffith and convinced him to transform *The Clansman* into an epic motion picture. The result, *Birth of a Nation*, undoubtedly became the most significant factor in perpetuating black stereotypes, glorifying the Ku Klux Klan, and condoning racial violence. Moreover, after a private screening, President Woodrow Wilson's remark that the film was entirely accurate history served to intensify anti-black hatred and violence.[11]

Leadership changes in the black community also contributed to changing patterns of race relations, and these changes influenced Bethune's developing racial philosophy. The emergence of Booker T. Washington following the death of Frederick Douglass in 1895 encouraged a new era of accommodation in race relations. Washington urged that African Americans accept

10. Madison Grant, *The Passing of the Great Race*, 80–81, 228.
11. These issues are addressed in several texts including Franklin and Moss, *From Slavery to Freedom*; Williamson, *A Rage for Order*; John Hope Franklin, *Racial Equality in America*; and Steven Mintz and Randy Roberts, *Hollywood's America: United States History through Its Films* among others.

the formal disfranchisement whites imposed upon them and improve their economic standing by means of industrial education and hard work. He told African Americans, "all forms of labor are honorable, and all forms of idleness disgraceful. It has been necessary . . . to learn that all races that have gotten to their feet have done so largely by laying an economic foundation, and, in general, by beginning in a proper cultivation and ownership of the soil."[12]

Washington encouraged African Americans to "cast down your bucket where you are," to make a new beginning wherever possible. For most blacks in the South, this meant work in agriculture, mechanics, and domestic service. According to Washington, the greatest need for the black man was to fit himself for the "opportunities of freedom." According to Washington, the way to do this was to connect knowledge to "every-day practical things in life, upon something that is needed to be done, and something which they [the masses] will be permitted to do" in their communities.[13] Washington's emphasis on hard work and the dignity of labor resonated with Mary McLeod Bethune, influencing her early educational philosophy.

While he claimed not to limit African American students, Washington argued that abstract knowledge meant little; industrial education prepared blacks to enter the commercial world. Economic development among African Americans would lead to respect for the black man and the end of white prejudice. Washington also tried to calm white fears about the social relations between the races. He told whites, "In all things that are purely social we can be as separate as the fingers, yet one as the hand in all things essential to mutual progress."[14] Publicly, Washington passively accepted legalized social separation, ignored political and civil rights, and championed interdependence in economic endeavors by embracing an approach based on gradualism, appeasement, and accommodation. Washington told blacks to *win* rather than *demand* their place in society.

However, Washington's racial philosophy was more complex than his public declarations suggested. He carefully designed his public speeches to gain and retain the support of white business leaders, philanthropists, and ministers. At the same time, Washington worked privately through his power-

---

12. Booker T. Washington, "Industrial Education for the Negro," 9; see also August Meier, *Negro Thought in America, 1880–1915,* especially chapters 6 and 7.

13. Booker T. Washington, "Chapters from My Experience"; Washington, "Industrial Education for the Negro," 10–12.

14. Louis R. Harlan, *Booker T. Washington: The Making of a Black Leader, 1856–1901,* 216–19.

ful white allies to fight against discrimination, segregation, and disfranchisement. For example, Washington raised money and recruited lawyers to legally challenge the Louisiana grandfather clause, although he publicly refused to associate his name with the case. Washington's white champions elevated him to the position of primary spokesman for black America and made him the sole administrator of white patronage. Washington's quiet work behind the scenes for black equality went unnoticed, but his public strategies and actions gained notoriety. His public pronouncements became the new ideological platform and shaped discussions on race relations for at least a decade.[15]

Bethune's strategies for racial advancement incorporated Washington's views on the importance of hard work. Yet, unlike Washington, she did not hide her work against segregation and did not disregard black political participation. She was outspoken in her defense of the race, particularly of black women, grounding her philosophy in her experience as a southern black woman. She believed in the importance of vocational training for making black women economically independent, "that they may be self-supporting," but championed liberal education so they could use their education to "help improve the communities in which they live."[16] Liberally educated black women ensured the progress of the race through the myriad tasks they took on and the service they provided. Liberal education allowed African American women to become teachers and to educate the next generation, but their contributions did "not end with the classroom." They also filled positions as supervisors, home-demonstration agents, and nurses. All types of education were necessary for black women because "no phase in the development of our people is being overlooked by our women."[17] Bethune needed philanthropic support, yet unlike Washington, she refused to accept philanthropist's ideas about boundaries for black education. In 1911, she openly challenged white Board of Trustee members at Daytona Institute when they sought to limit opportunities for black children, telling them, "I called you in here to assist me not tie my hands." She militantly fought for equal educational opportunities for black children (see chapter 2).

Washington's elevation to power by leaders of the white community met challenges in the black community. William Monroe Trotter, W. E. B. Du Bois, and other black leaders contested Washington's suitability as the sole

15. Harlan, *Booker T. Washington,* 297–98, chapter 16.

16. Quoted in Sheila Y. Fleming, *The Answered Prayer to a Dream: Bethune-Cookman College, 1904–1994,* 27–28.

17. Mary McLeod Bethune, "The Negro Woman in American Life," n.d., MMB.

spokesperson for black Americans. At first, Du Bois and Washington agreed on strategies for racial advancement that focused on racial solidarity and economic development. However, after Du Bois witnessed racial violence in the South firsthand and documented an increasing number of violent assaults against blacks, he questioned Washington's approach. By the early 1900s, Du Bois and Washington publicly disagreed over philosophies, strategies, and leadership for racial advancement. Du Bois's first public challenge to Washington's leadership was his publication of *The Souls of Black Folk*. In a chapter entitled "Of Mr. Booker T. Washington and Others," Du Bois criticized Washington for compromising with whites at the expense of blacks. Du Bois applauded Washington for encouraging interracial cooperation in the South, inspiring thrift, practical education, and the acquisition of property. However, Du Bois opposed Washington's program when he observed increasing black disfranchisement, the decline of public school education and the black college, and the reinforced implementation of a color caste system. Du Bois forcefully argued that Washington's racial philosophy was actually promoting racial dehumanization and taking the race backward. Moreover, Du Bois objected to Washington's heavy-handed approach toward anyone who disagreed with his philosophy.[18] Du Bois's work was the catalyst for a public division between those who endorsed gradualism and accommodation and those who championed a return to agitation and reform.

Du Bois effectively argued that Washington's compromise had cost blacks three important things: political power, opportunities for higher education, and civil rights. Bethune's views on black access to citizenship rights mirrored Du Bois's. She consistently worked to ensure that African Americans had free and open access to these three components of equal citizenship and encouraged African Americans along these same lines throughout her life. In Daytona Beach she organized black voters and worked to elect officials who would address black needs; she modified the curriculum at Daytona Institute and later Bethune-Cookman College to train young people for emerging employment opportunities; she used her position as a government appointee to coordinate activities to advance black equality. Bethune went beyond Du Bois's rhetoric; she coordinated and led African Americans and as a result expanded black social, economic, and political participation.

Historians have studied the controversy between Washington and Du Bois in depth and so the viewpoints of both men are well known. Yet, portray-

18. W. E. B. Du Bois, *The Souls of Black Folk*, 94; David Levering Lewis, *W. E. B. Du Bois: Biography of a Race, 1868–1919*, 273–77, 286–88, 501–3.

ing Washington and Du Bois as polar opposites distorts our understanding of African American history. While Washington and Du Bois disagreed on the means to achieve their objective, the goal—racial equality—was not in dispute. Both sought to gain inclusion for African Americans: Washington through economic means, Du Bois through political means. Unfortunately, historians have come to accept the notion that the ideas of these two men actually represented *all* of the opinions on race relations in black America at that time. New studies clearly show many other black Americans had their own ideas about improving race relations and achieving racial equality. These new works make it evident that a range of opinions existed and both black women and men used varieties of methods in their struggle for equality. Many of these new studies show that African American women were leaders in the fight for racial advancement.[19] Some women developed their own strategies for pursuing racial equality; others picked and chose from the alternative views as the situation warranted.

Whatever means and strategies these women used to fight for equality, one thing is certain—their notions of proper gender roles, a product of the time in which they came of age, played a central role. Moralists, ministers, popular media, and etiquette manuals disseminated the prominent gender ideology of the nineteenth century known as the "Cult of True Womanhood."[20] This ideology defined women as innately pure, pious, domestic, and submissive. Although it was meant to confine women to the domestic sphere, some women turned these attributes on their head and used them to justify a public place for themselves. Through an array of charitable, benevolent, and missionary societies, women carved out a public sphere in redefining America's social and economic systems. These women used the principle of women's innate abilities to nurture, their higher moral nature, and their self-sacrificing character

19. See Shaw, *What a Woman Ought to Be and to Do;* Evelyn Brooks Higginbotham, *Righteous Discontent: The Women's Movement in the Black Baptist Church, 1880–1920;* Glenda Elizabeth Gilmore, *Gender and Jim Crow: Women and the Politics of White Supremacy in North Carolina, 1896–1920;* Charles W. Wadelington and Richard F. Knapp, *Charlotte Hawkins Brown and Palmer Memorial Institute: What One Young African American Woman Could Do;* Adrienne Lash Jones, "Jane Edna Hunter: A Case Study of Black Leadership, 1910–1950"; Beverly W. Jones, "Quest for Equality: The Life and Writings of Mary Eliza Church Terrell, 1863–1954"; Jacqueline A. Rouse, *Lugenia Burns Hope: Black Southern Reformer;* Dorothy Salem, "To Better Our World: Black Women in Organized Reform, 1890–1920"; Deborah Gray White, "The Cost of Club Work, the Price of Feminism."

20. Barbara Welter first identified the construction of this ideology in the years 1820 to 1860 that defined the "true woman" as pious, pure, domestic, and submissive. Home was woman's "proper sphere" and was understood to be a shelter from the outside world of men. See Barbara Welter, "The Cult of True Womanhood, 1820–1860," 151–74.

to enter into social welfare work. Who was better suited to tend to the needs of the poor, the infirm, the young, and the elderly than women? African American women used this ideology as a justification for public work in racial uplift that soon propelled them into leadership positions in their communities. Although they did not adhere to notions of the "worthy" and "unworthy" poor as white women did, black women went about as members of groups dispensing aid, instilling "respectability" in the "lower-classes" through instruction in proper manners, homemaking, child-rearing, and sexual restraint, and establishing institutions to uplift the masses.[21] The "Cult of True Womanhood" justified public work and leadership positions for upper- and middle-class African American women. Inculcated with the tenets of this ideology largely through her exposure to missionary education, Bethune acquired a lifelong devotion to the idea of women's higher moral capacity.

Like most of her female contemporaries—churchwoman Nannie Helen Burroughs, educator Charlotte Hawkins Brown, clubwoman Mary Church Terrell, and community activists Lugenia Burns Hope and Jane Edna Hunter—Bethune was a pragmatist and a negotiator who pursued a course of action based on her confidence in women's higher moral capacity, the power of educational advancement, Christian responsibility, and community activism. Bethune believed in liberty, personal dignity, self-respect, and the power of the ballot—issues she emphasized in her speeches and writings. Through her involvement in education, women's clubs, and politics, Bethune reached a wide audience. Her themes reflected the issues that affected all African Americans—education, prejudice, segregation, and civil rights. Bethune's writings advocated racial pride and celebrated the moral strength and accomplishments of black women. She designed her writings to awaken the moral consciousness of whites and inspire black women and men to fight against all forms of injustice. Bethune, and her contemporaries, followed in the footsteps of other outspoken African American women.

Maria W. Stewart (1803–1879) of Boston was one model for Bethune. Stewart, a public speaker, teacher, and political activist, was an early advocate of African American women's right to have a public role in race leadership. She encouraged women to speak out, write, and teach to benefit the race. She

21. Shaw, *What a Woman Ought to Be and to Do*, 13–14, 21–28; Brooks Higginbotham, *Righteous Discontent*, 185–229; Deborah Gray White, *Too Heavy a Load: Black Women in Defense of Themselves, 1894–1994*, 21–24; Gilmore, *Gender and Jim Crow*, chapter 2; Linda Gordon, "Black and White Visions of Welfare: Women's Welfare Activism, 1890–1945," 168–74; White, "The Cost of Club Work," 252–59.

called upon women to "make a mighty effort and arise," to practice middle-class values of thrift, sobriety, and hard work and distinguish themselves through economic independence and education. Few women heard Stewart's appeals firsthand, but many nineteenth-century women imbued with the tenets of true womanhood organized benevolent associations, literary societies, mutual aid associations, church groups, and fraternal organizations to provide social services, entertainment, and financial assistance to the black community throughout the antebellum period. In the 1830s, this community activism merged with abolitionism as free black women began to recognize their obligation to and racial connection with southern slaves. Discrimination and prejudice made free black women aware that advancement for all blacks was intimately related to the progress of blacks as a group. Whatever denigrated one, denigrated all. As one teacher explained, "I am myself a colored woman, bound to that ignorant, degraded long enslaved race."[22] By working to end slavery and overcome ignorance, black women hoped to improve the lives of the entire race. The end of slavery became the beginning of a long-term commitment by African American women to ending racial oppression; when the abolitionist movement ended, black women stepped up their public work for racial equality.

Antebellum black women's commitment to ending racial oppression led to patterns of public participation that carried forward into the twentieth century. The young women of Bethune's generation followed the example set by their antebellum sisters; they too organized for a variety of reasons and developed a strong sense of responsibility for racial advancement. Yet, as Stephanie Shaw has recently argued in her study of black professional women, the women of Bethune's generation were unique, not because they organized or had a powerful sense of racial responsibility, but because of the systematic way in which family, community, and educators instilled this ideology. Shaw argues that families willingly sacrificed to educate these young women and encourage achievement. For some, this was a way to limit vulnerability to the economic and sexual exploitation inherent in agricultural and domestic work.

22. Dorothy Sterling, ed., *We Are Your Sisters: Black Women in the Nineteenth Century*, 154, 263; Shirley J. Yee, *Black Women Abolitionists: A Study in Activism, 1828–1860*, 85, 125–26, 139. For more detailed analysis of organizations founded by black women, see Sterling, ed., *We Are Your Sisters*; Paula Giddings, *When and Where I Enter: The Impact of Black Women on Race and Sex in America*; Sharon Harley and Rosalyn Terborg-Penn, eds., *The Afro-American Woman: Struggles and Images*; Gerda Lerner, ed., *Black Women in White America: A Documentary History*. Sharon Harley, "Beyond the Classroom: The Organizational Life of Black Female Educators in the District of Columbia, 1890–1930," 265.

For many others, however, education encompassed more than just reading, writing, and arithmetic. Their education reinforced an orientation toward individual achievement. Their family supplemented formal education with life lessons to assure these young women that race, class, or sex did not determine their ability and should not limit ambitions. More important, however, family members and mentors counterbalanced the emphasis on individual achievement by an equally powerful emphasis on mutual obligation. Since formal education was available to few African Americans, those fortunate enough to receive formal training were encouraged and expected to use their education in a socially responsible way—that is, to open new social, economic, and political opportunities for *all* African Americans and persistently carry on the fight for racial equality. This generation was encouraged to excel individually, but only in the context of *group advancement.* They were not to use the opportunities given to them for *individual* gain. Shaw refers to this as developing an ethic of *socially responsible individualism.* According to Shaw, parents, grandparents, and mentors *deliberately* instilled these young women with a sense of duty. Once assured they spoke for the voiceless masses, many women of this transitional generation became racial activists. Many black educated women believed they had a responsibility to the community that only they could fulfill, that "educational training meant that they had a special obligation to 'uplift' their less fortunate brothers and sisters." Self-confident and outspoken, frequently applauded by their communities as "race women" and role models for young people, they became the political and social vanguard for formal and informal movements within the black community.[23]

These postwar southern young women also differed from their northern antebellum counterparts in the way they viewed the black masses. Many young southern women were born into families with close connections to slavery; many of their grandparents, parents, and often their brothers and sisters, had been slaves. These personal connections to slavery taught them to see that poor social, economic, and political conditions among freed people were the result of limited opportunities within the institution of slavery, not some inherent weakness of character. A further difference between the two groups was the way in which they disseminated this ideology. In the antebellum period, women's associations were local in scope and designed to address

23. Shaw, *What a Woman Ought to Be and to Do,* especially chapters 1–3; Elsa Barkley Brown, "African-American Women's Quilting: A Framework for Conceptualizing and Teaching African-American Women's History," 925–26; Harley, "Beyond the Classroom," 257; Shirley J. Carlson, "Black Ideals of Womanhood in the Late Victorian Era," 62.

community improvement on a local level; they did not instill commitments to racial advancement. For example, although William Lloyd Garrison published several of Maria Stewart's essays in the *Liberator*, her speaking engagements reached only a limited audience in the Boston area primarily because her career as a public speaker was short-lived. Criticism by black male leaders pushed her to retire from public speaking by 1833.[24] The women who came of age in the post–Civil War era had greater opportunities to spread their messages. These women founded or participated in national associations and institutions specifically designed to advance the race and promote African American women's social, economic, and political activism. Mary McLeod Bethune was a member of this generation, and her early life reveals how family background, religion, teachers, and mentors consciously instilled in her an ethic of socially responsible individualism.

Mary McLeod's place as one of the first freeborn children in her family profoundly affected how she looked at the world and the intensity of her personal ambitions. The heroic actions of her maternal grandmother, Sophie, and her mother, Patsy, were the cornerstones upon which she built her life. Sophie's and Patsy's ability to survive the harshness and sexual exploitation of slavery became a foundation of young Mary's belief in the moral strength of African American women. Sophie told her grandchildren stories of her life in slavery—about the long hours of backbreaking work in the fields and the abuse slaves suffered at the hands of the cruel masters and overseers. In 1829, Sophie's first master sold her to a plantation owner near Mayesville, separating her from her three young children. On the new plantation, her African "husband" was sold to the first slave trader to come by the plantation for being "too proud" when her fourth child, Patsy, was just a week old.[25] Alone, Sophie not only became the sole caregiver to her daughter but also took on the role of protector for Patsy as well as herself. Strong and independent, Sophie resisted the sexual advances of her white master and overseer. She carried "stripes" on her back from the whip used to punish her when she refused to "become subjected to the indulgences of her master." Emancipation fueled her optimism for her grandchildren's future, as they would never have to endure the suffering she had in slavery. Although Sophie lived only until Bethune was about seven years old, she often reflected on her grandmother's stories and the "signs of great suffering" and "traces of sorrow in her face." Bethune interpreted the lesson in Sophie's stories as being to "hold and cling

24. Sterling, ed., *We Are Your Sisters*, 157.
25. Bernice Anderson Poole, *Mary McLeod Bethune, Educator*, 47–48.

to that which was right and honorable and true in womanhood."[26] Sophie deeply impressed young Mary as a model of the strong, moral black woman.

Patsy McLeod was originally a slave to the McIntosh family. When she was sixteen, McIntosh separated Patsy from Sophie when he gave Patsy to his daughter as a wedding gift. No one can confirm the specifics of Patsy's lineage, but Bethune often spoke of Patsy's "queen-like dignity" and her royal heritage as the great-granddaughter of a matrilineal West African ruling family. Based on Sophie's story about Patsy's father being a proud African who could not adjust to enslavement, this story may in fact have some validity. Whether the stories of a royal heritage are fact or fiction, Bethune respected and admired Patsy deeply, crediting her for disciplining "my life in order that I might know humility, stamina, faith, and goodness." She frequently spoke of her mother as having a "keen intelligence and great refinement," "a will of her own," and "great vision."[27] Bethune believed her mother's actions, appearance, language, and poise set her apart from others.

Patsy's stories of her life in slavery reinforced her daughter's respect. At the age of seventeen, Patsy met Samuel at a communal cotton harvest and a short time later, their masters granted them permission to "marry." A local prayer meeting leader performed the ceremony, and since Samuel's master refused to sell him, Patsy remained on the Wilson plantation and Samuel on the McLeod plantation. White masters often used economic reasons to justify this practice. In this case, McLeod claimed Samuel was much too valuable to sell to Wilson. Wilson, on the other hand, had no incentive to sell Patsy, since any children born to the couple legally became his property and increased his economic worth. In reality, white masters used abroad slave unions as a form of physical and psychological control. Marriage and family reduced the risk of flight. Masters spent less money on finding runaways and ensured an un-interrupted work cycle. Psychologically, this arrangement emasculated black men by denying them their rights as head of household. Black men had no power to provide for or protect their family from the actions of the master or overseer. Moreover, men had to ask permission to visit their family, usu-ally arriving on Saturday nights and leaving on Sunday. This was Samuel's

26. Williams interview, 7, 10.

27. "Autobiography," chapter 7; Untitled biographical interview of Mary McLeod Bethune with Charles Johnson (hereafter referred to as Johnson interview), BFC I, 7; Williams interview, 1; Fleming, *The Answered Prayer to a Dream,* 13; Elmer Anderson Carter, "A Modern Matriarch," *Christian Advocate Southwestern Edition,* 79–80 in MMB; Elmer Anderson Carter, "Within the Home Circle," *Christian Advocate,* Cincinnati, Ohio, reprinted from *Survey Graphic:* 116–17, MMB; Johnson interview, 5.

and Patsy's experience. Although Patsy gave birth to eight children during slavery—Sallie, Satira, Samuel, Julia, Kissie, Kelly, Carrie, and Beauguard—Samuel was not present for their births. Samuel was not the head of his "own" household, a point driven home when Patsy became the target of sexual exploitation. Like Sophie, Patsy resisted sexual abuse by an overseer and suffered the consequences. She told young Mary she refused "to permit her body to be persuaded by the desire of those who owned and controlled her," although her breast was scalded with hot soap as punishment. Bethune admired Sophie's and Patsy's courage and strength. She spoke of their "high spirited" nature and their "courage" in fighting for "their rights." Bethune claimed, "That courage has brought me right straight on through."[28] She credited Patsy's and Sophie's example for giving her the determination to work for racial equality. More important, these incidents had a deep-rooted impact on her perceptions of male and female relationships.

Sophie and Patsy were instrumental in shaping Bethune's perspective on women's physical and moral strength and their role in racial advancement, but her perceptions of Samuel's place in the family also contributed to her concepts of appropriate gender roles. While Bethune respected Sophie's and Patsy's strength of character and control, she described Samuel as "sympathetic, big-hearted, and indulgent." Her recollections of Samuel indicate a deep respect for his hard work on the farm; however, she did not see Samuel as "strong willed" like Patsy or having her "great leadership and determination." There were no stories of Samuel's resistance in slavery. After emancipation, he did not openly confront or antagonize whites. Samuel's resistance was less public.[29] He worked hard, provided for his family, and together with his wife managed to buy land and maintain a family and a farm at a time when it was risky for blacks to show signs of economic progress. Bethune saw Samuel as a good-natured and indulgent man who depended on his wife to organize, plan, and manage the household.

In the course of her lifetime, Bethune consistently portrayed women as heroic actors, while men became mere shadow figures. Family dynamics play

28. Williams interview, 1, 10; Johnson interview.
29. Carter, "A Modern Matriarch," 79; Carter, "Within the Home Circle," 116; Johnson interview, 6–7; *Washington Post*, "A Portrait of Mary McLeod Bethune: The Cotton-Picker Still Sings," BFC I, 1–2. James C. Scott has referred to this type of resistance as "infrapolitics" and argues that oppressed peoples develop "hidden transcripts" within their communities to articulate their discontent with oppression. This discontent can become public only when a fissure appears in the hegemonic discourse. See James C. Scott, *Weapons of the Weak: Everyday Forms of Peasant Resistance*; James C. Scott, *Domination and the Arts of Resistance: Hidden Transcripts*.

a significant role in explaining her views of gender relations. First are Sophie's and Patsy's experiences in slavery. Both women tell remarkably similar stories: slavery forced both women to effectively become single mothers; both assumed the role of protector for themselves and their children; both fought sexual exploitation by white masters or overseers; both endured punishment for their resistance; both worked to reunite families after emancipation. These incidents overwhelmingly emphasize an image of strong, independent black women, yet also speak to the powerlessness of black manhood. Sophie's first partner could not protect her from separation by sale, and her second relationship also ended in enforced separation by sale. It both cases, the white master controlled her personal relationships and left her to care for her family alone. Samuel was Patsy's husband, but could not assume his place as the head of his household. He lived separated from his slave wife and endured the sale of all of his children by the real head of his household—his wife's master, whose overseer repeatedly tried to violate Patsy while Samuel lived at a distance. White men succeeded in completely emasculating Samuel. He was psychologically impotent. Like Sophie, Patsy protected and cared for her family alone. The gender-and-race sexual triangle Samuel and Patsy experienced profoundly affected their personal relationship, and explained much about their marital relationship. Most certainly, it became a determining factor in Bethune's evolution as a strong black woman, and later would affect her personal relationships with men.

Like many women who had endured slavery, Patsy had high expectations for her freeborn children. She told young Mary that she was special because of her "unusual" birth. Patsy told her daughter that she came into the world with her "eyes wide open," which was a sign that she would see things before they happened. As Mary grew, Patsy continued to tell her of her "specialness"; "You are going to make mama proud. You are so smart" and "My lil [*sic*] Mary will grow up to be a great woman some day." Sophie further impressed young Mary with the idea that she was "special." Sophie told Mary she was different from the other children—that someday she would be a great woman and would make her parents very proud and bring them "great happiness." These expectations fueled Mary's ambitions and encouraged self-esteem. Bethune believed that a strong motivation for her race work came from "the realization of dense darkness and ignorance that I found myself [in] . . . with the seeming absence of remedy." She claimed this took place by the time she was seven years old, when she recognized the "lack of opportunity" and saw the "contrast of what was being done for the white children and the lack of what we got." Racial inequality resulted in unequal opportunity and trapped

African Americans in and around Mayesville in a tangled web of poor economic and social conditions. On market days, she claims to have noticed the contrasts between former masters and former slaves. White families wore fine clothes and soft leather shoes, lived in houses with glass windows, and rode in carriages. Black families had clean but ragged clothes, stiff leather shoes with brass tips, and lived in crude log cabins. However, the most distinctive difference was that the white children had books, piles of books. Bethune later noted, "I had no books. I could not even read!" Bethune says she saw African Americans as a "people still in darkness, unable, in spite of their being free, in spite of all their heartbreaking toil, to experience the good things in life. . . . Mr. Lincoln told our race we were free, but mentally we were still enslaved."[30]

The importance of books and literacy became even clearer when she picked up a book and a white child berated, "Put down that book, you can't read."[31] According to Bethune's recollection, this pivotal event drove home the connection between illiteracy and racial inequality. From that time on, Bethune claims she recognized education and literacy as inexorably linked to eliminating inequity and racism. Later she said these incidents galvanized her belief that there could be more in life for African Americans than continuing poverty. She became determined to read, but more important, she says she became determined to educate as many others as she could.[32]

It is highly unlikely that as a seven- or eight-year-old child, no matter how perceptive, Bethune could have made these links between education, poverty, service to the race, and the value of education as a means of racial uplift. These were, however, the premier educational assumptions of the time in which she came of age. Both the Peabody and Slater Funds, which channeled money toward industrial education for blacks, endorsed these views. They were the motivating factor behind the introduction of the Blair Bill in the 1880s and had a primary place in the educational philosophy of Booker T. Washington.[33] Most likely, Bethune developed this view as she reached adulthood and used this dramatic homily to explain her educational philosophy.

30. Williams interview, 2, 7–10, 13; Poole, *Mary McLeod Bethune*, 38; Johnson interview, 3–4, 5; "Autobiography," chapter 2; Bethune, "Faith That Moved a Dump Heap," 32.

31. Williams interview, 13; Johnson interview, 3–4.

32. Williams interview, 13.

33. Several times in the 1880s and early 1890s, Senator Henry W. Blair (R–NH) introduced a bill providing for the distribution of surplus federal monies to state schools in proportion to the level of illiteracy in the states. The bill never passed, thus ending the campaign for federal funding for public schools. See Herbert Aptheker, ed., *A Documentary History of the Negro People in the United States*, vol. 2, 648; Ward M. McAfee, "Reconstruction Revisited: The Republican Public Education Campaign of the 1870s," 150–53.

Forced separation during slavery reinforced the importance of family unity for many freedmen and women. This was true for the McLeods. Patsy's separation from her mother as an adolescent reinforced the importance of family connections, and Master Wilson's sale of each of Patsy's and Samuel's eight children when they reached adolescence was the catalyst for a strong emphasis on family obligation and loyalty within the McLeod household. Like many other freed people, after emancipation, the McLeods worked to reunite the family. Although the older children had married and begun families of their own, Patsy and Samuel sought them out and held family reunions regularly. The younger children remained in Mayesville, where they worked with their parents to build their small family farm known simply as "The Homestead." Patsy became the business manager of the family, and her "willpower and drive" held the household together.[34]

After emancipation, many former slaves left the plantations to strike out on their own, while others remained on the land and worked out tenant or sharecropping arrangements with former masters. In the McLeods' case, the family worked together pooling their earnings to become small landowners. Samuel did carpentry work in addition to farming. Several of the McLeod children found work in carpentry and other trades. Patsy worked out an arrangement with the Wilson family to stay on as a cook and housekeeper. She supplemented these earnings by taking in washing, cooking "special dinners," nursing, and acting as a midwife to both black and white families in the area. When they had earned enough money, Wilson agreed to sell five acres of land located across from the old plantation to Patsy and Samuel.[35] This was an unusual experience for former slaves. In many areas, whites had a pact not to sell or rent land to blacks. This suggests the McLeods had a special relationship with the Wilsons. This model offered young Mary another example of "good whites" helping poor blacks and most certainly would influence her future relationships with her white benefactors.

The McLeod family worked together to bring in crops and make improvements to their farm. Patsy assigned farm and household work to the younger children according to their age and ability. Tasks included doing fieldwork, milking cows, washing, ironing, cooking, and other household duties; responsibilities increased as age and ability grew. Neighbors also helped each

34. Johnson interview, 6, 9; Williams interview, 10–12; "Autobiography," chapter 7; Carter, "A Modern Matriarch," 79; Carter, "Within the Home Circle," 116.

35. "Notes for Rackham Holt," in BFC I, 2; Bethune, "Faith That Moved a Dump Heap," 31–35, 54; Williams interview, 7.

other through hard times. According to Bethune, Patsy nursed sick neighbors through epidemics and the family was "often awakened by someone knocking on the door at night." Through hard work, the McLeods were eventually able to increase their landholdings to thirty acres.[36]

Clearly, Patsy and Samuel modeled lessons in family commitment, shared responsibility, economic self-sufficiency, and hard work. Yet, as Bethune related the story, Patsy's work for the Wilson's, her "special dinners," and her nursing and midwifery were the central focus of the story. Bethune mentioned Samuel's (and her male siblings') contributions—farming and carpentry— only in passing. As Bethune recalled, "My mother was a consecrated, clear-thinking, careful woman, and my father was a principled man with more than average devotion to his family and to the best he knew."[37] In Bethune's memory, it was Patsy's selflessness, her sacrifices, and her hard work that allowed the McLeods to become small landowners and maintain that status while others remained tenant farmers and sharecroppers. This perception influenced Bethune's view of gender roles in the black family. The "special relationship" the McLeods had with the Wilsons was through the mediation of a black woman, not a black man. Apparently Bethune interpreted this as an indication that black women were better suited to negotiate with whites than black men, and were, therefore, largely responsible for black advancement. However, Patsy may have had another reason for taking on the role of negotiator. This may have been her way of protecting her husband's sense of manhood. By negotiating with Wilson, Patsy saved Samuel from being put in a situation where he would have to acknowledge Wilson, a white man and his wife's former master, as a superior. This would serve to keep Samuel's role as head of the household and man of the family intact, thus preserving the balance of power in the McLeod household.

Religion played an important part in family life for the McLeods, and again it was Sophie's and Patsy's religious conviction that Bethune claimed was most important to the development of her religiosity and spirituality. The McLeod family attended church each Sunday, and itinerant ministers were frequent visitors in their home. Before they were able to read the Bible, Samuel and Patsy led evening prayers, ending each family prayer meeting with the Lord's Prayer. While Sophie practiced a prophetic religion, Patsy was "more restrained," thanking God in her prayers for "giving her freedom,

36. "Autobiography," chapter 15; Williams interview, 3, 8, 12; Bethune, "Faith That Moved a Dump Heap," 32.
37. Quoted in Fleming, *The Answered Prayer to a Dream*, 13.

shelter, and the privilege of having her children with her." Bethune credited both women with first influencing her to "serious thinking" by the practice of morning and evening family prayers.[38]

Bethune also credited Bible stories and passages for reinforcing her notions about the acceptability of powerful women. She recalled the story of Queen Esther as particularly inspiring her to work for the race. King Xerxes I of Persia married Queen Vashti. When Vashti refused to obey Xerxes, he ordered that she be banished, and he sought another queen who would show him proper deference. After searching the kingdom, Xerxes takes Esther as his new queen. Queen Esther, however, hid her Jewish heritage from the king.[39] All goes well until Mordecai (a leading Jew and Esther's father) angers Haman, a viceroy of the king; Mordecai refuses to bow down to pay him homage. Haman manipulates Xerxes to order the destruction of all Jews, convincing Xerxes that he must eliminate all Jews, as they are a menace. (Haman does not tell Xerxes this is really retribution for Mordecai's insult.) After Xerxes issues the order to kill all the Jews, Mordecai implores Esther to intercede with the king on behalf of the Jews. However, Esther is afraid. She cannot go to the king of her own accord; she must wait until summoned. She refuses Mordecai's request, to which he responds, "Do not imagine that you in the king's palace can escape any more than all the Jews."[40] At this point, Esther realizes her duty to be the spokesperson for her people.

Still, Esther cannot approach the king directly. Instead, she uses her feminine wiles; Esther situates herself so that Xerxes will have to notice her and waits for his summons. Esther dutifully goes to Xerxes, who sees she looks troubled. He begs Esther to tell him the reason for her unease, promising her half of his kingdom if it will ease her mind and take away her troubled look.[41] Esther asks only one request of Xerxes: hold a banquet and invite Haman; there she will make her appeal. If Xerxes grants her wish, then her troubled look will disappear. Before the banquet, Xerxes discovers Mordecai saved him from assassination in the past but never received a reward. Xerxes orders his viceroy, Haman, to reward Mordecai, which Haman reluctantly does. Finally, the banquet begins. Xerxes asks Esther to make her request. Esther reveals her Jewish heritage, asking that Xerxes allow her people to live. She points to Haman as her personal enemy. The king goes out to the garden in a rage, as

---

38. Williams interview, 12; Bethune, "Faith That Moved a Dump Heap," 32.
39. Esther 1:19–22; Esther 2:8–16.
40. Esther 4:13.
41. Esther 5:6.

Haman begs Esther to change the king's anger against him. The king returns to find Haman clutching Esther, and orders his immediate execution.

As Bethune interpreted the story, Esther's intercession with Xerxes on behalf of her people saved the Jews as a race and improved future relationships between the Jews and the Persian kings. After hearing how Esther was "willing to risk her life and plead with the king for her people," Bethune vowed, "I could and would risk mine to do the same for my people."[42] In Esther, Bethune claims she found a biblical role model. Bethune used the story to justify her role as a spokesperson for black interests at the highest levels, working patiently to improve the social, economic, and political status of African Americans. The story of Esther also illustrates once again to Bethune that women, not men, have a superior capacity for special relationships with men of power.

However, the story of Esther illustrates even more clearly how powerless people can gain a measure of control over those in power. Vashti was a strong, forceful woman who clashed with Xerxes head-on, resulting in her banishment. Strength is a noble attribute, but those who are not present cannot bring change. Esther, on the other hand, uses a different method to get what she needs. Learning from Vashti's mistakes, Esther finds it more productive to dissemble and manipulate Xerxes to achieve her larger goal. Perhaps this is the real lesson Bethune took from the story. Bethune saw direct confrontation against segregation and discrimination in white-racist America was not likely to advance her race. To fulfill her social responsibility to racial uplift, she would have to be subtle and manipulative, as Esther had been with Xerxes. Throughout her long career, Bethune practices dissemblance with financially and politically powerful whites and uses the perception of herself as a diminutive black woman to navigate the corridors of power—not for personal power (although that is to some extent a by-product of her race work), but to discharge her duties as a socially responsible black woman.

When Bethune received a Bible from the local missionary school, she claims she found more inspiration for her future. She later recalled that it was John 3:16—"whosoever believeth in Him should not perish, but have everlasting life"—that first inspired her to no longer feel inferior to whites despite the obvious differences in their lives. John's use of the word "Whosoever" focused Bethune's attention on the fact that the passage did not mention "Jew nor Gentile, no Catholic nor Protestant, no black nor white; just 'whoso-

42. Bethune, "Faith That Moved a Dump Heap," 32.

ever.'" This meant that everyone was equal in the sight of God and all people, regardless of race, could achieve.[43]

Exposure to strong, independent female role models and religious beliefs allowed Bethune to develop an unwavering belief in the primary responsibility of black women for sustaining the race. Her grandmother and mother demonstrated how black women who embraced "a larger appreciation for good citizenship, cleanliness, beauty, thoughtfulness" could lead African Americans as "the mothers of the race, the homemakers and spiritual guides." Bethune believed African American women had an obligation to understand these responsibilities and use their status to fight for equality.[44] In true Victorian fashion, she publicly endorsed the notion of women's higher moral capacity and their obligation to use this virtue to perfect society. She also learned and exploited the subtle advantages that a culture with a strong slaveholding heritage gave clever black women to advance the cause of racial uplift. Female family role models and religious teachings became mutually reinforcing. Bethune perceived family life and religion as nurturing, advocating, and celebrating courageous women who fought for their rights and the rights of their people. Whether these stories are myth, the creative reorganization of fact, or perhaps a composite truth, one thing is clear—Bethune believed Sophie, Patsy, and the Bible presented her with examples of the strength, character, and responsibilities of African American womanhood.

In addition to all of these influences, Bethune claimed she was "just different" from the other children in her family. She often described herself as "the homely one" of the McLeod children because unlike her siblings—who had her mother's soft, fine features—she had dark, coarse skin and a very low hairline. However, Bethune contends that her physical appearance helped her become an individualist, and because she believed she was an individualist, she became the peacemaker among the children. When fights broke out during children's games, the children looked to her to settle disputes and determine the truth. She remembered always trying to be diplomatic, and it made no difference to her if the squabbles involved mixed groups of girls and boys. She tried to point out the faults on both sides and persuade everyone involved into apologizing and getting together. She maintained she never felt uncomfortable with or distrustful of boys, and was a "good mixer" with both boys and girls. She was comfortable dealing with men and women and never

43. Ibid., 33.
44. Ibid., 34; Mary McLeod Bethune, "A Philosophy of Education for Negro Girls," n.d., MMB.

thought of herself as inferior to men. She believed "I always had a mind."[45] If these incidents are true, then Bethune's willingness to act as an intermediary for older children nourished the assertive side of her personality, allowed her to have faith in herself and her decisions, and fostered a sense of independence. Likewise, these experiences would have made her less likely to adhere to standard views of hierarchy. Mediating childhood disputes would allow her to develop the ability to see both sides of an issue and negotiate agreements. Her ability to negotiate with both boys and girls would later permit her to be comfortable in dealing with men in business and politics.

Family and religion were fulfilling, but young Mary yearned to go to school. At the end of the Civil War, Freedman's Bureau agents who went into the South to educate the freed people found that through sheer determination the former slaves had made great efforts to educate themselves in "native schools." As early as 1860 in some areas of the South, slaves and free people of color had begun the systematic organization of black schools wherever possible. By 1866, the Freedman's Bureau estimated that there were "at least 500" of these native (or common) schools in operation. In fact, Sumter County, South Carolina, was reportedly one of the areas where, by 1867, African Americans had made "significant progress" in establishing and sustaining common and Sabbath schools. Yet, despite the efforts of the freed people, the Freedmen's Bureau, and religious denominations to advance education, not more than one-tenth of black children attended school on a regular basis.[46]

By the end of Reconstruction, educational opportunities for blacks were dismal in the South. Whites believed teaching blacks how to read, write, and cipher would "ruin" them as agricultural laborers, primarily by permitting them to read labor contracts and calculate their earnings and expenditures. Whites had strong economic incentives to keep African Americans illiterate, or at least limit how much education blacks received. Whites endorsed "industrial education," as developed by Samuel Chapman Armstrong at Hampton Institute and practiced by Booker T. Washington at Tuskegee. According to dominant white beliefs, education was to advance a moral, productive, and subordinate life, not produce freethinking scholars. At Tuskegee, Washington trained a cadre of teachers inculcated in the industrial education philosophy. These teachers spread throughout the South, establishing what amounted to satellite Tuskegee campuses, spreading the gospel of accommodation.[47]

45. Williams interview, 2–3.
46. Anderson, *The Education of Blacks in the South*, 7–8; W. E. B. Du Bois, *Economic Co-Operation among Negro Americans*, 79.
47. Litwack, *Trouble in Mind*, 52–113; Anderson, *Education of Blacks in the South*, 33–78.

The public education system was also inadequate. In South Carolina, by 1870, the legislature established a racially segregated public school system enrolling about sixty thousand students almost evenly divided between white and black. Unfortunately, corruption became a part of the system immediately, and the corruption had racial overtones. County treasurers delayed paying teachers and school officials, and some black Republicans serving in local positions for the school system began skimming off educational funds. Instead of receiving cash payments, teachers and administrators ended up with promissory certificates that speculators were more than willing to buy at significant discount. In 1872, Justus K. Jillson, South Carolina's Republican superintendent of public instruction, claimed that county treasurers and school officials had not dispersed one dollar of the three hundred thousand dollars appropriated for public education to meet school expenses. By 1874, Jillson publicly disparaged the teachers as "incompetent, inefficient, and worthless." In light of this corruption, the quality of school officers and the teaching staff declined rapidly.[48]

In rural Sumter County, these factors plus the declining economic status of African Americans led to a lack of adequate public or private schools. It was 1886, the year Bethune turned eleven, before the Presbyterian Board of Missions established the first common school for black children in Mayesville. That year, Emma J. Wilson, a young black missionary educated at Scotia Seminary in North Carolina, opened the Trinity Presbyterian Mission School with ten students at an abandoned cotton gin house near Mayesville. Like most local missionary schools, Trinity served the families of poor black tenant farmers, sharecroppers, and small landowners. Since money was scarce, Wilson accepted eggs, chickens, and produce for tuition. She raised extra money by asking for donations at northern black churches and camp meetings. She also worked as a laundress when necessary to support her and the school. Eventually she convinced the County Board of Education to give the school forty-five dollars each year in public aid. With this money, she hired an assistant, increased enrollment, and managed to build a schoolhouse. After years of begging, Wilson gained continuing support from northern philanthropists and began to receive two hundred dollars per year from the state in educational support. The school received accreditation in 1896.[49]

48. Ward M. McAfee, *Religion, Race, and Reconstruction: The Public School System in the Politics of the 1870s,* 100–101.

49. Francis R. Keyser, "Life of Mary McLeod Bethune," unpublished manuscript dated February 14, 1927, BFC I, chapter 3; Lerner, ed., *Black Women in White America,* 120–21. It is

Wilson visited each farm in the area, asking parents to send their children to school. The McLeods could only allow one of their children to leave the fields to attend school. Since Patsy believed Mary was destined for great things, and Mary longed to go to school, she was chosen to study at the missionary school. However, Patsy also made it clear to her daughter that when she returned from school, Patsy expected her to share her lessons with everyone in the family. Mary did this willingly, and on Sunday afternoons she gathered neighboring farm children together and shared her school lessons in poetry, reading, and song with them.[50] As with many young women of her generation, Patsy encouraged Bethune to achieve as an individual, but only in the context of family and community advancement.

Bethune learned more than reading and writing at the mission school. Bethune later remembered being in awe of Wilson, the first formally educated black woman with whom she had had contact. Wilson became the first example of how important one educated black woman could be to racial advancement. In building the Trinity Mission School, Wilson gave Bethune a model for institution building and a method to promote racial progress. Wilson also passed on a second meaningful legacy—she taught Bethune the importance of kindness, understanding, tenderness, and patience when dealing with impressionable children.[51]

After about four years at the missionary school, Bethune had learned as much as Wilson could offer and returned to work on the family farm. Although she wanted to continue her education, the family did not have the means to send her away to a more advanced school. Within a few months, a Quaker dressmaker in Denver, Colorado, Mary Crissman, became interested in the work of Wilson's missionary school. She contacted Wilson and arranged to furnish a scholarship for the higher education of one deserving girl. Wilson chose Bethune to enroll at Scotia Seminary in Concord, North Carolina.[52]

Founded in 1867 by Reverend Luke Dorland of Toledo, Ohio, Scotia Seminary was the first major Presbyterian boarding school established to prepare

---

very difficult to find documentary evidence that supports the story of Wilson's school founding. The dates Lerner cites in her account do not match with Bethune's account of going to school in Mayesville. For example, Lerner writes that Wilson returned to Mayesville in 1892 after attending Scotia Seminary to start the school. However, Bethune wrote that she began school when she was eleven years old, which would mean that the school had to be in existence by 1886.

50. Johnson interview, 11.
51. Johnson interview, 15.
52. Keyser, "Life of Mary McLeod Bethune," chapter 3.

black teachers and social workers. At the time of its founding, Scotia offered the highest level of training available to black women, who were largely excluded from higher educational opportunities. Modeled after Mount Holyoke Female Seminary in South Hadley, Massachusetts, although never as well funded, Scotia educated black girls in religion, arts and sciences, and domestic duties so that they would become "the highest type of wife, mother, and teacher." Like Mount Holyoke, Wellesley, and Oberlin, Scotia required students to do some manual labor to inculcate habits of industry and defer some cost of their education. However, "manual training" was not a part of the instructional program.[53] Scotia offered two curricula: the four-year grammar program included English, arithmetic, algebra, geography, science, history, and literature; and the three-year normal and scientific program included geometry, astronomy, physics, chemistry, history, Latin, and rhetoric. The curriculum also included training in refinement that emphasized using a gently moderate voice, displaying quiet dignity, and dressing conventionally. An industrial department taught sewing and cooking, and all students did housekeeping chores to control operating costs. The close relationship of the integrated faculty at Scotia reflected President David Satterfield's belief in promoting an egalitarian Christianity. Satterfield also believed that Scotia's educational philosophy of "head-heart-hand" would help each student develop her fullest potential and demonstrate spiritual and moral growth, integrity, and responsibility. Administrators and teachers specifically designed Scotia's program to stress egalitarianism and the development of social consciousness as well as to enhance knowledge.[54]

Bethune entered Scotia as a "good natured, earnest, ambitious young girl who was willing to do anything that was required of her to obtain an education." Mary chose the normal and scientific program. More important than the curriculum, however, was her exposure to the biracial teaching staff. Scotia gave Bethune her first experience with integration and promoted her developing notions of racial and gender equality. In contrast to the prevailing Social Darwinist ideology of the time, the faculty taught Scotia's students

53. Anderson, *Education of Blacks in the South*, 35.

54. Elaine M. Smith, "Scotia Seminary," 1016–17; Fleming, *The Answered Prayer to a Dream*, 10. For an extended discussion of the role of the American Missionary Association in black education see Joe M. Richardson, *Christian Reconstruction: The American Missionary Association and Southern Blacks, 1861–1890*; Ronald Butchart, *Northern Schools, Southern Blacks, and Reconstruction: Freedmen's Education, 1862–1875*; Jacqueline Jones, *Soldiers of Light and Love: Northern Teachers and Georgia Blacks, 1865–1873*; and Edmund L. Drago, *Initiative, Paternalism, and Race Relations: Charleston's Avery Normal Institute*.

that skin color had nothing to do with intelligence and that color, class, and caste distinctions were immoral. Because of these radical beliefs and the need to protect its students from the effects of popular racial ideologies, Scotia physically and psychologically isolated itself from the surrounding community. School authorities controlled all aspects of the student's academic and personal lives.[55]

The missionary spirit of Scotia's northern white teachers impressed Bethune. She saw them as noble and courageous, refusing to give credence to popular social and pseudo-scientific theories that espoused innate racial inferiority. These white missionaries saw it as their God-given duty to help African Americans develop: to see to their general well-being and encourage their talents through education. Scotia's white faculty also gave Bethune her first chance to have personal contact with white racial liberals. Bethune's experience at Scotia was "the first time I had a chance to study and know white people. . . . I can never doubt the sincerity and interest of some white people when I think of my experience with my beloved, consecrated teachers who took so much time and patience with me at a time when time and tolerance was needed." These contacts profoundly affected Bethune's ideas of race relations. For the first time, she saw whites as a group interested in helping African Americans to overcome the disadvantages of slavery. Like W. E. B. Du Bois, who recalled his years at Fisk as "years of growth and development" and his contact with white teachers as "inspiring and beneficial," Bethune's writings portray the faculty as reverent, gentle, modest, and caring. She saw the white teachers encouraging black students to think for themselves and discover their abilities, and motivating them to reach their full potential. Bethune's relationship with at least two white teachers was long-lasting. In 1946, Miss Mary Chapman and Miss Ida Catheart visited Bethune to see the school she founded.[56] These teachers so impressed Bethune that she selected white trustees for Daytona Institute who exhibited the same characteristics as her white teachers at Scotia and used this model of white involvement in black education in building her school.

55. Quote from an unnamed teacher at Scotia contained in untitled biographical notes, BFC I, 28. Fleming, *The Answered Prayer to a Dream*, 11. Bethune, "Faith That Moved a Dump Heap," 33; Carter, "A Modern Matriarch," 79; Carter, "Within the Home Circle," 116; Smith, "Scotia Seminary," 1016–17.

56. Johnson interview, 22–23; W. E. B. Du Bois, *Dusk of Dawn: An Essay toward an Autobiography of Race Concept*, 30–31. Du Bois reaffirmed this praise near the end of his life in his autobiography. See *The Autobiography of W. E. B. Du Bois*, 112–13. Letter from Mary McLeod Bethune to Miss Mary E. Chapman dated December 26, 1946, BFC II.

Of course, not all missionaries exhibited these attitudes. In 1874, the secretary of the Methodist Freedman's Aid Society referred to blacks as children who needed those "more favored" to "take them by the hand and lead them . . . up from debasement and misery." And not all African Americans had such high praise for the missionaries and their educational institutions. Many blacks, including Frederick Douglass, resented the patronizing attitude expressed by such missionaries. Douglass believed that blacks had been "more injured than we have been helped" by such men. He encouraged blacks to stop "begging" and establish independent black institutions.[57] Bethune was fortunate that her white instructors at Scotia were not this negative type.

The black faculty also affected the development of Bethune's views of her race and gender. In recalling her interaction with these black teachers, she said, "My contact with the fine young Negro teachers . . . gave me the confidence in the ability of Negro women to be cultured, gave me my very first vision of the culture and ability of Negro women and gave me the incentive and made me see that if they could do it I could do it too."[58] These black teachers provided additional role models for Bethune and further exposed her to the possibilities of educated black womanhood. Although we have generally recognized the positive impact of black educators on black students as occurring only in all black schools, Bethune's experience shows that this positive impact is also possible at a school administered by whites with an integrated, egalitarian-minded faculty—albeit in an environment isolated from outside negative influences. This integrated model could only work in a cocoon. Had it been tried in an open, public environment, the white reaction would have been inevitable and obvious. Bethune's perceptions of these black teachers fostered and strengthened her views of appropriate female conduct and women's ability to achieve. Bethune's positive interactions with the multiracial faculty at Scotia served to lay the foundation for a lifelong commitment to interracial cooperation.

Despite her overwhelmingly positive memories of the years at Scotia, the experience certainly had its more stressful moments. Bethune had been one of Wilson's favorite students at the Trinity Missionary School in Mayesville. She learned quickly, and Wilson paid special attention to her by choosing her for the scholarship at Scotia. However, when Bethune arrived at Scotia, she was no longer "special." She was poor and unsophisticated, and she was

57. James M. McPherson, "White Liberals and Black Power in Negro Education, 1865–1915," 1357–86.

58. Johnson interview, 22–23.

among many others who were more cultured and just as ambitious. Her poverty weighed heavily on her. Her parents could provide only the essentials, and neighbors or a missionary barrel provided most of her clothing. At first, several students ridiculed her clothing and made her even more self-conscious.[59]

Bethune was also disadvantaged in the educational sense. While Wilson worked hard at Trinity to provide a good, basic education to her students, the level of academic work could not compare to some of the better-funded schools. When Bethune entered Scotia, the drawbacks of her academic preparation became clear. Compared to many of Scotia's students her academic work was "adequate" but certainly not outstanding. She had to work harder and study much longer to compensate for her academic deficiencies.

Social distinction also weighed on Bethune. Mealtimes were highly stressful for her. Tables were set with starched white linens and elaborate place settings. No one in her family had ever had more than one fork, and Bethune was constantly afraid that she would use the wrong utensils. Fortunately, she quickly learned to adapt by watching and imitating others.[60] Although these situations were difficult, Bethune adapted quickly and on balance gained valuable life-lessons from the experiences. In a general sense, Scotia taught her that she would have to work harder if she wanted to be highly effective. Socially, she learned to interact comfortably with people of higher status without awkwardness. This ability served her well when she began dealing with wealthy philanthropists, dignitaries, and statesmen.

There was also a secondary effect to Bethune's experiences at Scotia. They awakened her long-suppressed yearning for "substantial things" and a craving for fine possessions. She began overcompensating for her insecurities by taking overt pride in her appearance; so much so that even her most ardent admirers would later describe her as quite "vain."[61] In fact, her vanity was one of the first things many people would later notice about her. Once she gained some level of economic security, she regularly indulged in having her hair "rolled," as well as in facials and pedicures. At Scotia, Bethune learned to hide her insecurities behind a façade of confidence that at times could be mistaken for pretentiousness.

Although some saw Bethune's careful attention to her appearance as "vain" or "pretentious," we must consider her attention to personal presentation in

59. "Autobiography," chapter 4; Johnson interview, 20; Keyser, "Life of Mary McLeod Bethune," chapter 4.
60. "Autobiography," chapter 4; Johnson interview, 20; Keyser, "Life of Mary McLeod Bethune," chapter 4.
61. Jeanetta Welch Brown, interview by Susan McElrath, July 10, 1992, NCNW.

the context of the times. Throughout the late nineteenth and early twentieth centuries, whites often characterized African American women as wanton, immoral, lazy, and slovenly. Overcoming these stereotypes became an important element in black women's activist agenda. African American women who became the representatives of the race to whites were especially careful of their appearance, dress, and manners. They incorporated lessons in personal hygiene and household cleanliness into their reform programs because they were well aware that whites judged *all* blacks by the lowest elements of the race. Bethune was no exception. As a representative of the race, she maintained a model of studied femininity, thus working to undermine negative perceptions of black womanhood.

Bethune's teachers and lessons at Scotia reinforced the concepts of socially responsible individualism. Furthermore, Scotia's teachers supplemented these concepts by teaching that this sense of responsibility had little to do with class distinction. Given the opportunity, even those of humble background were capable of becoming race leaders. Furthermore, formally trained leaders had no reason to consider themselves "superior." The masses were not mindless; in fact, quite the opposite was true. Their innate intelligence was strong but simply lacked the formal training necessary to develop formal organizations necessary for united action. Therefore, those fortunate enough to receive leadership training had an obligation to assume roles that promoted racial solidarity and improved the mental, moral, and material conditions of the masses.[62] Socially responsible young black women were not conditioned to see those they helped as "the other," rather they were trained to see all African Americans as part of an organic community bound together by virtue of their race.

The Satterfields, who headed Scotia, nurtured Bethune's passion for leadership. Bethune spent a great deal of time talking to Mrs. Satterfield about her desire to serve people and her wish to gain more experience "contacting people who did not live the normal life . . . I used to think of the people in jail and the people who lived in the red light districts and the poorer people of the alley who did not get a chance to go to the fashionable churches. The people out in the world not knowingly waiting, but waiting for somebody to come and teach them. I yearned for a preparation that would fit me to teach and awaken just such types." Since she was so intent on becoming a missionary to the masses, the Satterfields encouraged Bethune to continue her studies at Moody Bible

62. Sharon Harley, "The Middle Class," 786–89.

Institute in Chicago. Evangelist Dwight L. Moody founded Moody Bible Institute in September 1889. Moody planned to train students in basic theology
and then take on mission work among the urban poor and working class. The
emphasis at Moody was on practical applied Christianity designed to initiate
students into missionary activities while still in school. The two-year course
of study included the conservative, analytical study of the Bible and training
in Gospel singing. Teachers dedicated mornings to classroom training while
they divided afternoons and evenings between biblical study and practical
evangelistic mission work in the city. Practical training included rescue mission work, house-to-house visits, children's meetings, women's meetings, jail
work, and church visitations. Moody also held tent meetings on the streets
during the summer months and cottage meetings during the winter months.
After a somewhat rocky start, the school began to grow rapidly and in the
first decade of its existence thousands attended. In 1900, the school reported
202 graduates working in home, city, and rescue missions; 180 in evangelistic
work as preachers and singers; 38 in educational and philanthropic work; 64 as
superintendents of city missions; 368 pastors, pastor's assistants, and church
visitors; 58 Sunday-school missionaries; 25 Christian Association secretaries;
32 evangelists; and 186 foreign missionaries in its first decade of operation.[63]

After graduation from Scotia in 1893 and a strong recommendation from
the Satterfields, Crissman gave Bethune a second scholarship to attend
Moody Bible Institute to complete the two-year program in missionary training.[64] As Social Gospel reformers, the teachers at Moody promoted the idea
that human miseries resulted from systemic problems in society and not from
the personal failings of the individual. These teachers first introduced
Bethune to the Social Gospel ideology with its "application of the teaching of Jesus and the total message of the Christian salvation to society, the
economic life, and social institutions . . . as well as to individuals."[65] Students
at Moody took part in a variety of community outreach programs designed
to apply Jesus' teachings and uplift the less fortunate.

63. Mary McLeod Bethune, "A Yearning and a Longing Appeased," BFC I, 4–5. Untitled
partial autobiographical statement (hereafter referred to as autobiographical statement), n.d.,
BFC I, 1. James Findlay, "'Moody,' 'Gapmen,' and the Gospel: The Early Days of Moody
Bible Institute," 322–25; William R. Moody, *The Life of Dwight L. Moody*, 338–46.

64. If Bethune entered Scotia in 1890 after completing four years at Trinity Mission School
and enrolled in the four-year program, this date should be 1894. However, Bethune reports
the date as 1893 without explanation. "Mary McLeod Bethune (Biographical Sketch)," BCC.

65. White, Jr., *Liberty and Justice for All*, xvii.

Bethune was the only black student at Moody, but she never talked about being isolated from the white students. Rather, she recalled her stay at Moody Bible Institute as a "glorious one." In one statement, she recalled entering Moody "With no chip on my shoulder but as a student with an open mind" and being "received by all most graciously." She claimed her "classmates seemed to rival with each other in their attempts to make me happy" and went out of their way to greet and make conversation with her. Bethune's practical assignment was singing at the Pacific Garden Mission and visiting prisoners at the city prison. Every Thursday a group of students would visit the police station, sing hymns and read Scriptures to the prisoners, and go door to door proselytizing among the poor. Another assignment involved missionary work establishing Sunday schools in the rural districts of the Dakotas, Minnesota, and Wisconsin.[66]

Bethune's recollections of her days at Moody are too good to be true. This was Chicago in the 1890s when pseudo-scientific racism reached its high point and Social Darwinism became America's prevailing social ideology. Despite Bethune's recollections of complete acceptance, Moody officials treated her differently from white students. She was the only student assigned to proselytize in a relatively dangerous brightly lit mission room on Clark Street designed to attract wandering derelicts. She also worked alone in one of the worst slum areas in Chicago dispensing tracts about the Institute and urging the "lost souls" she encountered to come to Sunday services.[67]

According to Bethune, her evangelistic training at Moody taught her to deal with a diverse array of people and to return love for hate. She summed up her two years at Moody as the experience that helped her link "intellectual training and spiritual understanding in the service of mankind."[68] The Social Gospel ideology fit well with Bethune's experiences and outlook that the exclusion of African Americans, especially from the education system, was the cause of their poor condition. Teachers at Scotia Seminary reinforced the idea that African Americans were not innately inferior, while her experience as the only black student at Moody emphasized the systemic exclusion that limited black progress.

66. "Autobiography," chapter 6; Keyser, "Life of Mary McLeod Bethune," chapter 6; Autobiographical statement, 3–4; Bethune, "A Yearning and a Longing Appeased," 6; Rackham Holt, *Mary McLeod Bethune*, 41–42.

67. Autobiographical statement, 3–4; Holt, *Mary McLeod Bethune*, 41–42; "Autobiography," chapter 6; Keyser, "Life of Mary McLeod Bethune," chapter 6.

68. Autobiographical statement, 5.

By the time Bethune completed her course of study at Moody in 1895, she was intensely pious and deeply spiritual. Her lifelong dream was to serve as a missionary in Africa, and she applied for a position. By this time she had a high opinion of her capabilities—some would say she lacked humility—and was confident church officials would give her a position. However, church administrators denied her application. There were no openings for black missionaries in Africa. She was disappointed, but deeply imbued with a sense of racial responsibility, so she returned to Mayesville and took a position as assistant to Wilson at the missionary school, now the Mayesville Institute. Although this was not the missionary position she craved, the experience strengthened Bethune's early lessons in institution building. Bethune returned to Mayesville just as Wilson began her fight with state education officials for accreditation and increased funding. Wilson taught her how to approach government officials and northern philanthropists. Most important, Bethune learned how to supplement outside financial support through self-help. Mayesville Institute students raised their own food, built the main schoolhouse, and supplemented donations by operating a brick-making plant at the school.[69] Working with Wilson gave Bethune practical experience in the mechanics of building and operating a school.

Because of her deep-seated sense of family obligation, when Bethune returned to Mayesville, she watched over her parents' accounts with local merchants to make sure they were keeping honest accounts of the McLeods' transactions. She used her earnings from her first teaching position, as well as income earned from summer work as a laundress, cook, and nurse for local white families, to pay off the mortgage on the McLeod mule. Later, after she married and moved to Palatka, Florida, Bethune supplemented her teacher's salary by selling life insurance for the Afro-American Life Insurance Company after school hours and on Saturdays. She used some of that money to buy a comfortable home for her parents in Sumter, South Carolina, and to make sure they had comfortable furniture, plenty of linens, and "the good things in life." Samuel and Patsy McLeod remained in this home until their deaths in 1907 and 1914 respectively.[70]

69. "Mary McLeod Bethune (Biographical Sketch)"; "Autobiography," chapter 7; Keyser, "Life of Mary McLeod Bethune," chapter 7; Lerner, *Black Women in White America*, 120.

70. Williams interview, 9; "Notes for Rackham Holt," BFC I, 2; Williams interview, 2, 12, 16. In this interview, Bethune relates that her father (who was eight years older than her mother) died at age eighty-four and her mother at age eighty-three. Poole reports that Patsy was born in 1831, which means Samuel was born in 1823. This would make their years of death 1907 and 1914 respectively; see Poole, *Mary McLeod Bethune, Educator*, 47.

Bethune barely knew her older brothers and sisters, but she had a closer relationship with her younger siblings. She made certain her sisters Mazie, Hattie, and Marjorie studied at Scotia Seminary. Mazie married, and established a hand laundry that employed several women. Hattie married a carpenter and lived in a "beautiful home" in Sumter. Bethune also saw to the educational needs of her nieces and nephews. All three of Mazie's children studied at Bethune-Cookman College, as did Hattie's two children. Several of her nieces and nephews then completed advanced degrees at other colleges. Bethune's family ties pulled on her throughout her life. In late 1942, Bethune brought her mentally unstable niece Georgia to live with her in Daytona Beach, despite the objections of her son and closest women advisers. When they approached Bethune with their reservations, she insisted that Georgia was her "own blood" and she would bring her to Daytona Beach. After the death of her sister, Hattie, Bethune also watched over her niece Jerona, advising her on a variety of matters from establishing financial security to her spelling.[71]

After a year at Mayesville, Bethune requested an appointment from the Presbyterian Board of Education to Haines Industrial and Normal Institute in Augusta, Georgia. At Haines, Bethune came under the influence of Lucy C. Laney (1854–1933), a dynamic black pioneer female educator. Laney founded Haines in 1883 and devoted her entire life to protecting black children's rights to education. Laney essentially began Haines with no capital and seventy-five students, but traveled at length to secure financial support from missionary associations and individual philanthropists. In the second year of operation, Haines had 234 students and gained financial support from the Presbyterian Board of Missions for Freedmen. A donation of ten thousand dollars from Mrs. F. E. Haines allowed Laney to enlarge the school.[72]

71. "Autobiography," chapter 7; Keyser, "Life of Mary McLeod Bethune," chapter 7; Williams interview, 10–12; Unsigned letter to Arabella Denniston, October 21, 1942, BFC II; Unsigned letter to Arabella Denniston, November 21, 1942, BFC II; Unsigned letter to Arabella Denniston, December 9, 1942, BFC II; Mary McLeod Bethune to G. D. Rogers, June 20, 1945, BFC II; Mary McLeod Bethune to Dorothy Height, June 22, 1945, NCNW; Mary McLeod Bethune to Jerona Coffey, August 26, December 7, 1946, BFC II.

72. Bethune, "Faith That Moved a Dump Heap," 33; Carter, "A Modern Matriarch," 79; Carter, "Within the Home Circle," 116; Fleming, *The Answered Prayer to a Dream*, 20–21; Johnson interview, 37; "Autobiography," chapter 7; Keyser, "Life of Mary McLeod Bethune," chapter 7. See Benjamin G. Brawley, *Negro Builders and Heroes;* William Newton Hartshorne, ed., *An Era of Progress and Promise;* Mary White Ovington, *Portraits in Color;* Sadie Iola Daniels, *Women Builders;* Lerner, *Black Women in White America,* especially 122–23.

Although Haines was open to both boys and girls, Laney's primary interest was in the education of young black women, who she saw as the primary force for uplifting the race. Laney grounded her views in the nineteenth-century idea of "separate spheres" for men and women. This ideology saw women as more compassionate, nurturing, moral, and self-sacrificing, and men as aggressive, unemotional, and selfish. Women's special attributes made them the natural choice for educating children and doing social welfare work. Addressing an educational conference in 1899, Laney articulated her philosophy for the education and social responsibility of African American women:

> The educated Negro woman, the woman of character and culture, is needed in the schoolroom not only in the kindergarten, and in the primary and secondary schools; but she is needed in the high school, the academy, and the college. Only those of character and culture can do successful lifting, for she who would mould character must herself possess it. Not alone in the schoolroom can the intelligent woman lend a lifting hand, but as a public lecturer she may give advice, helpful suggestions, and important knowledge that will change a whole community and start its people on the upward way.[73]

Like many other black women educators of the time, Laney believed that women's most important power came through their roles as wives and mothers. In this capacity, a moral woman influenced her husband's behavior and molded the good character of her children. Adhering to "proper" (that is, white middle-class) manners and behaviors disproved the notion of innate racial inferiority. Racial uplift began at home. Unfortunately, by advocating that blacks adhere to a white middle-class model, black female reformers were reflecting white racist assumptions of black inferiority at the very time they were dedicating their lives to fighting those same assumptions. Still, female school founders held that well-educated, moral black women were necessary to racial advancement.[74] Schools such as Haines, Atlanta Baptist Female Seminary (later renamed Spelman College), and Hartshorn Memorial College in Richmond taught young women they had the authority to shape the character of the nation.

Laney's goal was to inspire, train, and prepare women for service and leadership through education by first establishing a training school for girls and

73. Lucy C. Laney, "The Burden of the Educated Colored Women," 296–301.
74. Brooks Higginbotham, *Righteous Discontent*, 19–46.

later a teacher training school.[75] Laney began Haines with a course in industrial training, but by 1887, the school also included primary, grammar, and normal departments. Over the next several years, Laney built up the normal program and developed a strong literary department. She also developed a well-equipped kindergarten and began a nurse-training program in association with the city hospital. Laney committed herself to preparing African American women to go into the community, build essential institutions, and take primary responsibility for uplifting the race. Her educational philosophy effectively combined industrial training, higher education, and character building—all essential for racial advancement.[76]

Laney was an important role model to Bethune on several levels. She not only offered a model for educating young black children and institution building but also was an advocate for black women. She was active in the National Association of Colored Women, the Southeastern Federation of Women's Clubs, the Georgia State Teachers Association, and the National Young Women's Christian Association. She also chaired the Colored Section of the Interracial Commission of Augusta. Through her work as an educator and activist, Laney passed on the possibilities of educated black womanhood and set an example for Bethune to follow. Working with Laney reinforced Bethune's early lessons in socially responsible individualism. Laney reminded Bethune that as an educated black woman, she had a significant responsibility to her race. Bethune credited Laney for giving her "a new vision: my life work lay not in Africa but in my own country." According to Bethune, Laney's fearlessness, humanity, energy, dedication, and influence inspired her to devote her life to improving opportunities for black children. Later, Bethune wrote that she was "drenched with inspiration from that rare spirit and my work with her was a joy." Bethune once said that she studied Laney, watched her every move, and then gave herself fully to "the cause" of the black community. During the year Bethune spent teaching at Haines she was able to translate the lessons of Scotia Seminary and Moody Bible Institute into action by organizing a "Mission School" on Sunday afternoons. Bethune took the girls in the science class and her own class out into the alleys and streets of Augusta, where she gathered about 250 young people to take part in a mission Sunday school. Bethune claimed that the mission school lasted for years and

75. Mary McLeod Bethune, "A Century of Progress for Negro Women," Address at the Chicago Women's Federation, n.d., MMB.
76. See E. P. Cowan, "Haines Normal and Industrial School"; A. C. Griggs, "Lucy Craft Laney"; Laney, "The Burden of the Educated Colored Women."

was a great asset to Haines Institute.[77] Under Laney's supervision, Bethune honed her programmatic and organizational skills as well as her educational philosophy. Bethune's year at Haines gave her experience in an essentially all-female educational environment with primary, grammar, and normal and industrial courses. By example, Laney offered practical lessons in developing a variety of curricula, running an educational institution on a businesslike basis, engaging in community programs, and building networks with other black female activists.

During the year Bethune taught at Haines, she maintains she began reading about Booker T. Washington and Tuskegee Institute, the leading black industrial school in the nation.[78] It was during this year that Bethune began to dream of building a school. Bethune modeled her educational philosophy on her educational experience, although moderated by black women's specific experiences. Black female educators saw the need to offer job-related training since white racism limited employment and wages for black men. Most African American women would have to work to help support their families. Because of this basic need, schools taught the essentials of homemaking and several skilled trades, but the majority of schools did not make this the central focus of the curriculum. To undermine the white notion of black female immorality, most schools founded by women also offered programs that included classes in the social graces, homemaking, and religion designed to raise public opinion of black women's morals and values. Concepts of the importance of the "Talented Tenth" were also in evidence at many of these schools. Schools founded by those educated at southern missionary schools did not ignore liberal education; rather they included programs focused on preparing teachers and other black professionals. Coursework included and encouraged instruction in history, math, economics, and English, as well as other liberal disciplines.[79]

Bethune's objectives for the education of black girls reflected her training at Scotia Seminary and her work with Lucy Laney at Haines Institute. It included economic mobility through job training and preparation for leadership

77. June O. Patton, "Lucy Craft Laney," 694; Bethune, "Faith That Moved a Dump Heap," 33; Carter, "A Modern Matriarch," 79; Carter, "Within the Home Circle," 116; Mary McLeod Bethune, "A College on a Garbage Dump," 135, 143; "Autobiography," chapter 7; Keyser, "Life of Mary McLeod Bethune," chapter 7; Johnson interview, 37, 38; Bethune, "A Yearning and a Longing Appeased," 7.

78. Several sources report that Bethune visited Tuskegee during her year at Haines; however, there is no documentation this visit ever occurred. She did meet with Booker T. Washington in 1912 when he visited Daytona Institute. Untitled biographical notes in BFC I, 23.

79. Anderson, *Education of Blacks in the South*, 67.

through service to the community. This was the *practical* part of Bethune's educational philosophy. Early in her career as an educator, she believed that industrial education should have a place in the school curriculum, albeit a small place. However, she did not believe that only blacks should receive industrial education, or that it should replace cultural development. In a speech addressing the causes of interracial conflict, she clearly called for developing a variety of educational programs for African Americans. She specifically wrote that the states that had developed programs of industrial and agricultural training were not relieved "of the responsibility of providing means for the ambitious Negro youth to find himself in whatever line of cultural attainment his natural aptitude may lead." All people, she believed, regardless of "color or condition of life," deserved to develop their abilities.[80] Bethune strongly believed that a well-rounded education was the basis for the solution to interracial problems. She held that educators had a responsibility to identify the most gifted students and give them every opportunity for higher education and the development of individual talents. Bethune's dream of building an educational institution capable of producing professionals in the sciences, medicine, and law as well as political leaders reflected her *idealism.*[81]

Women generally envisioned schools as a center of community life as well as a place of learning. Since publicly sponsored social services were almost nonexistent for African Americans, faculty and staff were also responsible for providing necessary services for the entire black community. Schools often operated as social settlements, offering day and night classes and providing literacy and hygiene instruction for adults, and free Sunday afternoon entertainment and lecture programs. Perhaps the most important and significant aspect of Bethune's vision of education was her view of citizenship training. Like Du Bois and other Progressive era reformers, Bethune did not believe in neglecting citizenship training or silencing protest. She emphasized the right and duty of exercising the franchise and the necessity of taking every legal step possible to secure that right.[82]

After leaving Haines, Bethune taught at several missionary schools throughout the South. In 1897, while teaching at Kendell Institute in Sumter,

80. Mary McLeod Bethune, "What Causes Chiefly Impede Progress in Interracial Cooperation and Can We Hope to Make More Rapid Progress during the Next Ten Years," n.d., MMB.

81. Perkins, "The Pragmatic Idealism of Mary McLeod Bethune," 30–35.

82. Bethune, "Faith That Moved a Dump Heap," 33; Carter, "A Modern Matriarch," 79; Carter, "Within the Home Circle," 116; Bethune, "A College on a Garbage Dump," 135, 143.

South Carolina, she met and married Albertus Bethune. Bethune was originally attracted to Albertus because of his "beautiful tenor voice, his active
church life, and his initial interest in teaching." The couple courted, fell in
love, and married. However, Albertus left Avery Institute one year before
finishing the teaching program to allow his brother, Jesse, to enter the program. Albertus found a job in Savannah as a haberdasher, and the couple
moved there soon after their marriage. While teaching in Savannah at a
small missionary school in 1899, Bethune gave birth to her only child, Albert
McLeod Bethune. After the birth of her son, Bethune gave up her work for
a short time, but soon became restless. Having a child made her race work
more personal to her. When Albert was nine months old, she took a position
at a mission school in Palatka, Florida, under the supervision of Reverend
C. J. Uggans. Albertus gave up his job in Savannah and followed his wife.
Bethune spent the next five years there putting the lessons of Moody Bible
Institute into practice. She established a mission school, aided prisoners in
the county jail, and worked with young people. However, Bethune was not
happy in Palatka. She remembered having "difficulties" and being in "hard,
hard places." There was "hard sledding here. So few people could see what I
wanted to do . . . I felt Palatka was not the place."[83]

Bethune continued to look for a place to build her school—a place where
she could do the most for the race. When Reverend S. P. Pratt returned from
a trip to Daytona Beach, he told Bethune about a new settlement of black
workers and their families near the Florida city and suggested she visit there.
She arranged to go to Daytona Beach although her husband, Albertus, did
not support her goal. Albertus believed she was a "dreamer" who was "too
anxious to give of myself." Bethune remembered him chiding her, "You are
foolish to make sacrifices and build for nothing. Why not stop chasing around
and stay put in a good job?" However, Bethune was not looking for nor did
she believe she needed Albertus's approval. She had saved a little money by
selling insurance for the Afro-American Life Insurance Company and used
her savings to finance her trip to Daytona Beach. Bethune believed, "This
married life was not intended to impede things I had in mind to do."[84] In

83. Bethune, "Faith That Moved a Dump Heap," 33; Johnson interview, 37–38; "Mrs.
Bethune: Spingarn Medalist," 202, MMB; "Autobiography," chapter 7; Keyser, "Life of Mary
McLeod Bethune," chapter 7; Johnson interview, 37; Autobiographical statement, 5–6; Flem-
ing, *The Answered Prayer to a Dream*, 12, 21–23.
84. Mr. Albert Bethune, Sr., interview by Barbara Grant Blackwell, July 8, 1977, 218; "Mrs.
Bethune: Spingarn Medalist," 202; Fleming, *The Answered Prayer to a Dream*, 24–25; Keyser,

other words, Bethune did not look at her marriage as something necessitating compromises on her part. Her family and religious background and her exposure to other strong black women vindicated her insistence on working for the race. Nothing dissuaded her, not even the prospect of undermining her marriage.

The irreconcilable difference between the Bethunes was essentially a difference in perspectives. After Albert's birth, Albertus became intent on fulfilling the goal of providing for his family—becoming the male breadwinner. He believed this was possible only through business ownership, so he wanted to settle in one area and begin a business. Albert's birth had quite the opposite effect on Bethune. Having a child made the work of racial advancement all the more compelling, reinforcing her determination "to build better lives for my people,"[85] and particularly her son. Bethune decided to pursue her race work in an area where African Americans had little access to education. She obviously prevailed for a time as Albertus followed her to Palatka and then Daytona Beach. He attempted to establish several business enterprises in Florida—he opened a taxi service, and became a tailor and then a real estate agent—but did not succeed in any of these ventures. Unfortunately, no records have survived so it is impossible to analyze Albertus's attempts to create and maintain an economically independent standard of living. The strain on the marriage increased and the couple continued to grow apart as Bethune's race work took more of her time and energy. By 1908, the marriage was effectively over. Albertus left Florida and returned to Wedgefield, South Carolina, to live with his sister until he died of tuberculosis in 1918.[86]

The separation highlights the gender tensions experienced between traditional men and "New" women. Albertus believed in the "traditional" family as modeled by a male breadwinner and a female homemaker. Although there is no explicit evidence to support this analysis, he appeared to believe that the best way to overcome racial prejudice was to "prove" to whites that African Americans were worthy of equality by creating stable nuclear families following traditional nineteenth-century gender roles. Domesticity for women and business ownership for men could raise the status of blacks in the eyes

---

"Life of Mary McLeod Bethune," chapter 7. Albert Bethune, Sr., recalled that Reverend Uggans told Bethune about Daytona Beach, but Fleming and Keyser write that it was Reverend S. P. Pratt. Partial biographical statement, 6; Bethune, "Faith That Moved a Dump Heap," 34; Johnson interview, 31, 39.

85. Bethune, "Faith That Moved a Dump Heap," 34.

86. "Notes for Rackham Holt," 3.

of the dominant white culture. This was not the family model Bethune experienced, nor did her education and mentors prepare her for this role. Her experiences had imbued her with the idea that as an educated black woman she was socially responsible for uplifting the race. This was not about *individual* achievement; this was about *group* advancement. She also understood that race prejudice made it impossible for even educated, prosperous blacks to escape discrimination and negative stereotypes. No African American could rise unless all African Americans rose. This was the fundamental and irreconcilable difference between the couple. Bethune continued her work in Daytona Beach, believing that working for racial advancement and equality took precedence over all else.

About the same time that Albertus left for South Carolina, Bethune sent young Albert to Haines Institute to attend boarding school.[87] Was Bethune imitating the white upper classes in doing this? If she believed Lucy Laney's assertion that race women were responsible for nurturing and teaching children through their roles as mothers, why did she send Albert away to school? The answer lies in the lack of good schools available in Daytona Beach. Albert could not attend the school she intended to build, at least for the long term, because she was intent on building a school for black girls. Perhaps Bethune did not think the few church-associated missionary schools in Daytona Beach would give Albert the type of education she wanted him to have. Having experienced the quality of small missionary school education and remembering her own academic struggles at Scotia, perhaps she wanted something better for her son: an elementary and secondary education to prepare him to enter college. Since Bethune had worked with and greatly admired Lucy Laney, it is completely logical that she would trust Laney to give her son the best possible education to prepare him for a higher education and instill the moral values Laney and Bethune shared. Bethune was not neglecting her son, nor was she trying to evade her responsibility as a mother. In fact, seen through the lens of her experiences, she was doing the very best she could for him in an era of worsening conditions for African Americans.

∞

Bethune's personal life did not measure up to the conventional notions of nineteenth-century femininity. For a race woman, this created a prob-

87. Mr. Albert Bethune, Sr., interview, 220–21.

lem. During the 1890s, African American women were subject to increasingly negative stereotypes as liars, prostitutes, and thieves. A large part of the educated black woman's agenda for racial uplift rested on disproving and overturning these images, particularly through sexual respectability and stable marriage. Bethune reconciled this tension by working to make her personal life *appear* traditional. She presented a model of decorum, femininity, and studied propriety. Her appearance was always impeccable and her good manners rarely faltered. During this time, it was common for educated black women to experience long separations from their husbands in pursuit of their race work, so despite the separation from Albertus, her married life appeared acceptable.[88] She consistently introduced herself as "Mrs. Bethune" and insisted that all refer to her as such. Although this was a charade, Bethune's actions constituted an act of cultural resistance. At a time when whites routinely addressed black women by their first names or used the term "Auntie," Bethune's insistence on the formal title "Mrs. Bethune" forced whites to address a black woman with respect and her behavior served to undermine the popular image of black women as wanton and immoral. Although Bethune separated from her husband to pursue her race work, she succeeded in maintaining the illusion that her personal life remained within "proper" boundaries as determined by white society.

Bethune was not alone in her inability to combine marriage with race work. This was a common problem for black women activists, including her closest associates Charlotte Hawkins Brown and Nannie Helen Burroughs. Women activists faced these dual responsibilities with a variety of strategies and met with varying degrees of success. Mary Church Terrell and Lugenia Burns Hope successfully combined marriage and community work, primarily by building their reform activities around their husband's careers. Others often spoke critically about men and marriage and feared that marriage would force them to limit their race work. Bethune, Brown, and Jane Edna Hunter separated from their husbands because of their dedication to race work. A few black women, such as Dean Lucy Slowe of Howard University, chose not to marry, but to spend their lives with other women instead. Burroughs and

---

88. See White, *Too Heavy a Load,* 21–141; Gordon, "Black and White Visions of Welfare," 169–70; Stephanie J. Shaw, "Black Club Women and the Creation of the National Association of Colored Women," 434–35; Giddings, *When and Where I Enter,* 89–95; Shaw, *What a Woman Ought to Be and To Do,* 21–26. For examples of long marital separations for educated black women, see Gordon, "Black and White Visions of Welfare"; Gordon, *Pitied but Not Entitled: Single Mothers and the History of Welfare, 1890–1935.*

Lucy Laney did not marry but still took on the obligation of caring for parents, nieces, nephews, and foster children. In addition to her responsibilities as a single parent, Bethune also chose to take responsibility for the education of her nieces and nephews and several foster children. In one instance, she fostered an entire family of children. Bethune brought Edward Rodriquez, his brother, and his sister to Daytona Beach, giving all three the opportunity to get an education even though they had no ties to Bethune, no family, and no money. Rodriquez completed his undergraduate education at Bethune-Cookman and went on to Morehouse College and Atlanta University, where he earned a master's degree. He later became a career counselor and placement officer for Bethune-Cookman College.[89] Whether these women married and had children of their own or not, they commonly saw all black children as being in their charge, and they often took on the responsibility of caring for children other than their own. Marriage and race work was often incompatible, but educating children *was* the essence of race work. In establishing Daytona Educational and Industrial School for Negro Girls, Bethune would fulfill her dreams of educating young African American women to carry on the work of racial advancement.

89. See Mary Church Terrell, *A Colored Woman in a White World;* Rouse, *Lugenia Burns Hope,* 124–25 and 129–35; Wadelington and Knapp, *Charlotte Hawkins Brown;* Jones, *Jane Edna Hunter;* Evelyn Brooks, "Religion, Politics, and Gender: The Leadership of Nannie Helen Burroughs"; Brooks Higginbotham, *Righteous Discontent;* Mr. Edward Rodriquez interview by Barbara Grant Blackwell, July 8, 1977, 186, 188–89.

2

Daytona Normal and Industrial Institute for Negro Girls

After five years of "rough sledding" in Palatka, Florida, Bethune traveled to Daytona Beach, arriving in September 1904, with $1.50 in cash and her dream of building a school. She found a small, four-room cottage that rented for $11 per month and talked the black owner, John Williams, into accepting her $1.50 as a deposit on the rent until the end of the month. To raise money, she visited ministers and persuaded them to let her to take up collections during Sunday services. She "buttonholed" every woman who would listen to her and asked for contributions. She sold ice cream and sweet potato pies to railroad workers to raise money. She burned logs and saved the charred splinters for pencils, mashed elderberries for ink, and scavenged the city dump and trash piles for old linens, cracked dishes, kitchenware, and broken chairs for her school. Then, on October 3, 1904, Bethune opened the doors of the Daytona Educational and Industrial Training School for Negro Girls to a total enrollment of five little girls aged eight to twelve whose parents paid fifty cents per week tuition.[1]

This legendary account of the establishment of Daytona Institute finds its way into articles and books written about Bethune's life. It is a celebratory

---

1. Johnson interview, 32. The five girls were Lena, Lucille, and Ruth Warren, Anna Geiger, and Celest Jackson. See Fleming, *The Answered Prayer to a Dream*, 23. Autobiographical statement, 23; Bethune, "Faith That Moved a Dump Heap," 34; Carter, "A Modern Matriarch," 79; Carter, "Within the Home Circle," 116; Bethune, "A College on a Garbage Dump," in Lerner, *Black Women in White America*, 135, 143.

tale reinforcing the image of the mythical black woman educator who relied exclusively on her distinctive abilities to build a local institution detached from the larger economic, social, and political questions of the day. This mythical woman with her story of individual success becomes "the exceptional Negro" of her era. She is safe and apolitical. But Bethune was not safe and apolitical. While she actually did buttonhole women, spoke at Sunday services, and made pies and ice cream to sell to raise money for her school, she engaged in very carefully calculated actions as well. Her interaction with community leaders and active participation in the political life of the community add substance and depth to her legendary exploit. In Daytona Beach, Bethune successfully tapped into an existing wellspring of community activism and threw herself into community work built upon a solid foundation. With community support, Daytona Institute quickly became much more than a school for black girls: it became a center of black political activism and the training ground for a new generation of black women activists. Community activism and solidarity in Dayton Beach empowered Bethune; within two decades, she rose from newcomer to political leader.

Bethune's choice of Daytona Beach as the place to build a school was not accidental; it was a carefully calculated decision. Reverend Pratt suggested the area, but that was not reason enough for Bethune to invest in building a school there. The five years of being in "hard, hard places" in Palatka had taught Bethune some very important lessons about community support. Upon her arrival in September 1904, Bethune met with several of Daytona Beach's most influential black leaders, where she learned a number of important things about the population, culture, economy, and politics. Since the town's incorporation in 1876, African Americans had been present in Daytona Beach. Many of the original black residents migrated from the all-black town of Freemanville, a few miles to the south. Two black men, Thaddeus Goodwin and James Tolliver, were among the founding fathers and remained a part of the Reconstruction city government; black men maintained their voting rights. They were not emasculated in Daytona Beach. African Americans constituted 45 percent of the population and lived in three black neighborhoods: Midway, Norcross, and Newton, located west of the railroad tracks. There were three main black churches, a black-owned drugstore and grocery store, a Masonic Lodge, and an Odd Fellows lodge. Among the longtime residents, black men worked as blacksmiths, carpenters, masons, and teamsters while women were primarily domestic servants or laundresses. The vast majority of the families were industrious and self-supporting. Moreover, Daytona Beach's black population was growing rapidly as hundreds more African Americans came to work for Henry Flagler on the construction of the Florida East Coast Railroad. These newer residents were mostly menial laborers, and their families tended to be uneducated. Bethune said she saw them enduring "dense ignorance and meager educational facilities, racial prejudice of the most violent type—crime and violence."[2]

In 1899, the wealthy white women of the Palmetto Club agreed to support black schools, believing it was in the best interests of the city to help educate black children;[3] still, educational opportunities were limited. The local school boards provided funding for a limited number of black schools. There was one public kindergarten, one public elementary school, and a few church-run schools. Within the entire state of Florida, there were only three or four state-supported public high schools for black students. Moreover, all black public schools had four- or five-month terms and only taught lessons through the sixth or seventh grade level. White schools held nine-month terms and public education for whites was available through the twelfth grade.[4]

The presence of wealthy white regular and winter residents originally from the "abolitionist strongholds" of Ohio, New York, Michigan, and Massachusetts tempered incidents of overt racial violence,[5] but Daytona Beach was home to an active chapter of the Ku Klux Klan. As in other American cities, the KKK hoped to intimidate blacks, to discourage them from demanding equal treatment and trying "to get out of their place." In 1907, the KKK lynched a local black man who "dared to stand up for his rights" and then paraded his body through the streets. In addition to select incidents of overt violence, African Americans suffered daily indignities as well. The railroad tracks and canals divided the town into black and white districts. While white store owners accepted African Americans as customers, they never allowed blacks to work in their stores. Most black women sewed clothes for their families, but when forced to patronize white-owned stores, African Americans had to

2. "Autobiography," chapter 7; Keyser, "Life of Mary McLeod Bethune," chapter 7; Autobiographical statement, 5–6; Leonard Lempel, "African American Settlements in the Daytona Beach Area, 1866," 108–24; Fleming, *The Answered Prayer to a Dream*, 23–24; Bethune, "Faith That Moved a Dump Heap," 34.

3. Lempel, "African American Settlements in the Daytona Beach Area, 1866," 108–24.

4. Autobiographical statement, 13; Lucy Miller Mitchell, interview conducted by Cheryl Townsend Gilkes on June 17 and 24 and July 1, 6, and 25, 1977, 13.

5. Lempel, "African American Settlements in the Daytona Beach Area, 1866," 108–24.

buy goods without knowing if they fit properly. If something did not fit, they could not return it. They either had to try to alter the item themselves, or try to sell it or give it to someone else.[6]

In spite of instances of physical, material, and psychological oppression, there were signs that Daytona Beach was the right place to begin building a new life and a new institution. The black community in Daytona Beach flourished. Mothers, fathers, grandmothers, aunts, and uncles built close-knit extended families. Children played hopscotch, baseball, and "house," and went to Sunday school. Existing black businesses were well established and seemed to be sound. Neighbors helped each other in times of sickness and death. Fraternal organizations served the needs of their members and worked to protect the community when race relations became strained. The church was a center of the community, with baptisms and revivals a major part of the religious and social life.[7]

Establishing Daytona Institute became a community effort from the beginning. Mrs. Susie Warren, a widow, laundress, and devoted Christian, housed Bethune and young Albert until she located a place for her school. When Daytona Institute opened its doors in October 1904, Lena, Lucille, and Ruth Warren were among its first five students. Warren also introduced Bethune to others who helped in starting the school, including John Williams, the black carpenter and real estate owner who rented Bethune the first cottage that served as the school. Later, Williams would help construct Faith Hall, the first building at Daytona Institute. Dr. Texas Adams and his wife, Ladosia, became Bethune's closest friends and confidants. Adams served as the physician at McLeod Hospital from 1911 to 1975 and on the board of trustees for more than fifty years. Reverend A. L. James of Bethel Baptist Church and Reverend J. Cromatia of Mount Zion A.M.E. Church served on the first board of trustees established in 1904. Local men built tables and benches from cast-off wood and orange crates. Several local women worked as primary school teachers, sometimes without pay for long periods, to show their support for the school. Women often sponsored chicken suppers to raise money to pay the grocery bills or teachers' salaries. They donated used dishware and clothing and offered vegetables from their gardens for food. It was a difficult financial period for Bethune, but she recalled that she did not see lack of money as a major obstacle. Bethune remembered, "I had faith in a loving God, faith in

6. Mitchell interview, 14.
7. Ibid., 15–16.

myself, and a desire to serve."[8] As she saw it, these were her greatest assets. However strong her faith and desire to serve, they were not the only things that pulled her through the hard times. Bethune received substantial support from the black community; the burden of establishing the school was not hers alone.

Daytona Institute expanded rapidly. Within two years, the school had 250 female students who Bethune believed were "hampered by lack of educational opportunity" yet needed a "distinctive education" because of the "unique responsibility" of these girls in the world. As the school grew, Bethune began implementing some of the institution-building techniques Wilson used in Mayesville. To control expenses, she slowly began to buy property and raise money to construct buildings rather than renting them. Reverend Cromatia, who was also a real estate agent, helped Bethune purchase her first piece of land, a field used as a dump called "Hell's Hole," near the school. The asking price was $250. Bethune made a $5 down payment and signed a note promising to pay the remaining $245 within two years.[9]

As a newcomer, Bethune knew she had to appeal to the black community at large to garner their support for the school, and most provided a great deal of material aid and gave their endorsement. Many community leaders knew education was important, and Bethune remembered they gave "their cooperation with my idea of starting a school."[10] However, black support for Bethune was not unanimous. There were members of the community who saw her as promoting an educational experience that would best fit young black girls for menial and subservient positions. When Bethune attended a service at one local church, the pastor saw her among the congregation and launched a scathing attack against her and the school. He told the congregation that Bethune wanted to teach her students to be servants and obedient to white masters. He castigated her methods and curriculum and then said he would rather see his daughter in hell and taught by Satan than under the influence of

8. Fleming, *The Answered Prayer to a Dream*, 23–24; Albert Bethune, Sr., interview, 218; "Mrs. Bethune: Spingarn Medalist," *Crisis*, 218; Mitchell interview, 16–17; "Contributions List, 11th year, Beginning June 1st 1914," BFC I; Bethune, "Faith That Moved a Dump Heap," 34.

9. Mary McLeod Bethune, "A Philosophy of Education for Negro Girls," n.d., MMB; Fleming, *The Answered Prayer to a Dream*, 24; Bethune, "Faith That Moved a Dump Heap," 34; see also Catherine Owen Peare, *Mary McLeod Bethune*; Emma Gelders Sterne, *Mary McLeod Bethune*; and Holt, *Mary McLeod Bethune*; Lerner, *Black Women in White America*, 134–43.

10. Johnson interview, 31.

Mary McLeod Bethune.[11] Although this specific incident is unverifiable, as a newcomer, Bethune undoubtedly faced opposition. There certainly would be opposition from those who saw Bethune as an "outsider" trying to dictate what was best for a well-established community in which black men played a dominant role. For those who opposed the Tuskegee idea, Bethune's decision to include "industrial" in the name of the school equated her educational philosophy with Booker T. Washington's accommodationism. There is no indication that Bethune challenged this opposition either publicly or privately. Perhaps she decided that it would be best to go about "fitting in" and not gain the reputation as an outsider who was responsible for internal divisions in the black community. Cultivating supporters and finding her place in this community without gaining the reputation as a divisive influence would be in the best interests of the children and most beneficial to the school. Or perhaps Bethune told this story to prove she was "safe" to white philanthropists in the area. Nevertheless, Bethune's intuitive ability to know when publicly to challenge others or move ahead quietly was one of her strongest assets.

Bethune took a realistic approach in founding the Daytona Educational and Industrial Training School for Negro Girls. She knew she needed as much support as she could possibly get from the local black community, individual philanthropists, and the larger educational funds available in the white world. Like many other black teachers, she declared her support for "industrial education," then quietly went about focusing the curricula on academic subjects and insisting that blacks receive the same kinds of education as whites.[12] Bethune did everything feasible to win the support of these diverse benefactors, even if that meant developing a creative flair for changing her presentation of the school, its students, and the curriculum to fit the expectations of her audience.

One of the most compelling reasons for Bethune to choose Daytona Beach was that many wealthy whites, such as James N. Gamble, president of the Proctor and Gamble Company of Cincinnati, Thomas H. White, president of the White Sewing Machine Company, and Harrison Garfield Rhodes, a playwright and author,[13] vacationed in Daytona Beach. Bethune's past experiences

11. Holt, *Mary McLeod Bethune*, 75. Holt offers no additional information about this incident. Other secondary sources are so complimentary they make no mention of any opposition, and the primary sources lack any information on any such incident.

12. Adam Fairclough, " 'Being in the Field of Education and Also Being a Negro . . . Seems . . . Tragic': Black Teachers in the Jim Crow South," 65–91.

13. James N. Gamble was the son of Proctor and Gamble founder James Gamble and a chemist who invented Ivory Soap in 1879. Thomas H. White was the founder of the White

taught her that despite strong support from black residents, it was unlikely the school would survive without philanthropic support. Philanthropists often provided the funds necessary to supplement teacher's salaries, buy equipment, and construct buildings as well as help with necessary day-to-day expenses. She was also aware that the General Education Board, the Slater Fund, the Jeannes Fund, and the Phelps-Stokes Fund all supported black education that reinforced the existing structure of the southern political economy and believed that the amount and type of education blacks received should be limited. In short, they endorsed a model of black education focused on developing the skills and habits necessary to a dependable, subservient workforce.[14] Booker T. Washington's model of industrial education best served their goals.

Washington publicly indicated his belief that the study of science, mathematics, literature, and foreign language was impractical for the vast majority of blacks. Rather than seek higher intellectual pursuits, they should concentrate on learning skills geared toward meeting what he called "community needs." Tuskegee Institute offered two types of instruction: an elementary academic program that prepared students to pass teacher certification exams, and a program focused on training in manual labor. All students were subject to a strict routine of social discipline. The goal of the teacher education program was to train black teachers who would then go out into the communities and start new schools modeled on Tuskegee. Teacher training was a means of spreading Tuskegee's industrial education philosophy and acculturating African Americans into the New South economy; to make sure they understood their place in this new economy. To achieve this, blacks could not be ignorant, as ignorance impeded the economic advancement of the region. But Tuskegee did not teach students academic subjects that were beyond their station in life, and moral and religious instruction fostered conservative tendencies. Supporters designed programs to build character and mold the ideology of prospective teachers. "Industrial education" glorified the dignity of common labor and celebrated hard work as the means to economic advancement. Advocates organized industrial education around a conservative sociopolitical ideology that discouraged blacks from seeking basic social and political equality. According

---

Sewing Machine Company in 1858. Harrison Garfield Rhodes wrote many travel books, plays, and short stories, including *A Guide to Eldorado; Marietta's Miracle; Marrying the Twins; The Escapade; The Felt Hat; The Flight to Eden;* and *Worldly Letters to a Debutante.*

14. Fred L. Brownlee, "Educational Programs for the Improvement of Race Relations: Philanthropic Foundations," 329–39; Anderson, *Education of Blacks in the South,* 80.

to historian James Anderson, "'Education for Life' meant training to adjust to a life carved out for blacks within an oppressive social order."[15]

At Tuskegee Institute, Washington urged his students to develop the habits and skills—good farm management, thrift, patience, perseverance, high morals, and good manners—that would win them an economic, and eventually a social and political, place in southern society. According to Washington, the greatest need for the black man was to prepare for the "opportunities of freedom."[16] Many whites liked what they saw as Washington's relative disinterest in political and civil rights for blacks. Most did not appreciate that Washington's public pronouncements merely indicated that because blacks were starting with so little they would have to work their way up to positions of power and respectability. They overlooked the implicit assumption of eventual acceptance and integration in Washington's message. Few recognized the expectation of full entrance into the professions, and they did not seem to notice that Washington sent his children to college. Hearing only what they wanted to hear, many major educational funds accepted Washington and the Tuskegee model of industrial education as the ultimate solution to the "Negro Problem." In time, industrial education became a euphemism for consigning blacks to inferior economic, social, and political status, and whites made Booker T. Washington the gatekeeper for the flow of philanthropic monies to black schools.[17]

Although Bethune publicly professed her admiration for Washington and Tuskegee, she did not adhere to the Tuskegee idea in founding Daytona Institute. Instead, Bethune quietly manipulated the situation rather than publicly

15. Washington, "Industrial Education for the Negro"; see also Meier, *Negro Thought in America*, especially chapters 6 and 7. In support of the view of the Tuskegee model described here, see Louis R. Harlan, *Separate and Unequal: Public School Campaigns and Racism in the Southern Seaboard States, 1901–1915*; Anderson, *Education of Blacks in the South*; Donald Spivey, *Schooling for the New Slavery: Black Industrial Education, 1868–1915*; Henry S. Enck, "Black Self-Help in the Progressive Era: The 'Northern Campaigns' of Smaller Southern Black Industrial Schools, 1900–1915," 73–87; Henry S. Enck, "Tuskegee Institute and Northern White Philanthropy: A Case Study in Fund Raising, 1900–1915," 336–48. For an opposing view, see Arnold Cooper, *Between Struggle and Hope: Four Black Educators in the South* and Robert R. Moton, *Finding a Way Out*; for a more complex assessment see Drago, *Initiative, Paternalism, and Race Relations*. Spivey, *Schooling for the New Slavery*, 26–28, 79. See Carter G. Woodson, *The Mis-education of the Negro*; Enck, "Black Self-Help in the Progressive Era," 79–80; Anderson, *Education of Blacks in the South*, 57.

16. Washington, "Chapters from My Experience."

17. See W. E. B. Du Bois, "Of Mr. Booker T. Washington and Others," in *The Souls of Black Folk*; Enck, "Black Self-Help in the Progressive Era," 79–80; Enck, "Tuskegee Institute and Northern White Philanthropy," 336–48; Spivey, *Schooling for the New Negro*, 81.

confront her benefactors. Washington publicly denounced programs that emphasized studying science, mathematics, literature, and foreign language; this type of education was useless. However, this is exactly the course of study Bethune pursued at Scotia Seminary. She could not have missed the direct connection between Washington's remarks and her educational experience, yet because she needed his support, Bethune did not challenge Washington outright. Rather, she quietly put her "useless" classical liberal education to use in service to the race. She made it her mission to found a school that would train black women as community leaders, empower them, and instill an intense commitment to racial advancement and social service in them. Her goals included teaching girls and young women to become professional teachers, nurses, librarians, and social workers; ultimately, they were to combine economic independence with community activism to uplift the race.[18] Daytona Institute's curriculum would strongly resemble that of Scotia Seminary, and Bethune would use actions, not words, to vindicate classical liberal education.

Missionary-based education differed significantly from the industrial education model. The principal focus of missionary schools was teacher training based on a classic liberal tradition, and centering on literary and professional training for the development of a black leadership class to fight for political and civil equality. Classical education imbued these intelligent, self-confident women graduates with race consciousness and a commitment to community. Female teachers became role models of economic independence, intellectual accomplishment, and race work. Schools such as Scotia Seminary included manual labor requirements, but only to the extent that this work would instill habits of industry and defer some costs of educating the students. "Manual training" was not a part of the instructional program. The inclusion of the term "industrial" in the names of many schools represents a pragmatic approach to fund-raising. After 1881, the John F. Slater Fund began offering financial help exclusively to those schools offering black industrial education. These small schools could not afford to turn their backs on funding from any source, so the number of schools adding vocational training to their curricula began increasing rapidly. However, the founders and teachers in many of these schools were products of a classic liberal education, and although the schools touted new courses in industrial training, industrial education never replaced

18. Beverly Guy-Sheftall, "Daughters of Sorrow: Attitudes toward Black Women, 1880–1920," 134.

the classical liberal curriculum. Like many blacks educated in the missionary schools of the South, Bethune's educational philosophy incorporated her missionary training at the Trinity Mission School and Scotia Seminary while adding Moody's emphasis on Christian democracy and Lucy Laney's concepts of public leadership roles for women. Her professed goal was to "train students to become strong, useful Christian women, to afford them an opportunity to learn a vocation, so that . . . they may be self-supporting, and by precept and example . . . help to improve . . . the communities in which they live. A sound body, a trained mind, hand and heart, is our idea of complete education."[19]

This decision significantly decreased Bethune's long-term chances of success, as by this time most of the larger educational funds did not endorse programs that emphasized leadership training for African Americans. If Bethune was unable to convince Washington to endorse her school, she would need independent wealthy benefactors who supported her vision of educating young black women to uplift the race; men such as Gamble, White, and Rhodes fulfilled that requirement. She also looked into women's groups in the area and found that upper-class white women of the Palmetto Club continued to support black children's education.[20]

Although her chances of successfully gaining Washington's endorsement were slim, Bethune dutifully paid court to him. She knew she would need his approval to obtain financial support from the larger education funds. In March 1912, Washington visited Daytona Institute as part of a tour of black schools in Florida. After this visit, Bethune used her association with Margaret M. Washington in the National Association of Colored Women's Clubs (NACW) as a tool to gain further notice from Washington. In March 1915, Margaret Washington visited the school. Her comments to Washington resulted in him sending his personal envoy, Charles Fearing, to visit Daytona Institute. On March 11, 1915, Fearing reported to Washington on the impressive progress the school was making in educating students and in its

19. Anderson, *Education of Blacks in the South*, 35, 67–68; Richardson, *Christian Reconstruction;* Butchart, *Northern Schools, Southern Blacks, and Reconstruction;* Jones, *Soldiers of Light and Love;* Drago, *Initiative, Paternalism, and Race Relations;* Carlson, "Black Ideals of Womanhood in the Late Victorian Era," 62–65; *Southern Workman* 14 (March 1885): 25; James D. Anderson, "Historical Development of Black Vocational Education," 181–85; Robert G. Sherer, *Subordination or Liberation? The Development of Conflicting Theories of Black Education in Nineteenth Century Alabama,* 64, 133; Autobiographical statement, 22; Fleming, *The Answered Prayer to a Dream,* 27–28.

20. Johnson interview, 31.

involvement with the "rural people." He also commented on the quality of teaching, the facilities, the farm and hospital, and the support of the local black and white people. In light of Fearing's positive assessment, on March 15, 1915, Washington replied, expressing his interest in Bethune and Daytona Institute. Washington wrote to Fearing, "I wonder if it would not be worth while for us to consider taking this school somewhat under our control and treat it in the same way as we treat Snow Hill, etc. Supposing you 'feel' Mrs. Bethune on this point, if you are there."[21]

Fearing completed his follow-up visit to Daytona Institute in April 1915. He reported to Washington that Bethune had left for New York the day before his arrival, but he spoke to Harrison Rhodes, who was then vice-president of the board of trustees. Rhodes assured Fearing that the board and Bethune wanted to "secure Tuskegee's backing in the work" and wished Washington to consider becoming a trustee. Fearing suggested Washington take this under serious consideration as Bethune had surrounded herself with a "strong and helpful board of trustees." He also noted that the school was currently debt free and Bethune was beginning to make "permanent improvements . . . in the way of more substantial buildings." He also noted that Bethune had made an application to the General Education Board (GEB) for help, and "Mr. Rhodes wonders if you are willing to write Dr. Buttrick concerning this." Fearing pointed out to Washington that "There is a large population of Northern people who spend the winter in Daytona, some of whom are wealthy, and a visit on your part to Daytona would be very helpful, not only to Mrs. Bethune's work, but to your own work as well."[22]

Despite Margaret Washington's encouragement and Fearing's assessment of the possible benefits of a working relationship between Washington and

21. Perkins, "The Pragmatic Idealism of Mary McLeod Bethune," 32; "A Press Release of Washington's Tour of Florida," dated March 8, 1912, in *The Booker T. Washington Papers,* vol. 11, 482–86; Bethune, "Faith That Moved a Dump Heap," 34; *Booker T. Washington Papers,* vol. 13, 256; Booker T. Washington to Charles H. Fearing, March 15, 1915, in *Booker T. Washington Papers,* vol. 13, 255. Snow Hill was one of a number of small, independent, nondenominational black private institutions. By the early 1900s, educational funds such as the General Education Board, Slater Fund, and Phelps-Stoke fund were embarking on a campaign to transform existing black secondary and normal schools into Hampton-Tuskegee–style industrial teacher training schools. See Anderson, *Education of Blacks in the South,* 136–37.

22. Wallace Buttrick was an original member of the Southern Education Board. He was also among the original trustees of the General Education Board, established by John D. Rockefeller in 1902, to promote the Hampton-Tuskegee model of industrial education throughout the South. Charles H. Fearing to Booker T. Washington, April 16, 1915, in *The Booker T. Washington Papers,* vol. 13, 272–73.

Daytona Institute, Washington did not become involved. On May 25, 1915, just five weeks after Fearing sent his letter, Bethune wrote Washington asking for his help in raising twelve thousand dollars. She asked for a personal donation of one hundred dollars as well as his assistance in obtaining money "from any of the Funds."[23] Washington's reply left no doubt that his refusal was retribution for Bethune's decision to use a northern organization for fundraising:

> I have been under the impression lately that the expenses of your school were being taken care of by an organization in New York of which your school is a member; that is, I understand the organization has agreed to be responsible for all current expenses so that the principles of schools will not have to spend their time in traveling about seeking money for their individual schools. If an organization is to be supported with headquarters and then each individual is to travel and incur the same expense as heretofore in getting money for schools, I can see no advantage in the organization. But, as I have stated, my understanding is that in the future you are to be relieved personally from collecting money and traveling in the interest of the school.[24]

Unfortunately, no records survive naming the organization for which Washington had such an aversion. The records that remain of contributions to Daytona Institute for 1914–1915 do show one contribution of "Cash N.Y. Meeting $46.00" and is followed by a list of individual contributions from New York residents ranging from two hundred dollars to fifty cents, but indicates no fund-raising organization. There is some indication, however, that Bethune was considering joining such a group. Notes from a meeting that took place on March 31, 1915, clearly show that a Dr. Watson from New York made a presentation to southern educators about fund-raising strategies and goals including publicity, building a constituency, systematic applications for raising money, and employing a field agent.[25] Moreover, when Fearing arrived on April 16, 1915, to meet with Bethune, she had left for New York the day before his visit. Most likely, this is what Washington referred to in his reply to Bethune's request for help. Since any monies raised in this way

23. Mary McLeod Bethune to Booker T. Washington, May 25, 1915, in *The Booker T. Washington Papers*, vol. 13, 292–93.
24. Booker T. Washington to Mary McLeod Bethune, May 31, 1915, in *The Booker T. Washington Papers*, vol. 13, 297.
25. "Contributions List, 11th year, Beginning June 1st 1914," BFC I.

would be beyond his control, he would be unable to use the threat of funding cuts to influence Bethune's operations or curriculum. Since his stated goal was to make Daytona Institute another Snow Hill, Bethune's interest in Dr. Watson's arrangement destroyed Washington's plans. Washington's death in November 1915 resolved the issue.

Harrison Rhodes's interaction with Fearing is also contradictory. It would appear that both Fearing and Rhodes were using this visit to advance their individual agendas: Fearing to gain additional wealthy contacts for Washington, and Rhodes to secure Washington's endorsement for Daytona Institute's funding request to the General Education Board. Rhodes was close to Bethune and he certainly understood her ambitions for the school. Just a year earlier, Bethune had threatened to walk away from the school if the board of trustees did not approve her plan to expand the curriculum to include high-school-level education. Bethune did not promote an educational program that relied on industrial training. While she believed practical training was necessary to ensure economic self-sufficiency, she insisted that all children should be educated to the level of their unique abilities and capabilities. In 1911, several white members of the board of trustees challenged Bethune's educational vision. Black education was in transition in Florida. As an increasing number of elementary facilities became available for black children, Bethune wanted Daytona Institute to expand its curriculum to focus on high-school-level work. Many students at Daytona Institute were ready for a high school curriculum, but high schools for black students statewide were few in number. If Daytona Institute's curriculum remained at the elementary level many young women in the area would be limited to an eighth-grade education. This situation had serious implications for the future of the race in general and these young black women in particular. When Bethune presented her new curriculum to the board, several trustees argued against her plan to expand the curriculum, contending that eight grades were enough for blacks. Bethune rose to the challenge. She told the members of the board that she would not tolerate any attempt that impeded her from teaching her students to the full measure of their capabilities. She went on, saying, "I called you in here to assist me not tie my hands. In my estimation, my people need just what in your estimation your people need. I am not going to permit anybody to say that. . . . Before I will let you tie my hands, I will give you what I have done this far, and I will go in the Palmetto and start another." Bethune stormed out of the meeting as Gamble called on the board to form a committee to study the need for an expanded curriculum. Several hours later Gamble appeared at Bethune's home to apologize for the actions of the board and to assure her that they would not stand in the way of her plans or handicap her in any way.[26]

Bethune's approach was quite different than that of her friend Charlotte Hawkins Brown at Palmer Memorial Institute. Brown depended entirely on northern philanthropists for financial contributions, and particularly on Galen Stone, a Boston broker and businessman. Brown allowed Stone to guide Palmer's development by directing Brown to cultivate local white businessmen, sending accountants to Palmer to "set her books in order," and securing a per capita payment from the county for each child attending Palmer. When Stone decided that Palmer was too dependent on Brown, he forced Brown to undertake negotiations with the American Missionary Association to "provide control and regular support for Palmer."[27] Bethune knew that inequality in state funding for black education made white philanthropic support essential. She saw white philanthropy as a means to an end, drew prominent whites into her corner, and tried to get whatever she needed from them. When necessary, she could be very diplomatic and accept some things that she found condescending, and even objectionable, to advance black education. She also found that at times quiet manipulation was ineffective; she learned that sometimes it was more effective to be confrontational. She firmly believed that educational decisions that affected the lives of black children belonged in the hands of black parents, educators, administrators, and professionals. Donating money or materials did not give white philanthropists the right to make life-altering decisions for black children. Bethune believed that the time for white paternalism had passed, saying, "the white man has been thinking for us too long; we want him to think with us now instead of for us."[28] While she strongly advocated interracial cooperation, she abhorred and refused to tolerate whites making decisions for black children that would profoundly affect the course of their lives. Rhodes was well aware of this incident, so his comments to Fearing regarding the desirability of a close relationship between Tuskegee and Daytona Institute were pragmatic. Daytona Institute would be more secure with GEB funding; Rhodes sought to secure that funding.

26. Johnson interview, 13–14.

27. Sandra N. Smith and Earle H. West, "Charlotte Hawkins Brown," 195; See also Gilmore, *Gender and Jim Crow*, especially chapter 7; Wadelington and Knapp, *Charlotte Hawkins Brown*.

28. Elaine M. Smith, "Mary McLeod Bethune and the National Youth Administration," 153.

Bethune did what she needed to do to secure new buildings, better books, equipment, or money for salaries.[29] She did manage to get a limited amount of support on an individual basis from philanthropists such as John D. Rockefeller. White philanthropists possibly believed they could use their wealth and influence to coerce her into adopting the Tuskegee model. According to historian James Anderson, in the early twentieth century, philanthropists often donated money to small private schools like Daytona Institute that were not under the influence of missionary societies, religious organizations, or state authorities. Their goal was to acquaint the school founders with the educational funds, then use the threat of cutting their financial aid to take control and transform the schools from classical liberal education to the Tuskegee model. Such was the case of Fort Valley High and Industrial School in Fort Valley, Georgia. Founder John W. Davidson worked hard to establish the school and put it on solid financial footing between 1890 and 1896, to no avail. In 1896, Davidson brought in James Torbert to assist him and act as financial agent for the school. In his capacity as financial agent, Torbert made monthly trips to the North, eliciting between three and five thousand dollars annually. This helped with normal expenses, but was insufficient to create an endowment or construct additional buildings. Hoping to put the school on a more stable financial footing, Torbert stacked the board of trustees with white northern industrialists. In what appeared to be a stroke of genius, he convinced philanthropist George F. Peabody to serve. This brought Fort Valley to the attention of the General Education Board; the institution was touted as the prospective Tuskegee of Georgia's Black Belt.[30] This changed the course of Fort Valley's history.

Davidson assured Peabody that from the beginning it was his desire to make Fort Valley an industrial school on the model of Hampton and Tuskegee. This was untrue. Davidson's real desire was to create a secondary and normal school modeled on the Atlanta University system. For reasons known only to him, Torbert wrote Peabody that Davidson was not interested developing an industrial program; he was using that pretext to attract funds that he diverted into building a liberal arts institution. Consequently, "school inspectors" from the philanthropic funds began visiting Fort Valley and quickly began guiding the school down the Hampton-Tuskegee path. When David-

29. According to Adam Fairclough, a significant number of African American male and female teachers often transformed themselves in order to gain white funding. See Fairclough, "Being in the Field of Education and Also Being a Negro . . . Seems . . . Tragic," 65–91.

30. Anderson, *Education of Blacks in the South,* 115–17.

son realized his position was in jeopardy, he struggled to convince fund directors that he had been converted and now worshiped at the altar of industrial education, but they had lost faith in him, ultimately removing him from the school he had founded. After a careful search, and in consultation with Booker T. Washington, the GEB hired Henry Hunt as Fort Valley's new principal. They watched Hunt carefully to ensure his commitment to industrial education, and rewarded him for his compliance with large grants well into the 1930s.[31]

Bethune had to tread lightly. She played the game well with individual industrialists, but received no support from educational funds in the early years. When inspectors visited Daytona Institute, Bethune was careful to focus on the industrial departments and talk about training "her girls" in domestic science, farm work, and food preparation. However, like Davidson at Fort Valley, Daytona Institute's "industrial" departments were actually departments in name only, existing primarily to reduce day-to-day operating expenses. By this time, inspectors were more careful in ferreting out "sham" schools.[32] Daytona Institute did not receive any support from any educational funds until the 1935–1936 fiscal year when the Slater Fund and the GEB contributed to salary and building accounts.[33] This was long after Daytona Institute merged with Cookman College under the auspices of the Methodist church, and well after the educational funds began assisting black colleges. Bethune maintained control over curriculum and mission of the school, but funding often fell far short.

Because of these circumstances, Bethune saw that the most important job was "to be a good beggar!" and she had to do her best work among the prominent white visitors in the area. Like many other school founders, she made door-to-door appeals to wealthy whites in the area. She wrote personal letters to northerners, emphasizing her humility, hard work, self-sacrifice, and strong character. These appeals told of her difficulties and her faith in education as the means to uplift the race, and asked for donations to help educate African Americans so they could make the transition from a dependent people to independent citizens of the nation. She sent school publications and newsletters that stressed the virtues and industriousness of the students as well as the graduates' success in racial uplift. These publications

31. Ibid., 120–27.
32. Ibid., 118.
33. "Contributions List, 11th year, Beginning June 1st 1914," BFC I; "Contributions List September 1935–March 1936," BFC I.

also told of the school's immediate and long-term financial needs, implying that their donations would solve the "southern problem." Bethune made numerous trips to the North where she met with philanthropists and wealthy whites, speaking at churches and clubs, and organizing local chapters of the Mary McLeod Bethune Circle and Birthday Clubs to disseminate information and raise money for the school. In 1937, Bethune hired Gerald W. Allen as a financial agent to raise funds in the North for the school. Like at Fisk University, she organized a choir and arranged for the children to present programs at local resort hotels. After the choir performance, she talked about the school and its mission to the prominent winter visitors and solicited funds. In the winter of 1914–1915, the choir performances at local resort hotels raised almost four hundred dollars for the school. Daytona Institute secured additional funds from selling their farm produce and crafts, and realized a small profit from operating the McLeod Hospital. Bethune accepted donations of books, kitchen items, food, cleaning supplies, material, and clothing. She was impeccably polite and gracious when she approached upper-class whites, and proud of her ability to cajole, praise, and charm them into making donations and becoming members of her board of trustees or advisory board. As with other small private school founders, Bethune packed her boards with wealthy white members; of the original twelve board members only Reverend James and Reverend Cromatia were black. In addition to Gamble, White, and Rhodes, over the years the list of advisers and trustees included Jane Addams of Hull House; Robert Moton, successor to Booker T. Washington at Tuskegee; Theodore Roosevelt; Robert Vann, owner of the *Pittsburgh Courier;* and Senator Frederick Walcott of Connecticut.[34] By giving these prominent people a visible role, Bethune hoped to increase their interest in the school, and, in turn, the size of their donations.

However, with so many "worthy" causes competing for their donations, many philanthropists were careful to "test" the worthiness of those asking for funds. Bethune rigorously kept track of all contributions through meticulous records, treating each donation as important no matter how small. According to Bethune's recollections, in two cases Daytona Institute reaped enormous

34. According to Enck, Bethune's efforts reflected common forms of fund-raising for almost all small schools in the South. See Enck, "Black Self-Help in the Progressive Era," 76–78; "Contributions List, 11th year, Beginning June 1st 1914," BFC I. There is no available evidence to supply the first names of James and Cromatia. However, it is likely that they both strongly supported Bethune and Daytona Institute, thus their appointment to the first board of trustees. Advisory Board and Board of Trustees lists dated 1928, 1936, and 1938, BCC.

benefits because of her insistence on keeping such accurate records. One day a Mr. J. S. Peabody visited the school to "look around." He seemed quite interested and told Bethune he would be "in again sometime to see you." He reached into his pocket and gave her a twenty-five-cent donation. Although greatly disappointed, Bethune graciously thanked him, gave him a receipt, and then duly entered his donation in her account book. Three years later Peabody visited Bethune and asked her if she remembered his donation to the school. After asking his name and the date of his visit, she looked him up in her account book and said, "Oh yes, Mr. Peabody, you gave us twenty-five cents." Peabody was so impressed that she had bothered to keep track of such a small donation that he handed her a check for two hundred dollars and arranged to provide a scholarship for the education of one girl each year. When Peabody died a few years later, he bequeathed Daytona Institute ten thousand dollars.[35]

Another story Bethune often told was about Mrs. Flora Curtis, a wealthy white woman who wintered in Daytona Beach. Each day Curtis would come to the student-operated farm to buy ten cents' worth of carrots. Frank Taylor, the farm manager, would pick the vegetables for Curtis, who insisted on inspecting every vegetable before she accepted it. Curtis would then go to the office and pay Bethune for the carrots. She watched as Bethune recorded each individual transaction in her account book. Although the story is somewhat unclear, at some time during the summer of 1921, Bethune sent Curtis a newsletter and asked for a donation that she apparently did not make. However, when Curtis passed away the following year, her will specified that Daytona Institute receive eighty thousand dollars for the construction of a new building, which Bethune appropriately named Curtis Hall.[36]

The lesson in the stories Bethune related about her experiences with Peabody and Curtis was straightforward. Her careful record keeping led to great financial gains for the school, and Peabody and Curtis demanded nothing in return for their generosity. Bethune needed to court philanthropists simply to cover annual expenses, increase staff and salaries, and donate money for new buildings. She used her dealings with white philanthropists to hone her diplomatic skills. This was her political training ground, and it served her well for her later work within the New Deal. Thomas White donated the cottage for McLeod Hospital in addition to sewing machines and beds for students. Both James Gamble and White gave substantial sums for running

35. Autobiographical statement, 20.
36. Ibid., 34.

the hospital and purchasing Bethune's home, Faith Hall, and additional land. White lobbied the city council on Bethune's behalf to provide city electric and water services to the school and bequeathed it seventy-nine thousand dollars upon his death. Harrison Rhodes organized the first Christmas carolers of the school and helped Bethune win Carnegie Foundation grants to purchase books for the school library. Moreover, Bethune used her relationships with her white trustees to open new funding doors. Rhodes introduced her to the Astors, Guggenheims, Vanderbilts, and Pierponts. Mrs. Frank Chapman, a regular wealthy winter resident, invited the Carnegies, Mellons, and Rockefellers to the Ormond Hotel to hear the choir sing and Bethune speak. Eventually, these meetings lead to sizable grants from the General Education Board authorized by John D. Rockefeller, Jr. Bethune also organized the wives of wealthy industrialists into an advisory board that worked to furnish living quarters and the infirmary for the students. In 1911, the women's advisory board organized an annual bazaar to raise funds for the school.[37]

Yet, no matter how hard she worked compared to schools like Tuskegee, Daytona Institute wallowed in poverty. Washington founded Tuskegee in 1881 with a meager annual state subsidy of $2,000 and a first-year fundraising return of $855.83. By 1900, however, cash contributions totaled $236,163.40, which did not include the endowment fund (begun in December 1899) of $152,232.49. By the time of Washington's death in 1915, annual cash receipts totaled $379,704.83, while the endowment fund swelled to $1,970,214.17. In comparison, between June 15, 1914, and May 15, 1915, Bethune raised a total of $11,831.68 plus material donations of books, wood, clothing, and bandages. As of June 30, 1933, the school had a $9,958 deficit. Even with support from the GEB, Board of Education of the Methodist Episcopal Church, and Slater Fund, receipts for September 1935 through March 1936 totaled only $23,603.17.[38] There were no funds for an endowment, and no stable sources of money for growth and expansion. As a black woman educator, Bethune had to work harder to get less.

Bethune believed her duty to the race was preparing young black women to use their "heads, hearts, and hands" to shape opportunities for African

---

37. Rackham Holt, *Mary McLeod Bethune,* 135–39; Fleming, *The Answered Prayer to a Dream,* 23–25.

38. Enck, "Tuskegee Institute and Northern White Philanthropy," 336; "Contributions List, 11th year, Beginning June 1st 1914," BFC I; Accounting records to the General Education Board, September 30, 1933, BCC; "Contributions List," September 1935–March 1936, BFC I.

American men and women. She taught young black women in her charge to become a force that was eminently qualified to take on administrative, managerial, and professional positions. Following Laney's example at Haines, Bethune used the school to advance an informal curriculum designed to instill a commitment to racial progress. During Daytona Institute's first year of operation, Bethune was principal, guardian, nurse, cook, maid, and educational mentor, passing along the principles of social responsibility mastered from family, religious, and educational experiences. The school became her workshop for forging intergenerational networks. She once commented that each generation should be free to move in its own direction, but if it "does this without roots or without hooking onto something, pretty soon it becomes disillusioned, it becomes deradicalized, it becomes much more conservative."[39] Throughout her life, Bethune worked with young black women to ensure their sense of history, to make sure they had a solid footing. African American women could not afford to become complacent or conservative. Bethune encouraged her students to fight inequality by example, and her school reflected Bethune's beliefs about the role of African American women in society.

One of the original students at Daytona Institute, Lucy Miller, recalled Bethune's firm belief in empowerment through community action, unselfish concern for others, and an unwavering insistence on self-respect. Bethune developed community outreach programs designed to undermine racial inequality. By 1911, she established the Tomoka Mission for children of workers in a turpentine camp located about five miles from the school. She assigned students to teach the children at the camp. After running the school for five years, Bethune convinced the county superintendent of schools to visit. After his inspection, the county took over running the school, although it held classes for only three months a year. Bethune also set up a reading room, a community center for men, a Better Boys Club modeled on the white YMCA, a summer school and playground, and a farmer's institute. She instituted racial uplift projects that aimed to make women better wives and mothers, such as classes in home hygiene and child care. Bethune built the McLeod Hospital and Training School for Nurses after a white superintendent at a sanatorium refused to admit a sick child unless Bethune took her through the back door. Bethune looked the woman in the eye and reportedly said, "I will *never* go to your back door; I will put my girls on my back and walk to St. Augustine, where I can go in at the front door—so Good bye." Soon after, Bethune began fund-raising to build the hospital and began a visiting nurse service in

39. Dorothy Irene Height, interview conducted by Polly Cowan on April 10, 1974, 73.

Daytona Beach.[40] While these programs did not question inequality directly, they did serve to undermine black oppression and improve the quality of life for many African Americans.

Under Bethune's direction, Daytona Institute made significant contributions to community life in Daytona Beach considering its precarious financial position. Yet, Bethune's insistence on personally overseeing to every detail of its day-to-day operations and management hindered its possibilities for growth and expansion. Bethune's workday stretched from 5 A.M. until after midnight. She taught class, saw to the administration of the school, personally conducted individual and group fund-raising campaigns, and did community work. She began each school term by quieting the fears and anxieties of the children and began each day's activities with a prayer. Besides daily prayers, Bethune conducted weekly "chapel talks" to encourage her students to develop spiritual growth and integrity. One of her most common expressions was, "You are being trained to serve, go out into your community and be an example of what education and training can mean to the individual. Help your fellow man." Bethune passed on her absolute belief that "through God's power all things are possible," and trained "her girls" to become aware of their moral responsibility to their community and their race. To paraphrase one of Bethune's mottoes, students at Daytona Institute entered to learn and departed to serve. She often told her students, "This is not just for you, this is for you to take back to the women who could not come." Education was not something individuals kept for themselves; educated black women had an obligation to share what they learned with others. Students became "strong, useful Christian women" trained and able to improve their communities.[41]

In 1912, Bethune began hiring formally trained administrators and teachers to assist in running the school. The first college graduate she hired was Frances Reynolds Keyser, who served as the first academic dean and laid the foundation for serious academic work at Daytona Institute. Keyser had run the White Rose Mission for delinquent black girls in New York before taking the job with Bethune at Daytona Institute. Keyser was also responsible for Bethune's involvement in the National Association of Colored Women, and

40. Mitchell interview, 16; Fleming, *The Answered Prayer to a Dream,* 29–30; Dr. T. A. Adams, "As I Recollect," n.d., BFC I; Lerner, ed., *Black Women in White America,* 142; Holt, *Mary McLeod Bethune,* chapters 10 and 12.

41. Mitchell interview, 17, 20; untitled autobiographical notes, 31; Autobiographical statement, 30; Henrine Ward Banks interview by Barbara Grant Blackwell, July 7 and 8, 1977, 180; Fleming, *The Answered Prayer to a Dream,* 27–28.

introduced Bethune to Margaret Murray Washington and Mary Church Ter-rell (see chapter 3). By 1915, there were eight women teachers and one male farm manager on the staff: Portia Smiley, superintendent of industries; Lucille Jenkins, history and geography; LaUrsa W. Snelson, teacher and stenogra-pher; W. Belle Davis, primary teacher and penmanship; Lucinda M. Jeffer-son, sewing; Harrietta E. Reynolds, domestic science; Alice Van Derezee, music; Anita Pickney, matron and housekeeper; I. E. Bryan, farm manager. The school provided classes in history, geography, mathematics, penman-ship, music, religion, and speech as well as sewing, cooking, and domestic sciences.[42]

Despite hiring a well-trained and competent staff, Bethune continued to personally oversee every detail; she did not allow any shortcuts. She encour-aged students to do every job to the best of their ability. She told them, "Any work is honest however humble," and "In whatever you do, strive to be an artist."[43] Bethune understood that not every student was destined for a college education. She encouraged those not bound for higher education by stressing that manual labor was honest labor and encouraging these students to strive to be the best at whatever kind of work they chose. After all, blue-collar work required almost as much education as professional work. Brickmasons, elec-tricians, and other blue-collar workers had to know how to read blueprints, create designs, use mathematics, and complete an apprenticeship. Rather than favor one type of training over another, Bethune encouraged full training in a student's chosen field.[44]

Bethune also personally attended to students' problems. She had a natural rapport with young people, and according to former student Lucy Miller, she invariably knew when something was wrong, or if something was upset-ting a student. She was sensitive and understanding of any problem, seeming instinctively to know and understand the behavior of adolescents. Students respected Bethune, and felt comfortable taking their problems to her.[45] In return, the students supported Bethune. In 1930, students signed and sub-mitted a resolution to the faculty to remove a trustee, Dr. Seth J. Hills, as he "grossly insulted" Bethune causing her to "suffer a very humiliating or un-deserved impertinence." Students also resented Hills for trying to "use his office as Trustee to wield undesired influence in the administration of student

42. Fleming, *The Answered Prayer to a Dream,* 27–30.
43. Mitchell interview, 19.
44. Albert Bethune, Jr., interview by Barbara Grant Blackwell, July 7 and 8, 1977, 227.
45. Mitchell interview, 17–20.

affairs."[46] Unfortunately, no record exists regarding either the nature of Hill's insulting behavior or his ultimate fate, yet it is obvious that Bethune's unique qualities made the educational experience at Daytona Institute extraordinary.

Still, Bethune hampered the institution's potential growth through her inability to delegate routine tasks. As academic dean, Keyser should have controlled curriculum development, guided teachers, and seen to student problems. Under Keyser's guidance, teachers should have instructed and mentored students. Bethune was a charismatic speaker, captivating audiences with her life story; fund-raising should have been the centerpiece of her efforts. By delegating routine tasks, she would have had more time to work with the board of trustees and advisory board, make new contacts, develop an endowment fund, and expand the physical plant. Her inability to "let go" put the school at financial risk for many years.

Bethune's experience in building Daytona Institute was also her political training ground. The ratification of the Nineteenth Amendment giving women the vote marked a turning point in women's political participation. Bethune's personal transition from informal to formal political leadership in Daytona Beach came during the 1922 mayoral election. Two candidates competed for mayor; one promised to build a new high school for the black community, and the other had the endorsement and support of the Ku Klux Klan. Bethune, as well as other progressive black and white citizens, supported the first candidate. On the eve of the election, Bethune learned that the KKK was going to retaliate against the black community for its opposition to the Klan-endorsed candidate by destroying Daytona Institute. Miller recalled Bethune telling the faculty that the Klan intended to march on the campus and burn some buildings. She said that the black men in the community had been advised, would be on campus, hundreds strong, with ammunition, and if there was any move by a Klansman to set a fire, there would be violence. "But God is not going to let that happen," she said. "I am going to be there to protect this campus."[47]

Miller, who had graduated from Talladega College and returned to Daytona Institute to teach, and other faculty members made sure the students were safely in the dormitories and then stationed themselves around the campus. In the bright moonlight, Bethune stood in the quadrangle at the entrance

---

46. Resolution to the Faculty of Bethune-Cookman College from the Class Officers and the Student Council dated January 9, 1930, MMB.
47. Mitchell interview, 20.

to the school with her arms folded as the Klansmen entered the campus. Ac-cording to Miller, Bethune's actions exemplified the courage of black women in the face of danger. She reportedly stood in the center of the quadrangle while the hooded Klansmen marched in the front gate, around her, and out the other entrance of the campus. Despite KKK intimidation, Bethune rallied the five hundred black voters at six the next morning and led them to the polls, where they waited until they cast their ballots. They voted for their candidate and got their high school.[48]

In 1938, Bethune related a slightly different version of the same story. She remembered seventy-five or a hundred hooded Klansmen walking around the grounds trying to intimidate and frighten her from leading black voters to the polls the next day. According to Bethune's version, the Klan members marched around the campus chanting "white supremacy, white supremacy!" After the students began to sing a hymn, the Klansmen left campus. The next day Bethune "was out in the street with a band of women as far back as you could look." She led them up to the polls where they "stood for hours and hours until we got our chance to cast our votes."[49] Bethune's courage in facing the Klan was beyond question. However, this incident also illustrates Bethune's deep commitment to changing the social and political practices in Daytona Beach and her insistence on the right of African Americans to the ballot. Moreover, her understanding of the use of the ballot as a political weapon and her mobilization of the community in defense of individual and civil rights despite threats of physical violence and material destruction were certainly her most important accomplishments that night.

Bethune's commitment to formal protest was growing, but she was selec-tive in its use. The resurgence of the Klan in the 1920s made it unwise to be indiscriminate in mounting public protests against segregation. Bethune did not openly endorse integration, and informal political actions continued to be her primary weapon to effect change. Daytona Institute's Sunday community program was one such tool. On Sunday afternoons, students presented pro-grams for the community that featured musical selections and poetry readings.

48. Ibid., 20–21.
49. Minutes of business meeting held on November 26, 1938, Series 2, Box 1, Folder 4, NCNW, 54–55. This business meeting was a National Council of Negro Women's meeting that in part addressed advancing women's participation in the government. As such, it is likely that Bethune used it as a platform for emphasizing the importance of *women's* role in the political process. This does not mean that male voters were absent in Daytona Beach at the time this incident took place.

After the student program, Bethune always spoke about such things as improving current standards of living, black history, and the contributions of the race. She used these meetings to instill a sense of race pride in her students, as well as in the community. She consistently urged audiences to "Hold your heads up high! Look every man straight in the eye and make apology to no man because of his race or color." She would always tell the audience, "Look at me, I am Black, I am beautiful."[50]

White philanthropists and tourists heard about the musical and literary programs held on Sunday afternoons, and asked to attend. Again, Bethune used these opportunities to make her position on southern racial practices clear. She answered that everyone was welcome, but there would be no segregated seating. Miller remembered that in 1922 whites and blacks sat side by side in Daytona Institute's auditorium in spite of state segregation policies. They enjoyed the folk music, heard students speak or read a poem, and listened while Bethune talked of her hopes and ambitions for African Americans.[51] Bethune's stand on this issue was legendary. In 1948, a National Urban League representative reported that Bethune-Cookman "has maintained a firm position as a bulwark of democracy down through the years. . . . Her visitors have subscribed to her philosophy apparently without any outward signs of opposition."[52] Throughout the years, Bethune steadfastly refused to conform to southern racial segregation practices on the Bethune-Cookman campus.

Bethune's refusal to conform to local segregation laws was her way of publicly expressing her antipathy to Jim Crow laws. This incident illustrates a fundamental dilemma faced by all school founders: how to attract white support and maintain self-respect. Reconciling these two goals was often difficult, and at times founders sacrificed their ideals to ensure financial survival. Charlotte Hawkins Brown at Palmer Memorial Institute chose to obey public segregation rules. When arranging concerts by Palmer Musical groups, Brown reserved "the entire middle aisle for our white friends," and asked local sponsors to arrange ticket sales to African Americans "if you have a balcony or gallery."[53] Northern supporters demanded this behavior as the price of their

50. Mitchell interview, 22.

51. Ibid.

52. Report of Southern Field Division from George L. Edwards to Nelson C. Jackson, April 7, 1948, NUL, 1–2.

53. Smith and West, "Charlotte Hawkins Brown," 199; Tera Hunter, "The Correct Thing: Charlotte Hawkins Brown and the Palmer Institute," 38–40.

financial support. Disparaging them in private correspondence as tying "my hands so I can't speak out when I am being crushed," Brown publicly assured outsiders and reduced southern hostility by declaring that Palmer was not infusing "social equality into the veins" of the students.[54] Brown could not long tolerate what she considered as affronts to her personal dignity and became more aggressive, but she remained cautious longer than Bethune in dealing with southern segregation.

Bethune's insistence on integrated seating at Daytona Institute was only one of the stories that circulate about her refusal to accept segregation. She often told a story about being a passenger on a train when a conductor became traditionally familiar by saying, "Auntie, where is your ticket?" Bethune ignored him and kept reading, which she intended to be an affront. He went through the car a couple of times, each time asking for her ticket in the same way. Finally, he came around and shook her arm and said, "Auntie, where is that ticket? Get that ticket out. I've been asking you for that ticket." Bethune looked up at him and said, "Well, which one of my sister's boys are you?" He did not call her "Auntie" again and retreated from the car in a hurry.[55] In 1946, Bethune refused to attend a Women's Action Committee in Louisville, Kentucky, because black delegates were not allowed to stay in the hotels.[56] Throughout her life, Bethune consistently fought segregation. She never validated this policy through passive acquiescence. She often openly traversed racial boundaries. Her constant denial of inferiority based solely upon race reaffirmed an inherent race consciousness, and a sense of self-esteem and self-respect in the students and the community.

As educational facilities for younger students began to expand, Daytona Institute enlarged its high school and junior college training, and its curriculum changed accordingly. By 1922, Daytona Institute offered two courses of study: academic and vocational. All students took courses in home economics. Students not bound for college trained in the necessary skills to find a good-paying job. The school introduced clerical courses for those interested in pursuing a career. What was more important, Bethune used changing state requirements for teacher certification to expanded the curriculum and include courses necessary for college admission, including the addition of Latin and modern languages. Daytona Institute sought to offer a well-

54. Smith and West, "Charlotte Hawkins Brown," 200; Wadelington and Knapp, *Charlotte Hawkins Brown*, 57–58.
55. Vivian Carter Mason interview by Barbara Grant Blackwell, July 8, 1977, 183.
56. Mary McLeod Bethune to Charlotte Hawkins Brown, April 4, 1946, BFC II.

rounded curriculum.[57] According to a news release, "The graduates and former students of the school enter the fields of teaching, the ministry, the professions, nursing, agriculture business, journalism, law and statesmanship, or seek advanced technical or collegiate training."[58]

By the early 1920s, Bethune realized that she could no longer carry all of the responsibility for the school alone. She was now in her mid-forties and worried that if she became ill or incapacitated, the school would have to close. She handpicked Lucy Miller to assume her role and administer Daytona Institute. Bethune constantly told Miller that she wanted her to assume the "mantle of leadership" and continue "to give service to your people" through the administration of the school. When Miller decided to marry Joseph Mitchell and move to Boston rather than take over at Daytona Institute, Bethune was very upset and openly expressed her disappointment. Frustration and disapproval over her protégés' choice of marriage over activism became a pattern in Bethune's interactions with the young women she mentored. Bethune openly expressed the same feelings of disapproval to Jeanetta Welch Brown, who decided to marry during Bethune's tenure as president of the National Council of Negro Women. Remembering her husband Albertus's insistence on eliminating community work after the birth of her son, Bethune feared that "when a young girl takes a husband to herself she must take another course. Husbands come first." In 1946, she commented, "If some of you girls could only stay single long enough to do some of the important things that I have in my mind, but you must take unto yourselves your husbands and then it is necessary for you to see after them and administer to them. The two free-est [sic] women in the world at the present time are Eleanor Roosevelt and Mary McLeod Bethune."[59] According to Bethune, marriage undermined a young woman's strong commitment and dedication to race work even when these young women married men who were also committed to race work. Bethune believed these women would put their husband's race work above their own and assume support roles rather than leadership roles.

Despite the fact that Miller-Mitchell and Brown decided to marry and despite Bethune's misgivings, these marriages did not deter their community work. Miller-Mitchell dedicated a large part of her life to improving conditions for children in Boston. She worked to set state standards for adequate training for day care and nursery school teachers. She served as an

57. Mitchell interview, 25.
58. "News-Release," n.d., MMB.
59. Mitchell interview, 24–25; Mary McLeod Bethune to Jeanetta Welch Brown, December 15, 1945, May 23, 1946, BFC II.

original member of the board of directors of Freedom House, a community action program designed to involve local people in the improvement of neighborhood conditions in the predominantly black Roxbury area. Miller-Mitchell was also active in local chapters of the United Negro College Fund (UNCF), the NAACP, the Urban League, Alpha Kappa Alpha Sorority, and Links. Brown became executive secretary of the National Council of Negro Women (NCNW). After moving to Detroit in 1946, Brown helped organize the United Auto Workers (UAW) at the Ford automobile plant in Detroit, worked in conjunction with the Detroit Metropolitan Council of the NCNW, was active in women's associations, and campaigned for the Michigan state legislature.[60] Both credited Bethune for instilling them with a strong commitment to community service and racial advancement.

Bethune knew that to ensure Daytona Institute's continuation, she needed secure, businesslike support. However, she knew that state aid was not a viable alternative for her. She did not want the school to come under control of the state legislature. The state could then demand segregation in extracurricular activities such as the Sunday literary and musical programs, something Bethune had fought so hard to undermine. She also wished to maintain the freedom to conduct religious programs. Her main objective in looking for financial stability became to preserve Daytona Institute's status as a private institution. With that goal firmly in mind, Bethune decided that even insecure private funding was preferable to state funding, and in 1923 Daytona Institute merged with Cookman Institute of Jacksonville, Florida, under the auspices of the board of education of the Methodist Church. The merger created Bethune-Cookman College, an accredited coeducational college with more than four hundred regular students, a thirty-two-acre campus, property worth more than $800,000, and an operating budget of $70,000.[61]

Under this arrangement, the Methodist Church administered financial affairs and Bethune retained her full freedom of expression in school policy. Bethune liked this merger because of the financial arrangement, and she could retain full control over Bethune-Cookman's educational mission. However, she also remained responsible for the bulk of the fund-raising activity, personally raising nearly $85,000 each year to meet operational expenses. During the depression years of the 1930s, Bethune solicited funds from all quarters. She wrote to trustees, such as Senator F. C. Walcott of Connecticut,

60. Mitchell interview, 65–80; Jeanetta Welch Brown to Halena Wilson, October 16, 1943, NCNW; Jeanetta Welch Brown to Mary McLeod Bethune, May 10, 23, 1946, BFC II.
61. Carter, "Within the Home Circle," 116.

literally begging for pledges. She sent each board member a letter outlining the four main goals she hoped to achieve in the next year, including securing $300,000 for an endowment, buildings, and maintenance, along with a copy of the financial report. In 1936, Bethune was still sending these "begging letters" to the trustees as well as letters about specific problems to the board of education of the Methodist Episcopal Church. Bethune's contacts and resources at the National Youth Administration also benefited Bethune-Cookman. By the 1936–1937 academic year, students were receiving NYA funds. In 1937, the Log Cabin, a social center and cafeteria, became an NYA work project, and in 1938 Bethune-Cookman received a $2,700 NYA grant to begin a cafeteria training program. In 1942, Bethune-Cookman was operating a $35,000 workshop as part of the NYA program, and Bethune announced a plan whereby the college would become self-sustaining through increased food production as part of a war conservation effort in exchange for NYA funding for a student work-study program. At the end of the war, the school was named as a Veterans Administration Guidance Center.[62] Government funding kept Bethune-Cookman going during the Great Depression and increased its fortunes during and after World War II, although all means of securing funds, including hiring a financial agent, fell short of Bethune-Cookman's needs.

In 1937, Bethune hired financial agent Gerald E. Allen to solicit funds in the North. Allen dutifully sent reports to Bethune about his efforts, but by September 1937, there were few tangible results from his work. Bethune wrote Allen that it was "difficult for me to convince my trustees and business men and hold their faith" in furnishing his salary and expenses without returns. She suggested that Allen becoming a member of the college staff until the end of his contract would better serve Bethune-Cookman. Bethune frankly told Allen that if "we cannot find the money to cover our field work we cannot carry it on."[63] Another problem Bethune had with Allen was his propensity to enlarge his activities without her knowledge or consent. After a report arrived from Allen in early October 1937, Bethune was furious. Allen

62. Banks interview, 183; Dr. Florence Lovell Roane interview by Barbara Grant Blackwell, July 7 and 8, 1977, 216; Liliane R. Davidson, "Bethune-Cookman College Gears to New War Production Program"; Mary McLeod Bethune to Senator F. C. Wolcott, January 28, 1930, BCC; Form letter to Trustees from Mary McLeod Bethune March 25, 1930, BCC; Mary McLeod Bethune to Emmett J. Scott, November 4, 1936, BCC; Mary McLeod Bethune to Merrill J. Holmes, November 19, 1936, BCC; Fleming, *The Answered Prayer to a Dream*, 62; William T. Comer to William H. Gray, Jr., April 29, 1946, BFC II.
63. Mary McLeod Bethune to Gerald E. Allen, September 11, 1937, BCC.

had taken it upon himself to approach a Mr. Schiefflin to act as treasurer for the endowment fund. She wrote:

> Mr. Allen, I very definitely requested you to remain in the field of our maintenance and that the program for the endowment will be worked out by our Executive Committee and the committee we had appointed in New York . . . I am very frank to say that I just don't quite grasp your attitude in this matter. We need your services, Mr. Allen, to secure funds for our daily running. . . . There are certain people we do not want tampered with at this time. . . . I asked you when you were going out in the field that if there were certain people who should be approached, you would notify me, and I just can't understand the attitude you are taking in this whole thing.[64]

By February 1938, the board of trustees dismissed Gerald Allen.[65] But Allen was not alone in raising Bethune's ire.

Dr. Abram L. Simpson became acting president of the school in 1937. Within two years, he learned about the high cost of questioning Bethune's educational vision. Simpson and Bethune corresponded routinely about school operations, curriculum, and funding. Although Bethune selected Simpson for his position, she was not entirely happy with his performance. Disaster could possibly have been averted, but Simpson made a fatal mistake. In January 1938, an interviewer from the General Education Board visited the school (then Bethune-Cookman College) to assess the amount of funding, if any, the board should offer for a new library. During the visit, Simpson told the interviewer the school put "undue emphasis upon a college-preparatory course and too little emphasis upon 'terminal' occupations." He insisted the school needed more "emphasis on industrial arts" and expressed his desire for an "activities building" rather than a new library. He wanted space on campus to teach "painting, carpentry, masonry, etc." He also candidly told the interviewer that his "biggest problem was learning how to work with Mrs. Bethune and carry on constructively and with her approval."[66] Two issues in the report sealed Simpson's fate. Programs and curriculum were subjects not open to debate or question, particularly with "outsiders." Bethune was adamant about developing student's maximum capabilities. For Simpson to suggest that the

---

64. Mary McLeod Bethune to Gerald E. Allen, October 12, 1937, BCC.
65. Gerald E. Allen to Mary McLeod Bethune, February 25, 1938, BCC.
66. Elizabeth L. Ihle, ed., *Black Women in Higher Education: An Anthology of Essays, Studies, and Documents*, 213–14.

school should focus on vocational training not only jeopardized funding for the new library but also repudiated thirty-four years of Bethune's work. Another thing Bethune could not abide was a public show of disunity. She often reminded her colleagues to keep their disagreements "inside." Airing "dirty laundry" weakened the entire school in the eyes of outsiders. Simpson's allusion to the difficulty of working with a headstrong, domineering woman violated that edict. In March 1939, as Simpson's contract as acting president was about to expire, he received a letter from Bethune that said, in part

> Your coming to Bethune-Cookman College was my own dream and request, and certainly no-one [sic] would be more eager for your success than I. I have given careful study to your administrative ability as it has been reflected in the Institution, to your business ability, as you have followed through the business program of the school. I have found, through unbiassed [sic] study, that your administrative ability, your business follow-up and your ability to check on the details of the school's operation, do not fit into the pattern of this Institution. They do not indicate that you are the person we are seeking here.[67]

Under the circumstances, for Bethune to invite Simpson to stay on for the following year was "hypocritical"; therefore, she dismissed him, effective July 1, 1939.[68] Bethune brooked no challenge to her authority in defining the mission of the school and seeing that mission fulfilled. On July 1, 1939, despite her full-time work as director of Minority Affairs in the National Youth Administration, her continuing efforts to build and lead the National Council of Negro Women, her continuing duties as chair of the Headquarters Committee of the National Association of Colored Women, and increasingly severe and long-lasting bouts of asthma, she again took the reins of Bethune-Cookman and the search for a new president ensued.

Bethune continued her personal fund-raising efforts for the school. As late as October 1942, she was traveling to raise funds. In October she embarked on a fund-raising trip to California with First Lady Eleanor Roosevelt. Mr. and Mrs. Garfield Merner, philanthropists concerned with helping blacks and other underprivileged people of the South, opened their home to fifty friends who came to hear Mrs. Roosevelt speak about Bethune-Cookman's role in developing "wise leaders among colored people." Bethune told the Merners and

---

67. Letter from Mary McLeod Bethune to Abram L. Simpson, March 10, 1939, BCC.
68. Ibid.

their friends of the problems of black education. After returning to Florida, she wrote to Mrs. Ferris J. Meigs that it was "a glorious meeting" and was "sure of results."[69]

In late 1942, Bethune-Cookman finally found a new president, installing James A. Colston to that post in January 1943. Colston understood that Bethune would find it difficult to "let go," yet took on the challenge, asking just one thing of the board of trustees and Bethune: to make him president in fact, not just name. Two years later, Colston resigned because his "service had not satisfied Mrs. Bethune." According to Bethune, Colston took her "suggestions and explanations of the motives of the school" too "lightly." Like Simpson, Colston was never free of Bethune's "guiding hand" in operating Bethune-Cookman. He found himself in the position of constantly answering to Bethune and addressing her viewpoints on college matters, although Bethune insisted she did not expect Colston to consider all of her ideas. Nevertheless, she insisted she did expect him to "welcome from me suggestions and recommendations particularly for the working out of these points for your own strength and permanency."[70] Bethune criticized Colston for his "secretiveness" and unwillingness to confer with other long-term college staff. This was particularly evident during one episode. According to Bethune,

> I can never forget the evening in the dining room, when I made a plan for an appreciable number of stronger women whose influence and administrative power on the campus might be felt among the girls and young inexperienced teachers. The tone of your voice when you said so cold-bloodedly to me—"What is it that you want women to do on this campus that they are not doing now? The girls are being cared for and the women's council is going."[71]

Bethune's first reaction was to stop advising Colston, but she reconsidered after thinking about the "forty years of my life blood that I have poured into the building of that institution." She then decided it was her right to advise the president, trustees, and alumni association of the things she wanted incorporated into the program "until her dying day." Although she admitted

69. "Mrs. Roosevelt Guest at Merner Home, Hillsborough," *Times and Daily News Leader,* San Mateo, California, October 3, 1942; Mary McLeod Bethune to Mrs. Ferris J. Meigs, October 15, 1942, BFC I.

70. Form letter from Mary McLeod Bethune, December 31, 1943, BCC; Fleming, *The Answered Prayer to a Dream,* 77; Mary McLeod Bethune to James A. Colston, January 26, 1945, BFC II.

71. Mary McLeod Bethune to James A. Colston, January 26, 1945, BFC II.

Colston had the ability to get the school accredited, and she appreciated his "earnest efforts," she doubted his ability "to build from this point the institution my soul has unfolded." Like Simpson, Colston could not measure up to Bethune's standards in meeting the administrative needs of the college.[72]

No matter what Simpson or Colston did, neither was going to meet Bethune's standards for Bethune-Cookman for two reasons. First, by this time it was impossible for Bethune to separate herself from the institution. She had become the institution; everything that happened at the school reflected on her personally. Any failure in the program became a personal failure. Consequently, Bethune became increasingly assertive, demanding, and dominating when it came to administrative decisions and maintaining the public perception of the school. Simpson and Colston were unable to develop a working relationship with Bethune. Perhaps they did not consider her attachment to the institution she built, or they may have believed they knew what was best for Bethune-Cookman. More likely, they wanted freedom from Bethune and the main privilege of the office of the presidency: primary authority. This was the one thing Bethune was unwilling to relinquish. No matter what Simpson and Colston did or did not do, ultimately Bethune was unwilling to accept them because she never wanted a male president at Bethune-Cookman. She wanted Lucy Miller Mitchell, her handpicked successor and personal protégé, or at least some other strong, young woman, to take the position as president of the school. Apparently Bethune sought suggestions from her closest friends, including Charles S. Johnson, director of the Department of Sociology at Fisk University. Johnson offered Bethune the names of four women he believed qualified for the position "offhand" and promised to follow up with more suggestions. However, by July, Bethune seemed to have abandoned the idea of a woman president and wrote asking Johnson to speak to a Mr. J. C. Evans, who was to be at Fisk the following week, about "the importance of a strong well prepared man to carry on the work of the college."[73] There is no explanation for this change of heart, but it is likely that the board of trustees insisted on a male president to carry on the work. If that was the case, it was one of the few times the board prevailed over Bethune's wishes.

☙

72. Ibid.; Mary McLeod Bethune to Herbert Davidson, March 18, 1945, BFC II.
73. Mitchell interview, 24–25; Mary McLeod Bethune to Charlotte Hawkins Brown, April 4, 1946, BFC II; Charles S. Johnson to Mary McLeod Bethune, April 18, 1946, BFC II; Mary McLeod Bethune to Charles S. Johnson, July 9, 1946, BFC II.

Bethune worked to create her role as an educational and political leader in Daytona Beach. The role she created was grounded in her family, community, and educational experiences. Her grandmother, Sophie, and mother, Patsy, provided models of strength, character, and community responsibility. Emma Wilson at Mayesville Institute and Lucy Laney of Haines Institute had taught her the art of institution building. Teachers at Scotia Seminary reinforced ideas of equality and the possibilities of educated black womanhood. Experiences at Moody Bible Institute demonstrated the application of religious teachings to society. Using these relationships and experiences as her foundation, Bethune created the Daytona Educational and Industrial Training School for Negro Girls to promote female education. Yet, Daytona Institute was more than a school for black girls. Under Bethune's guidance, the school became a "protopolitical" tool.[74] Young women, such as Lucy Miller Mitchell, learned organizational skills, how to define community interests, develop networks, pool resources, and build a stronger sense of collective consciousness. Bethune used Daytona Institute to prepare a new generation of female political activists.

Founding Daytona Institute and transforming the school into a political training ground was an impressive accomplishment, yet this was a time of transition for Bethune. On the one hand, portions of the curriculum that she created indicated her belief in the cultivation of certain middle-class values for racial advancement and a gradual acceptance of blacks into white institutions and society. Throughout this period, she never demanded inclusion for blacks in white institutions. Rather, she emphasized black self-determination through building black institutions. Bethune saw, and used, racial separation a means to extend and strengthen racial cohesiveness. Moreover, her politics emphasized the redistribution of social resources, not the redistribution of power. On the other hand, overt challenges to white authority also seemed to be a part of her approach to racial advancement. In dealing with white trustees at Daytona Institute who sought to limit black education, she mili-

74. According to Louise A. Tilley and Patricia Gurin, "protopolitical" activities include "direct collective appeals to authorities (unmediated by organization), often in defense of customary rights or statuses, and membership and action in organizations that work outside the formal political arena." They argue, as does Estelle Freedman and others, that these associations allowed women to develop parliamentarian skills, build networks, accumulate resources, and develop a group consciousness. See Louise A. Tilley and Patricia Gurin, eds., *Women, Politics, and Change;* Estelle Freedman, "Separatism as Strategy: Female Institution Building and American Feminism, 1870–1930," 512–29; Anne Frior Scott, *Natural Allies: Women's Associations in American History.*

tantly demanded change and insisted on the right of blacks to determine educational choices. Under her direction, Daytona Institute increasingly moved toward helping students develop marketable skills outside the menial trades, gain training in higher education, and enlarge the number of female African American social and political leaders. In her encounter with the Ku Klux Klan, Bethune exhibited an essential commitment to direct action techniques as well as a strong conviction in the power of block voting and political activism. She was a leader who could be firm or pliant as the situation warranted.

Throughout her more than four decades in public life, Bethune would continue to redefine her notions of racial solidarity, self-help, and political action based on demographic, economic, and social change taking place in American society. And, although she retained her belief in black women's moral superiority and unique responsibility for racial uplift, she used that idea as a justification for moving African American women into decision-making positions in the body politic. Bethune's first steps in working in this latter arena began with her involvement in the black woman's club movement, the subject of the next chapter.

| 3 |

Mutual Aid, Self-Improvement, and Social Justice

In 1912, Mary McLeod Bethune became connected with the black women's club movement, thus initiating her opportunity to pursue collective race work on the state, regional, and national level. Although a new experience for Bethune, for generations black women had come together in local and regional associations to express concerns and confront issues affecting the race. Collectively, benevolent and mutual aid societies, church groups, and fraternal organizations provided social services, entertainment, and financial assistance in time of need. Specific programs promoted cultural improvement and helped African American communities to carry on in a racist society. More important, these associations worked to bring like-minded African Americans together while making demands for reform on the white community. On a personal level, associations offered black women a place to exercise and develop their individual talents. Outwardly, membership in voluntary organizations allowed women publicly to exercise traditional familial, religious, and community roles. Yet, on a broader level, working through voluntary associations also politicized many African American women. Organizing voluntary associations offered more civic-minded women a method for widespread mobilization and afforded them access to crucial support from like-minded women. Female activists used their associations to create relationships, develop and improve leadership skills, hold management positions, and refine their political talent and skills in a supportive environment. More important, the actions and accomplishments of organized black women leaders became a source of inspiration for new generations of young activists. Through their work in voluntary associations, pioneering black women organizers motivated younger women to continue working for the advancement of *all* African Americans.[1]

The beginning of Bethune's experience in communal activism was in Mayesville. Neighbors worked together to harvest the crops by holding "cotton picking parties." People would gather together from the surrounding area to pick cotton, have a picnic "dinner," and play games and sing. According to Bethune, these parties gave a "great spirit of helpfulness" and built "social relationships" that "laid the basic principles" of sharing and helping others. Her mother, Patsy, reinforced these principles through her commitment to neighbors. As local nurse and midwife, Patsy would go to neighbors whenever they came asking for help. Bethune remembers often being awakened by neighbors knocking on the door asking for help and Patsy being gone many nights. This dedication to the community was not unusual among former slave women. In fact, it was one of the lessons women learned in slavery: community survival rested upon cooperation and collective strength.[2]

These concepts carried over into both religious and secular women's associations after emancipation, and membership in these associations would add a new dimension to Bethune's social activism. Through church-related activities in mutual aid and benevolent societies, Sunday schools, missionary societies, and fund-raising organizations, African American women gained leadership skills, sharpened organizational abilities, and gained recognition and moral authority for active public roles that promoted social change. As the elite of the black community, the wives and daughters of ministers, teachers, and businessmen, they believed social change came through "mutual improvement" and moral reform. Literary associations formed to "cultivate the talents" of black women and emphasize "good" virtues that would "break down the strong barrier of prejudice" in the white community. To achieve equality

1. Freedman, "Separatism as Strategy," 512–29; Shaw, "Black Club Women and the Creation of the NACW," 10–25; Gilmore, *Gender and Jim Crow*, 150–57; Giddings, *When and Where I Enter*, 89–95; Cheryl Townsend Gilkes, "Holding Back the Ocean with a Broom: Black Women and Community Work," 217–32. Additional studies on the club movement include: White, *Too Heavy a Load*; Jones, *Jane Edna Hunter*; Jones, "Quest for Equality"; Cynthia Neverdon-Morton, *Afro-American Women in the South and the Advancement of the Race, 1895–1925*; Rouse, *Lugenia Burns Hope*; Salem, "To Better our World"; Ann Frior Scott, "Most Invisible of All: Black Women's Voluntary Associations"; Gerda Lerner, *The Majority Finds Its Past: Placing Women in History*; White, "The Cost of Club Work."

2. Williams interview, 1–5, 8; see Deborah Gray White, *Ar'n't I a Woman? Female Slaves in the Plantation South*; Deborah Gray White, "Female Slaves: Sex Roles and Status in the Antebellum Plantation South," 20–31.

required African Americans to promote specific values such as thrift, sobriety, cleanliness, and hard work among the "lower classes" because the perceived "vice and immorality" of *any* black woman reflected negatively on *all* black women. They worked to inculcate middle-class values among the "vicious" masses while distancing themselves from the "lower" classes in order to secure their social status. African American women's response was in reaction to Social Darwinism, the prominent racial ideology of the period, and to the pseudo-scientific practice of phrenology—the practice of studying character and mental capacity from the conformation of the human skull. Adherents and practitioners argued that African Americans were biologically and innately inferior, inclined to criminality, and unable to comprehend anything above a basic education.[3] These women were purposefully multiple in their thinking. While working for racial advancement, they created and maintained a racial identity for elite black women free of negative stereotypes created by white society.

This church-related activism was popularly known as the Social Gospel movement. The goal of the movement was the "application of the teaching of Jesus and the total message of the Christian salvation to society, the economic life, and social institutions . . . as well as to individuals." Through their work, Social Gospel reformers helped promote the idea that human miseries resulted from systemic problems in society and not from the personal failings of the individual. The Social Gospel movement helped break down the barriers between sacred and secular reform and led African American women into Progressive era reform. Black women's involvement in church-related associations put them among the ranks of Social Gospel reformers, and black progressive reform grew from the ranks of educated black women who adapted their church-related activities to deal with secular reform issues. Exclusion from white-dominated organizations, increasing racial discrimination, and an increasing sense of racial consciousness led black women to

3. See Darlene Clark Hine, "Lifting the Veil, Shattering the Silence: Black Women's History in Slavery and Freedom"; Jacqueline Jones, *Labor of Love, Labor of Sorrow: Black Women, Work, and the Family from Slavery to the Present*; Giddings, *When and Where I Enter*; Cheryl Townsend Gilkes, "W.E.B. Du Bois, Nannie Helen Burroughs and 'The Intellectual Leadership of the Race': Toward a Theory of African American Women and Social Change"; Sterling, *We Are Your Sisters*, 105; Grant, *The Passing of the Great Race*; Charles Carroll, "The Negro a Beast"; Robert W. Shufeldt, *The Negro: A Menace to American Civilization*. African American women embarked on a program of respectful self-representation to disprove theories of innate black inferiority and show black respectability. See Kevin Gaines, *Uplifting the Race: Black Leadership, Politics, and Culture in the Twentieth Century*, 67–93; White, "The Cost of Club Work," 252–59.

transform these religious organizations into social service agencies. This black women's network in the South included clubwoman and educator Margaret Murray Washington, churchwoman Nannie Helen Burroughs, settlement house founder Jane Porter Barrett, educator and clubwoman Lucy C. Laney, educator Jennie Moton, educator and clubwoman Charlotte Hawkins Brown, community activist Lugenia Hope Burns, YWCA organizer Mary Jackson McCrorly, clubwoman Marion B. Wilkinson, and Fisk registrar M. L. Crosthwait.[4] Bethune became an active member of this network, working with these women to establish state and regional associations that addressed the needs of blacks.

While the Social Gospel movement broke down the barriers between sacred and secular reform, southern urban development and the first great migration of blacks from the rural South to the urban North gave black women practical experience in addressing social problems. Black women were in the forefront of reform in initiating, funding, and implementing programs such as vocational training, poor relief, kindergartens, day-care facilities, industrial schools, job placement, and recreation. Black settlement houses operated programs to clothe and feed the poor, and offered medical care, adult education, recreation, mother's clubs, and legal representation to working-class black women. State women's clubs built facilities that sheltered black juvenile delinquents from adult criminals. They also built, supported, and managed playgrounds, kindergartens, nursery schools, orphanages, and old folks' homes. They worked for public health and temperance, and supported social purity and social hygiene programs. Involvement in social welfare programs moved black women from an emphasis on rescuing the poor to preventing poverty and encouraging programs that worked toward good character formation rather than the reformation of poor character. Like their white counterparts, these efforts among black women reflected an interest in new social scientific methods, an emphasis on the importance of trained professionals, and a belief in the power of statistical data. However, unlike their white counterparts, African American women did not distinguish between the "worthy" and "unworthy" poor. Black women recognized white racism, not inherent characteristics, as the cause of poverty and worked to help all blacks. Moreover, black women took their reform ideology further than their

    4. White, Jr., *Liberty and Justice for All*, xvii; Elisabeth Lasch-Quinn, *Black Neighbors: Race and the Limits of Reform in the American Settlement House Movement, 1890–1945*, especially chapter 2; see also Ralph E. Luker, *The Social Gospel in Black and White: American Racial Reform, 1885–1912*; Rouse, *Lugenia Burns Hope*, 35–40.

white counterparts. While incorporating the methods of the new social sciences, they also mounted a challenge to the prevailing theories of race and inferiority, and implemented strategies for change.[5]

African American women increasingly turned their attention to community development projects in organizations such as the Independent Order of St. Luke (IOSL). Under the direction of Maggie Lena Walker, IOSL began working for community uplift through economic independence by organizing the St. Luke Penny Savings Bank, the *St. Luke Herald* (a weekly newspaper), and the St. Luke Emporium (a department store). As secular organizations such as black insurance companies and banks began taking on the burdens of mutual aid societies, IOSL began to support a more diverse mix of community development projects. In the era of progressive reform, IOSL instituted a scholarship fund and founded a home for delinquent girls, fought for woman suffrage, protested black disfranchisement, organized boycotts, and condemned lynching.[6] The IOSL was the first African American association to take such a holistic approach to community development and racial advancement, and, more important, it became a model for the work of several other African American women's organizations. Some historians would describe this as a "feminist" approach to social reform; indeed, women's activism in the Progressive era has often been described as "social feminism." Others who focus primarily on African American women's activities, however, have argued that the term "feminism" is inappropriate to describe African American women's activism as "feminism" puts a priority on gender equality. Author Alice Walker and historian Darlene Clark Hine, among others, have used the term "womanist" and "womanism" in describing the black female experience. Walker defined womanist as a consciousness that incorporates racial, cultural, sexual, national, economic, and political considerations for *all* people.

5. See Gilkes, "Holding Back the Ocean with a Broom"; Hine, "Lifting the Veil, Shattering the Silence," 246–50; Cynthia Neverdon-Morton, "Self-Help Programs as Educative Activities of Black Women in the South, 1895–1925: Four Key Areas," 209; Gerda Lerner, "Early Community Work of Black Club Women," 159–60; Scott, "Most Invisible of All," 11–17, 20; Anne Frior Scott, "On Seeing and Not Seeing: a Case of Historical Invisibility," 18; Shaw, "Black Club Women and the Creation of the NACW," 440–41; Salem, "To Better Our World"; Jones, *Quest for Equality;* White, Jr. *Liberty and Justice for All,* xviii; Higginbotham, *Righteous Discontent,* 177; Gordon, "Black and White Visions of Welfare"; Gordon, *Pitied but not Entitled;* White, "The Cost of Club Work," 248–59; V. P. Franklin and Bettye Collier-Thomas, "Biography, Race Vindication, and African American Intellectuals: Introductory Essay," 8–11; Harley, "Beyond the Classroom," 265.

6. Elsa Barkley Brown, "Womanist Consciousness: Maggie Lena Walker and the Independent Order of Saint Luke," 610–33.

According to Hine, womanism describes the double legacy of oppression and the resistance to that dual oppression among black women. According to historian Elsa Barkley Brown, this "womanist" approach to community uplift flowed from a "both/and" worldview that emphasized interdependence, interaction, and wholeness and saw resistance to race, class, and sexual oppression as one and the same struggle.[7] African American women's organizations were engaging in a broader range of activities that included self-help, community development, and racial advancement. Women's organizations attempted to promote both a social welfare and civil rights agenda.

Despite some hailing Bethune as "one of the chief exponents of feminism," she did not describe herself as a "feminist." Indeed, she is best described as a "race woman" with a womanist consciousness as her activism addressed issues of race, gender, culture, economics, and politics. For Bethune, this work fit distinctly within woman's sphere of influence; it involved community advocacy with the on-going struggle for social justice, race uplift, and gender equality. It celebrated collective activity and multiple commitments that allowed black women to create a positive self-image. Sociologist Cheryl Townsend Gilkes has used the phrase "lots of small pieces" to describe the interconnected affiliations that African American women used to effect interracial cooperation, political empowerment, economic advancement, education, cultural enhancement, and community survival.[8] "Lots of small pieces" aptly described Bethune's womanist race work.

Bethune served as president of the Florida Federation of Colored Women's Clubs between 1917 and 1924. During her tenure, the club faced four pressing issues: internal organization, American involvement in World War I, woman suffrage, and interracial cooperation. She confronted these issues by organizing the federation on an efficient businesslike basis. She presided over several productive conventions, drafted a constitution, recorded and published minutes of the clubs' meetings, and created a newsletter. World War I ex-

---

7. On the use of the terms "feminism" and "womanism" see Phyllis M. Palmer, "White Women/Black Women: The Dualism of Female Identity and Experience in the United States," 151–70; Rosalyn Terborg-Penn, "Discontented Black Feminists: Preludes and Postscript to the Passage of the Nineteenth Amendment." On the use of "womanism" see Alice Walker, *In Search of Our Mother's Gardens: Womanist Prose;* Darlene Clark Hine, *Speak Truth to Power;* C. Ogunyemi, "Womanism: The Dynamics of the Contemporary Black Female Novel in English," 63–80; Barkley-Brown, "Womanist Consciousness," 630–33.

8. Radio station KFOX, "National Council of Negro Women," July 14, 1946, interview of Mary McLeod Bethune by Fay M. Jackson; Higginbotham, "African American Women's History and the Metalanguage of Race," 251–74; Cheryl Townsend Gilkes, "Building in Many Places: Multiple Commitments and Ideologies in Black Women's Community Work," 53–76.

panded Bethune's affiliations with other activist women. As a field representative for black women on the Women's Committee of the Council of National Defense, Alice Dunbar-Nelson, widow of black poet and literary figure
Paul Lawrence Dunbar, traveled throughout the South gathering information
about black women's war efforts. Dunbar-Nelson found that the most active black women were "for the most part teachers and college women, with
a keen sense of responsibility" or a "leading Negro club woman." Florida's
black women were among the most active and organized of all southern states.
Under the direction of black state chair Eartha M. White, each county had
appointed a black woman chair and organized a complete set of committees.
Bethune was a part of this organizational work in Volusia County, encouraging members to participate in the war effort at home through a host of
patriotic services. She established the Daytona Beach chapter of the Circle
of Negro War Relief (CNWR) to promote black women's participation in
the war effort. Like other groups throughout the South, Florida club women
and CNWR members worked to meet specific individual and local emergency needs. Members canvassed neighborhoods for donations, participated
in voluntary food conservation and production programs, taught canning and
food preservation techniques, and raised money through food sales. They established home demonstration programs, pushed for improvements in public
health, improved recreational facilities and playgrounds for children, and lobbied for measures to protect women in industry through the Mutual Protection League for Working Girls. They also established Hostess Houses, became Traveler's Aid workers, knitted goods for soldiers, supplied comfort kits,
gum, records, phonographs, and home-cooked dinners, and gave lectures on
social hygiene and race pride. Women raised money for Liberty Bond drives
and worked with Red Cross chapters to promote the inclusion of black nurses
whenever possible.[9]

When the Nineteenth Amendment passed in 1920 and voter registration
opened to women in Daytona Beach, Bethune organized a voter registration drive for the staff at Daytona Institute and local black women despite
intimidation by white supremacist groups. Woman suffrage, increasing participation in the women's club movement, and, most important, American

9. William J. Breen, "Black Women and the Great War: Mobilization and Reform in the
South," 424–25, 434–35, 437–39. Although no direct correspondence exists linking Bethune
and Eartha M. White, in a letter to Ruth Atkinson, Bethune asks if Atkinson has been in
contact with Eartha White. See Mary McLeod Bethune to Mrs. Ruth W. Atkinson, June
22, 1943, BFC I. Dorothy Salem, "World War I," 1286–87; Lerner, *Black Women in White
America,* 498–500.

involvement in World War I, participation in the International Council of the Women of the Darker Races, and a European tour in 1925–1926 worked to change Bethune's concept of "community" activism. These specific events widened Bethune's range of interest and made it apparent to her that people of color faced similar political and economic problems worldwide and that this global community must unite to achieve racial equality. Bethune began to move toward global activism by expanding her activities and taking on the responsibility for organizing black women on a regional level.

As president of the Southeastern Federation of Colored Women's Clubs (SFCWC) Bethune united state club federations from Alabama, Florida, Georgia, North Carolina, South Carolina, Tennessee, Mississippi, and Virginia in an effort to make their work to combat school desegregation and poor health facilities more effective. Her leading cause was the founding of a state home for delinquent and dependent young black women. Under Bethune's leadership, the SFCWC established and oversaw the administration of the Home for Delinquent Girls in Ocala, Florida, in 1921. The "Industrial School" offered an alternative to incarceration with adults for up to twelve young black girls and women. Between 1921 and 1923, Bethune personally took on the responsibility for the operation of the school, including paying the wages of two matrons from her own pocket when funding ran short.[10]

Through the SFCWC, Bethune worked with other regional club leaders, including Charlotte Hawkins Brown, Lucy C. Laney, Margaret Murray Washington, Janie Porter Barrett, and Lugenia Burns Hope, to establish a working relationship with egalitarian white women's groups, particularly those within religious denominations. By working together on a regular basis, the women lobbied state legislatures for annual appropriations for the operation of several delinquent girls homes, fought for the improvement of educational facilities and better travel conditions, instituted anti-lynching campaigns, demanded control of negative media portrayals of blacks, outlined improved working conditions for domestic workers, and advocated for woman suffrage as a means to end racial oppression. This cooperative effort opened the way for women to assume leadership positions on the Committee for Interracial Cooperation.[11]

10. Elaine M. Smith, "Mary McLeod Bethune," 118.

11. "Recommendations to the Committee on Interracial Relations to the Women's Missionary Council of the M.E. Church South," MMB; Gilmore, *Gender and Jim Crow,* 150–56; Smith, "Mary McLeod Bethune," 125–26; Glenda Gilmore, "Southeastern Association of Colored Women's Clubs," 1089.

Bethune's work in the Florida Federation of Colored Women's Clubs, the SFCWC, and World War I mirrored the work of many black women throughout the South in the first two decades of the twentieth century who initiated community projects designed to improve an array of conditions including housing, health, and education. During this period of increasing racial hostility, these black women became diplomats to the white community. Successful programs, however, required women to enter the public sphere by lobbying white legislators and appearing before local white bureaucrats. Black women increasingly assumed this responsibility for two reasons: they were not vulnerable, as black men were, to accusations of using public space to try to gain sexual access to white women, and they could approach officials as clients seeking relief for their family's social needs.[12] Informally, black women continued a tradition of African American political involvement at a time when social segregation and disfranchisement advanced black political invisibility.

As legal and customary segregation became more widespread, black women increasingly saw the importance of establishing a national organization to systematically address social segregation, economic inequality, and political disfranchisement. The creation of the National Association of Colored Women (NACW) in 1896 nationalized black women's racial and community work and gave black women a national infrastructure. This venture represented the first "nationalized effort exclusively created and controlled by black women." To publicize their efforts, NACW members established the first successful and cohesive national communication network among black women through a monthly newsletter—the *National Notes*. In addition to its own newsletter, the NACW placed columns in the national black press designed to increase public awareness of the club and its program. The newsletter channeled important information to local chapters quickly while biennial conventions brought black women together and created a cadre of elite women who headed local affiliates. The NACW stressed race pride, defended the black home and community, and fought for antilynching legislation, equal accommodations, and racial advancement.[13] In short, the NACW addressed problems faced by black women and the race.

Two separate incidents spurred African American women to come together to form a national organization. The first was the exclusion of black women's

12. Gilmore, *Gender and Jim Crow*, 151.
13. Beverly W. Jones, "Mary Church Terrell and the National Association of Colored Women, 1896–1901," 20, 25–26; Lerner, *Black Women in White America*, 435–37.

groups from the Columbian Exposition in 1893. The exposition was an international demonstration of progress celebrating the discovery of America. When separate black women's groups from Chicago and Washington, D.C., applied for inclusion in the planning process, white women denied them a place in the program because they had no national organization to represent them. The second catalyst was concern with increasingly harsh, scathing attacks by conservative whites against the moral character of black women. These assaults were not new, but in the late nineteenth century, they gained credibility because of their widespread circulation and increasing racial chauvinism. By 1895, the American press used attacks on the moral character of black women in an effort to discredit successful black antilynching activities, especially those of black activist Ida B. Wells-Barnett. James W. Jacks, president of the Missouri Press Association, sent a letter to a British reformer denouncing all blacks, and particularly denouncing the credibility of black women. Jacks wrote that African American women "were prostitutes and all were thieves and liars." In response to Jacks's letter, black clubwomen met in a national conference and founded the National Federation of Afro-American Women "for the sake of our own dignity, the dignity of our race, and the future good name of our children."[14]

From its inception, black women organizers designed the NACW as a political and social channel primarily for elite black women. In instituting its programs, the NACW succeeded in defining a role for educated black women in social reform, fostering the development of leadership skills among its members, and shifting its member's interests to areas outside the home.[15] These accomplishments notwithstanding, by feminist standards the NACW was a conservative organization. Leaders never called for social equality for women, nor did they call for any change in the domestic role of women. Rather, the NACW promoted political activity among black women for the explicit purpose of improving the lives of families and children and defending the dignity of black women against charges of wantonness, immorality, and social inferiority. The NACW sought to make African American women better wives and mothers through "a program that addressed racial problems through the elevation of black women" and sought to prove the moral, mental,

14. Dorothy Salem, "The National Association of Colored Women," 842–51; Scott, *Natural Allies*, 127, 147–48; see also Lillian Serece Williams, ed., "Introduction to the Records of the National Association of Colored Women's Clubs, 1895–1992."

15. Charles Harris Wesley, *The History of the National Association of Colored Women's Clubs: A Legacy of Service*, 57–59.

and material progress of people of color.[16] Illustrating its acceptance of Victorian ideology, the NACW believed improving the status of black women was essential to advancing the race as a whole since women were the arbitrators of family morals. The NACW did not call for any essential change in women's position in the public sector.

The women of the NACW did not directly challenge the status quo. Instead, they took it upon themselves to institute programs designed to train the "lower classes" to adapt the manners, attitudes, and behaviors acceptable to the white middle class. Instilling selected middle-class values and acquiring a middle-class lifestyle was supposed to improve white perceptions of the race. To accomplish these goals, chapters of the NACW organized voluntary teachers who began adult night schools that taught literature, language, and other subjects. Other reform measures focused on programs for children. Local affiliates began day-care centers and nurseries that provided care for children of working mothers and established kindergartens, schools, and mother's clubs. The NACW provided social services to the community as well, founding hospitals, old folks' homes, and orphanages. Women of the NACW worked to improve conditions for the race by redistributing social resources and providing community services through programs that emphasized its belief in women's moral primacy and the obligation of the elite to work for the betterment of the lives of the masses.[17]

This emphasis on proving that African Americans were making material, mental, and moral progress marked a turning point in African American definitions of "racial uplift." Historian Kevin Gaines has argued that in the antebellum period and during Reconstruction, African Americans used the term "uplift" to describe a group struggle for freedom and social advancement against the planter class and the slave system by all African Americans. In this sense, racial uplift contained a democratic vision—inclusion for all without class differentiation—and a sense of liberation. In the early twentieth century, industrialism, immigration, migration, segregation, anti-black violence, and particularly the growth of the black middle class contributed toward this new focus on demonstrating racial progress.[18] Gaines's argument is flawed, however, because he makes no distinction between social elite and middle-class African Americans. Indeed, there was a distinct difference.

16. Jones, "Mary Church Terrell and the National Association of Colored Women, 1896–1901," 24.
17. Ibid., 23.
18. Gaines, *Uplifting the Race,* 1–4, 19–21, 31, 80–99.

Historian Sharon Harley has argued the black middle class was not a monolithic class. Employment discrimination against African Americans meant that income or job description did not solely determine black middle-class status. According to Harley, in the early part of the twentieth century, racial restrictions in the job market often meant that for black women decorum, respectability, and moral refinement were more important than income, professional status, and family background in determining class position. In general, middle-class black women were college or normal school graduates, working in the professions, in white-collar jobs or in business, and were active in the organizational and institutional life of their communities. However, many black women found themselves excluded from professional positions based on race and gender. Forced to work in domestic service or semi-skilled positions, these women nevertheless considered themselves as middle-class. During this period, middle-class black women came from a wide variety of family backgrounds, income levels, and occupations. As the twentieth century progressed, class distinctions within the middle class became more distinct, and the black middle class became divided into three basic, although sometimes overlapping, groups: the social elite, the professional middle class, and the lower middle class.[19]

Women such as Mary Church Terrell, Margaret Murray Washington, and Josephine Silone Yates belonged to the social elite. These women differentiated themselves from most of the middle class as well as the masses based on their prominent family backgrounds, income, and light skin color. This numerically small group frequently portrayed themselves as the true representatives of black womanhood in order to destroy racist theories about the immorality of black women. It was the social elite who redefined "racial uplift" as their personal duty to aid the "lowly" in developing good character traits and managing their behavior through an emphasis on self-help, temperance, thrift, chastity, and purity. Socially elite women promoted an ideology of class differentiation, often referring to the lower classes as the "most illiterate and vicious representatives" of the race while holding themselves up as "the more intelligent and worthy classes."[20] Terrell made this distinction clear in 1900 when she remarked, "To our poor, benighted sisters in the Black Belt of Alabama we have been both a comfort and a help to these women, through the

19. Harley, "The Middle Class," 786–89; see also Evelyn Brooks Barnett, "Nannie Burroughs and the Education of Black Women"; Willard B. Gatewood, *Aristocrats of Color: the Black Elite, 1880–1920.*

20. Harley, "The Middle Class," 786–89; Brooks Barnett, "Nannie Burroughs and the Education of Black Women"; Gatewood, *Aristocrats of Color.*

darkness of whose ignorance of everything that makes life sweet or worth the living, no ray of light would have penetrated but for us. We have taught them the ABC of living by showing them how to make their huts more habitable and decent with the small means at their command and how to care for themselves and their families."[21]

Socially elite women distanced themselves from "the masses" in an effort to force whites to recognize their upper-class status and reinstate citizenship rights for those who had "proven" their worthiness for such rights. Although unforeseen by elite women at the time, "racial uplift" in this context had two fatal flaws—it implicitly blamed African Americans for their low status and reaffirmed whites' negative portrayals of African American life and culture. The black elite assumed that proof of moral, material, and mental progress would alleviate white racism and lead to inclusion. In fact, it did quite the opposite. Class differentiation actually served to reinforce malevolent white concepts of blackness and seriously limited democratic visions of social progress.[22]

A much larger group of women entered the middle class through their educational and professional achievements as teachers, white-collar office workers, small-business owners, and government employees. Women such as Maggie Lena Walker, Nannie Helen Burroughs, and Bethune are representative of the professional black middle class. Family background differentiated this group from the social elite. Most of the women on this level were born and raised in poverty (often to newly freed slave parents) with cultural values of the "folk." Some came from mixed ancestry, while others were fully African American. Because of their family backgrounds, these women had a very different perception of the "masses" than the social elite. They were personally familiar with the capabilities and virtues of the hard-working, religious "masses" and did not assume that education, occupation, or family background were the primary indicators of good moral character. They were active in community organizations but did not distance themselves from those with less formal education. Rather, their socialization stressed the importance of racial solidarity and compelled them to join with and acknowledge the innate capabilities of all members of their community. Their duty was to work with the masses, to represent them when they could not act on their own behalf and further racial advancement by taking on a wide variety of community roles. Middle-class status was a call to duty, and many middle-class

21. Mary Church Terrell, "Club Work among Women," *New York Age,* January 4, 1900, quoted in Gordon, "Black and White Visions of Welfare," 169. According to Gordon, Terrell used virtually the same rhetoric in another speech given in 1928.
22. Gaines, *Uplifting the Race,* 1–4, 74–77; Harley, "The Middle Class," 786–89.

women saw themselves as servants to their people.[23] Indeed, a consistent element in Bethune's educational, organizational, and government work was her emphasis on her *duty* to the race. She steadfastly believed that educated black women should not separate themselves from the masses, but should work *with* the masses and use their knowledge to *empower others*. This point of view often put her at odds with the socially elite element in the NACW.

Bethune's first contact with the NACW came about in 1912 when Frances Keyser, academic dean at Daytona Institute, suggested she attend an NACW meeting at Hampton Institute as a means of calling attention to and support for her work at Daytona. Bethune was immediately impressed, and somewhat intimidated, by the socially elite women who headed the association. Women such as Terrell, Washington, and Yates were sophisticated, older than she, and dressed in the finest clothes. While Bethune carefully worded her speech before the NACW meeting to gain their support and approval for Daytona Institute, she also wanted personal acceptance. Moreover, this event triggered Bethune's dormant desire for the finer things in life. She began pursuing the approval of the NACW leadership by reinventing herself. She became clothes-conscious. Whenever possible, she replaced her neat, somber missionary attire with more sophisticated styles. She struggled to create an image of herself as young and appealing, routinely referring to herself as "small" even though in reality she could never be described as an unsubstantial woman. As soon as her financial situation allowed, Bethune began dressing in velvet and lace, and in time became the epitome of a well-dressed, sophisticated woman, an image she seemed to thoroughly enjoy.[24] Although Bethune attempted to cross the invisible line that marked entry into the social elite, she was not able to do so. Outwardly, Bethune seemed to have crossed the class line. She dressed, spoke, and acted as if she were a member of this group. She could associate with Terrell, Washington, and Yates through her club affiliations, but those born into it did not accept her as a member of that class. Bethune's family background, financial position, and dark skin color prevented her complete acceptance by these women and her entry into the ranks of their class. Perhaps this subtle rejection fueled Bethune's social consciousness even more,

23. Harley, "The Middle Class," 786–89; Harley, "Beyond the Classroom," 265; Lerner, "Early Community Work of Black Club Women," 167; Elsa Barkley Brown, "Negotiating and Transforming the Public Sphere: African American Political Life in the Transition from Slavery to Freedom," 352; Barkley Brown, "African American Women's Quilting," 925–27; Franklin and Collier-Thomas, "Biography, Race Vindication, and African American Intellectuals," 11.

24. Holt, *Mary McLeod Bethune,* 105–7.

spurring her determination to prove that she was as essential as they were in the struggle for black equality.

From 1912 on Bethune carefully worked her way up through the ranks of the NACW. In 1919, she served as the chairperson of the NACW's Department of Education, as president of the Southeastern Section, as vice-president-at-large from 1922 to 1924, and as president from 1924 to 1928. Bethune expressed a very clear commitment to uplifting the masses by instilling certain values, as she did in 1925 when she called on the women of the NACW to bring "refinement and thrift and morality" into "thousands and thousands of homes and lives." Unlike Mary Church Terrell, however, Bethune's writings did not blame the masses for their shortcomings; rather, she believed racism had prevented them from progressing. The elite could not match Bethune's sense of duty. Her commitment to the concept of educated women possessing a duty to the race was clear: " 'Not for Ourselves, but for Others,' should be our great slogan." Bethune also expressed a strong belief in the enormous potential of *all* women in terms of their own development and their contributions to the community. Bethune often talked of harnessing "the great power of women into a force for constructive action."[25] She worked continuously to clarify her ideas and develop her own objectives for club work.

Bethune examined and reexamined her thoughts in an effort to eliminate "abstract lines of demarcation" and artificiality. In a speech given before the NAACP in 1935, she called for class unity and expressed her fears that future historians would see African Americans as a people who had had potential and resources, but were "unable to capitalize them because of their racial non-cohesiveness." She repeatedly reassessed the legitimacy of the social elite concept of uplift. Bethune believed, "Racial cohesion meant making a road out of all the achievements" of the race and harmonizing "conflicting idealism's" within the race. She began to question the notion articulated by Terrell that women should remain in the background and show support by electing "just men into positions of responsibility and power." Citing the work of Lucy Laney, Maggie Lena Walker, Jane Edna Hunter, and Lugenia Hope, Bethune argued that in the past racism and sexism forced black women to play a subtle and indirect role in racial advancement. Nevertheless, black

25. Wesley, *The History of the National Association of Colored Women's Clubs*, 93–100; Records of the NACW; Mary McLeod Bethune, "President's Address," in *National Notes*, vol. 27, no. 4, January 1925, NACW, 1; Mason interview, 191–92; Henrine Ward Banks, "The Purpose of the National Council of Negro Women"; Blackwell, "The Advocacies and Ideological Commitments of a Black Educator," 174.

women had "touched the most vital fields" and been a "contributing factor" to advancing interracial relations.[26] In the end, she concluded that racial unity should take precedence over class distinctions and that commonly accepted gender boundaries were too confining.

Bethune believed that collectively there were no limits to what women *could* do once they overcame impediments and prejudices, including intraracial class biases. Once African American women achieved intraracial unity, they could be more effective in building interracial female coalitions that would ally with male-led groups and hasten the end of racism, prejudice, segregation, and discrimination. Bethune was articulating her vision of what civil rights activists would later term "the beloved community": black and white men and women of all classes using their talents and abilities harmoniously and collectively to improve the quality of life for all Americans. Once this notion took shape, Bethune focused more intently on overcoming intraracial class cleavages and creating new opportunities for African American women in education, employment, and leadership roles.

In 1924, Bethune made a larger transition from regional to national organizational activity when she defeated Ida Wells-Barnett in her bid for the presidency of the NACW. The NACW membership elected Bethune because they thought she was less confrontational than Wells-Barnett. They soon discovered that despite her outwardly conciliatory and conformist attitude, Bethune's vision for the NACW was very different from that of past leaders and the majority of its members. She wanted to transform the association, making it a clearinghouse that could speak as one voice for the interests of *all* black women to the rest of the world. She envisioned state members working in the interests of the *national* organization first, and putting their state work second. In 1924, Charlotte Hawkins Brown wrote to Bethune with the names of eight North Carolina women who *might* be willing to work for the national. Brown told Bethune, "The women of N.C. are not enthusiastic in their interest in the National" but "believe in their State Work." Unfortunately, many members followed the same line of thinking as the women of North Carolina. They found Bethune's ideas threatening to their individual power, and Bethune found unity easier to talk about than to achieve.

---

26. Banks, "The Purpose of the National Council of Negro Women," 174; Speech at the 26th Annual Conference of the NAACP, June 28, 1935, MMB; "President's Address to the 15th Biennial Convention of the National Association of Colored Women," Oakland, California, August 2, 1926, MMB; Mary Church Terrell to Mary McLeod Bethune, September 28, 1926, MCT; "A Century of Progress of Negro Women," address given at the Chicago Women's Federation, June 30, 1933, MMB.

Bethune's presidential messages are continuous pleas to the membership to put aside their differences and be more cooperative. In August 1926, she wrote that the biggest problem facing the association was finding the "connecting threads" that united women nationwide. Again, in June 1928, she wrote that the main problem for women seemed to be unity—whites exploited black women because they were unable to present a united front. In July 1928, she urged the women to put aside their differences, be more cooperative, and realize "that in union there is strength." She pleaded with NACW women to "forget everything that looks like individualism, and seek only the work before them, that of building for posterity." She hoped that the women of the NACW could develop a national vision. She called on members to work to make the state affiliates a clearinghouse for individual clubs, the regional affiliates a clearinghouse for state affiliates, and the national a clearinghouse for the regional affiliates.[27]

By the mid-1920s, Bethune had become a part of a growing national network of black women activists. Women had begun to travel widely and were developing strong ties that offered mutual support across regional boundaries. However, this was largely an experience for those in the upper echelons of the NACW. The rank-and-file members remained closely tied to their local affiliations. As president, Bethune tried to make the membership recognize that all African American women faced the same types of problems nationwide—racial discrimination was not confined to any one region. This, she argued, was the "connecting thread" that should encourage women to unite across regional boundaries. She called on members to "help me draw fast the sisterly cords of love, the RACIAL cords that are bigger than our state organizations, our sectional organizations and even our own glorious National; for, as a RACE we must reach the topmost round of success, where we shall meet all other peoples on common ground."[28]

Her presidential addresses recorded in the *National Notes* are constant reminders of the importance of "united efforts" and a strengthened "spirit of

27. Charlotte Hawkins Brown to Mary McLeod Bethune, October 7, 1924, NACW; Mary McLeod Bethune, "Fifteenth Biennial Report National Association of Colored Women 1924–1926," *National Notes*, August 1926, vol. 28, no. 10, NACW; Mary McLeod Bethune, "President's Message," *National Notes*, June 1928, NACW; Mary McLeod Bethune, "The President's Biennial Report for 1926–1928," *National Notes*, July 1928, NACW.

28. Mary McLeod Bethune, "President's Biennial Report," *National Notes*, vol. 28, no. 10, August 1926, NACW; Mary McLeod Bethune, "President's Greetings," *National Notes*, vol. 27, no. 4, January, 1925, NACW.

co-operation and harmony" among black women.[29] As eighth president of the NACW, Bethune put her considerable talents to work by serving a national constituency concerned with lynching, declining industrial and rural conditions, job training, and women's status.

Bethune began her tenure in office by reorganizing and redefining the NACW departmental structure to eliminate overlapping functions. She personally assigned women to the committees and subcommittees concerned with the association's seven-plank program. She deplored the lax record-keeping that previous presidents had allowed and during her tenure as president required the committee leaders to submit quarterly reports directly to her on the first day of October, January, April, and June. She used her natural powers of persuasion to press influential members to support her four main objectives. First, she asked members to increase the scholarship fund. Bethune believed that higher education was critical to racial advancement, and her emphasis on increasing the scholarship fund reflected this belief. She proposed increasing the fund in order to help more young women attain the education they would need to aid in the "educational emancipation of the masses." Second, members needed to raise enough money to construct a caretaker's cottage and pay for a full-time caretaker at the Douglass Home to keep the property well maintained. If the property was in disrepair whites could criticize all "Negro womanhood." Poor maintenance reflected negatively on all African American women. Third, Bethune wanted to publish the first official directory of the association. In many cases, the association did not even have a record of its members' street addresses. This situation hindered the effectiveness of the NACW. In her four years in office, Bethune garnered enough support to achieve these three goals, in addition to her most significant accomplishment—the acquisition of a national headquarters at Twelfth and O Streets, N.W. in Washington, D.C. Bethune saw the acquisition of a permanent headquarters as the first step toward her goal of making the NACW the official authoritative voice for the concerns of black women. A permanent office would give the NACW legitimacy and set it on an equal

---

29. Mary McLeod Bethune, "President's Greetings," *National Notes*, vol. 27, no. 4, January, 1925, NACW; Mary McLeod Bethune, "Fifteenth Biennial Report National Association of Colored Women, 1924–1926," *National Notes*, vol. 28, no. 10, July–August 1926, NACW; Mary McLeod Bethune, "President's Message," *National Notes*, vol. 28, no. 14, December 1926, NACW; Mary McLeod Bethune, "President's Message," *National Notes*, June 1928, NACW; Mary McLeod Bethune, "The President's Biennial Report for 1926–1928," *National Notes*, July 1928, NACW.

footing with similar white women's organizations such as the General Federation of Women's Clubs (GFWC). It would give black women a place for making international contacts, become the official archive for NACW records, and give the *National Notes* a permanent home. Bethune envisioned the building in Washington as a foundation from which African American women could "force ourselves upon the notice of our government, so that it will recognize our worth and repay our efforts."[30]

As Bethune's reasons for establishing a national headquarters suggest, she also saw the NACW as a vehicle for making black women a force in national politics. She wanted the NACW to work to prepare African American women to enter places of responsibility. She believed that black women would see "political and social emancipation" in the twentieth century and must be thoroughly prepared in "civic and political matters." To be prepared to play a part in "the emancipation of our race from injustice and inequality," she urged women to read books on local government, political economy, and financial and economic questions.[31] Bethune also wanted to broaden the NACW's political agenda. It was Bethune's work toward this end that engendered tension between her and Mary Church Terrell, the first president of the NACW, and then National Legislative Chairman of the group.

The friction between Bethune and Terrell stemmed, in part, from their different points of view about the objectives of the NACW. Both women based their distinct vision for the organization on their vastly different personal experiences. Bethune had had humble beginnings, while Terrell's life had been one of comfort and privilege. Terrell's parents had been favored light-skinned slaves of wealthy white masters. However, unlike Bethune's family who celebrated their ability to survive the slave system, the Churches worked to do away with any trace of their slave beginnings. Terrell was born into the black elite in Memphis, Tennessee, in 1863. After emancipation, her father, Robert Church, quickly became an influential businessman in Memphis and by 1900, many considered him the richest black man in the city. Terrell's mother, Louisa Ayers, became the first black woman to operate a successful

30. "Fifteenth Annual Report National Association of Colored Women 1924–1926," Mary McLeod Bethune, *National Notes*, vol. 28, no. 10, July–August 1926, NACW, 4; Hazel Garland, "NACW Served as Vanguard for Women s Club Groups," in *Pittsburgh Courier*, September 17, 1960; Mary McLeod Bethune, "Editorial Page," *The Urban League of Pittsburgh*, MMB; Wesley, *The History of the National Association of Colored Women's Clubs*, 70, 92–98; Bethune, "President's Message," 4–5.

31. Mary McLeod Bethune, "Feminism in France and Elsewhere," n.d., NACW.

hair salon in the city. In 1869, when Terrell's parents divorced, she left Memphis with her mother, who sent her to school in Ohio. Terrell encountered a less virulent type of racism and discrimination while at school. According to her autobiography, some students and teachers questioned her intellectual abilities because of color, but she apparently did not witness racial violence firsthand. Terrell graduated from Oberlin College in 1884, then returned to Memphis to live with her father for a year. She traveled to Europe, studied in Germany, and in 1886 took a teaching position at Wilberforce University. One year later, she began teaching at M Street High School in Washington, D.C., where she met her husband. As first president of the NACW, Terrell molded the association into a vehicle for self-help whose objective was to improve the moral standards of the "less favored and more ignorant sisters." According to historian Beverly Jones, under Terrell's leadership the NACW sought to enhance the lives of the masses and provide "a vehicle for the emergence of middle-class women."[32] Terrell believed the NACW should remain a decentralized association that responded to local, state, and national self-help projects.

Bethune believed the organization should go beyond these limited goals. She wanted to focus on broader issues that did not pertain to African Americans alone. Bethune saw the NACW moving away from social service work and toward fighting for social justice. To accomplish this, the women of the NACW had to develop a unified political voice at the national level. Bethune clung to her belief in women's innate moral goodness and intuitive understanding of the social needs of the race; she used those ideas as the basis for pushing women toward greater political involvement. Women must realize that they should no longer confine their duties to the home, but instead "must have some voice in the laws which shall govern her and her children and send her sons to death."[33] Bethune advocated women of the NACW taking an active role as representatives to Congress on *all* legislative issues, since all legislation in some way affected the race. During her administration, the NACW began sending delegates to congressional hearings and lobbying elected officials. One-third of her address to the 15th Biennial Convention of the NACW in 1926 addressed problems within the race; one-third spoke of the national environment, and one-third articulated her international vision.

Within the race, Bethune called on women to harmonize what she termed "conflicting idealisms." She called on her audience to work to combine "brain

32. Mary Church Terrell, *A Colored Woman in a White World*; Jones, *Quest for Equality*.
33. Bethune, "Feminism in France and Elsewhere," 15.

and brawn power" to stimulate production that she saw as the way to "wealth, power, and influence."[34] In other words, black women of all classes should work together. Each had something to offer in the struggle for racial advancement. These calls for harmony among women reflect Bethune's ongoing efforts to achieve a cross-class unity among African American women so that they could gain political advantage and make a substantial impact on American policy-making.

The second part of the speech is most significant because it marks an important turning point in Bethune's evolving thought on how to best achieve racial progress. This speech clearly indicates that as early as 1926 Bethune was moving away from gradualism and conservatism. She no longer believed that changing individual behavior would substantially improve the lives of African Americans. Bethune began to advocate for systemic change to improve conditions for African Americans. She explicitly condemned the national government for not removing barriers to racial equality and castigated the United States for disregarding "its plain, moral, social, economic, political and spiritual obligations" to more than twelve million African Americans simply because of their "heritage of African blood." Bethune called on the NACW members not to accept separatism and to "invade every field of activity in America, contribute in every way we can to fostering and perpetuating" America's professed ideals.[35] Bethune was now insisting that American democracy live up to its principles not only in theory, but in reality and in practice as well.

In order to force the United States live up to these democratic ideals, members of the NACW had to have a political voice and become more involved in legislative issues. As an organization representing the interests of black women, Bethune believed the NACW had a responsibility to "assume an attitude toward all big questions involving the welfare of the nation, public right and especially the present and future of our race." Bethune believed the questions facing the women of the NACW were both national and international, and included humanitarian, moral, social, and economic world problems. Bethune said, "This brings forward the 'color question' belting the world, colonial dominions and their attendant evils; political freedom and territorial problems of governments. The future of our people is wrapped up

34. Mary McLeod Bethune, "President's Address to the 15th Biennial Convention of the National Association of Colored Women," Oakland, California, August 2, 1926, MMB, 16–18.
35. Ibid., 20–21.

in their proper adjustment. Bred, born and living here under the American Flag, we nevertheless bear a relation to others of our blood. Their problems are ours and vice versa."[36]

According to Bethune, the international mission of the NACW was to become a significant link between people of color worldwide, and under her administration the NACW "made contact" with women's organization in nine European countries. Terrell disagreed. She considered it the role of the NACW and her duty as legislative chairman "to emphasize the necessity of doing one's duty to her country, her State and the city or town in which she lives by learning all she can about the practical situation and then doing everything in her power to have wise, just laws enacted." According to Terrell, the best way to do this was to "put just men into positions of responsibility and power." Women's duty was to "have the right type of men nominated for the various offices" and "urge their representatives to vote for bills which will help improve our condition as a race."[37] African American women had a duty to support black male leaders. They should not strike out on their own and assume leadership positions.

Bethune articulated a different vision of African American women's roles and their "proper place" in American society and politics. According to Bethune, a woman had a "duty to prepare herself for the highest service for home and country, her duty [was] both to know and to do." Bethune foresaw that women "will be called upon in the future to take an active part in the political world" but she feared women would be unprepared "to assume the new duties and obligations involved." She believed "no women need preparation in civic and political matters more than our colored women" and urged women to study and prepare for this day as "Our women have a great part to play in the emancipation of our race from the injustice and inequality under which it labors today." The responsibility of women leaders included promoting qualified black *women* for decision-making positions in local, state, and national governments. Bethune believed that increasing the number of women in leadership posts would benefit the public welfare as these women could work toward ensuring the equitable distribution of social resources. Although she respected black men's efforts, she argued, "black women intuitively understand the social needs of the race and use more direct methods in fulfilling those needs." Bethune was advocating independent public roles for African

36. Ibid., 22–29.
37. "The President's Biennial Report for 1926–28," *National Notes*, July, 1928, NACW; Mary Church Terrell to Mary McLeod Bethune, September 28, 1926, MCT.

American women in the black community. This was untenable to Terrell, who like Lugenia Hope Burns and Margaret Murray Washington built her reform activities around her husband's career, not independently of him.[38]

Terrell did not believe the NACW should expand its legislative program to include issues that were not directly related to racial discrimination in America such as proposals to ban intermarriage and require segregated streetcars in Washington, D.C. Terrell advised Bethune to let other more qualified organizations attend to the larger international issues. Bethune strongly disagreed with Terrell's position, believing that it was acceptable, even desirable, for every organization to join on particular issues to present a strong, united front. Bethune insisted that the NACW inform its members on all "BILLS in Congress affecting the ECONOMIC, SOCIAL, MORAL and POLITICAL WELFARE of citizens" to advise them on the most effective way for securing the passage or defeat of these bills. Moreover, Bethune inserted a clause in the description of the legislative department requiring that members must submit all plans and methods for presenting bills to Congress to the president of the NACW for sanction or disapproval before members took any action.[39] Bethune wrote to Terrell expressing her desire to have the NACW openly support several bills before Congress, including the Dyer Anti-Lynching bill, the Child Labor Amendment, and the World Court bill. While Bethune's call to support the antilynching bill mirrors Terrell's insistence on supporting bills dealing with African American issues, supporting the Child Labor Amendment and the World Court bill reflect Bethune's broader vision.

Bethune's championing the Child Labor Amendment reflected Progressive-era reform analysis. Like white reformers such as Florence Kelley, Bethune believed releasing young children from intense and often debilitating labor gave them the opportunity for longer, healthier lives and access to education. This was a significant reason for Bethune. Her deep-seated faith in the effectiveness of education as a means of racial uplift led her to equate passing the Child Labor Amendment with race work. Moreover, eliminating child labor would open more jobs for adult workers and raise adult wages, as employers used child workers as a reserve labor source to keep wages low.[40]

38. Bethune, "Feminism in France and Elsewhere," 1–3; Rouse, *Lugenia Burns Hope*, 124–25, 129–35.

39. "Departments and Their Functions," in *National Notes*, January 1925, NACW.

40. On Florence Kelley's fight to end child labor see Kathryn Kish Sklar, *Florence Kelley and the Nation's Work: The Rise of Women's Political Culture, 1830–1900* (New Haven, Conn.: Yale University Press, 1995), 156–58.

Bethune's support for the World Court bill stemmed from her commit-ment to the peace movement beginning at the end of World War I. She held the same convictions about war as many progressive reformers, including fu-ture First Lady Eleanor Roosevelt, Elizabeth Read, Esther Lape, and Jane Addams. Bethune believed women " should . . . form a solid phalanx against war." The World Court was an instrument for international arbitration to "secure peace through mediation, negotiation, international law" promoted by peace advocates. After the "world conflagration" of 1914–1918 peace activists argued that war was an obsolete idea, a notion that gained legitimacy in the interwar period. If the stated objectives of the "Great War" were to preserve democracy, prevent the rise of despotic governments, and end all future wars, then World War I was a complete failure. By the 1920s Germany was rearm-ing, fascism was on the rise, and the settlements reached under the Versailles Treaty were fostering new hostilities. The outcome of the war at home was even more disappointing for African Americans. During World War I, more than 370,000, or 13 percent, of all draftees were black men who were subject to rigid military segregation and discrimination as well as civilian violence. Only about 3 percent (42,000) went into combat (the rest were used in labor battalions, as stevedores, in construction, and as cooks or bakers), but most compiled exemplary records. As discussed previously, black women supported the war by buying Liberty Bonds, laboring on the home front, and giving vocal support for American war aims. Yet, despite military and home front loyalty and President Woodrow Wilson's rhetoric that the war would make the world safe for democracy, African Americans endured increased discrimi-nation, prejudice, and violence at the end of the war. America did not achieve racial democracy. Like other race leaders, Bethune was disillusioned with the outcome. She saw the World Court as an instrument to establish peace and goodwill based on respect for human liberty and social justice. But she also cautioned that before America could achieve this understanding with other nations, they had to "find that spirit among the various races and classes that constitute her own population."[41] In Bethune's mind, American participation

41. Bethune, "Feminism in France and Elsewhere," 15; see, for example, Blanche Weisen Cook, *Eleanor Roosevelt, 1933–1938,* vol. 2 (New York: Viking Press, 1999), 236; Franklin, *From Slavery to Freedom,* 291–309; Robin D. G. Kelley and Earl Lewis, *To Make Our World Anew: A History of African Americans* (New York: Oxford University Press, 2000), 399–401; Darlene Clark Hine, William C. Hine, and Stanley Harrold, eds., *The African American Odyssey* (Upper Saddle River, N.J.: Prentice-Hall, Inc., 2000), 376–78; Mary McLeod Bethune, "In-terracial Goodwill Throughout the World," address to the NAACP, November 14, 1934, MMB, 4.

in the World Court could be a means for achieving social justice for African Americans.

In a letter dated February 16, 1926, Terrell firmly objected to Bethune's expectations and reiterated her belief that "as colored women we could do no more than powerful organizations of other women were already doing."[42] She continued:

> We should not try to spread ourselves over too wide a surface and thus dissipate our influence and strength. The measures which are strongly advocated by the powerful and strong will be well looked after, but the measures which concern our welfare as a race should be our special concern and we, as colored women, should concentrate all our strength upon them. Very few are interested in the measures which promote our welfare as a race, it seems to me, so that we should bend all our energies to win friends for our cause and not run after "strange gods," so to speak.[43]

On March 30, 1926, Bethune caustically replied, thanking Terrell for the information her letter "contained concerning my shortcomings, and for the corrections you have made. I am always happy to have my friends point out my errors. I know how full of them I am."[44] Bethune continued to push her own agenda. Obviously, she had a fundamentally different outlook on the objectives of the NACW. Terrell believed the NACW should not veer from its original path. It should continue to respond to local, state, and national self-help projects that focused strictly on racial issues. In short, Terrell saw the NACW as a social settlement. Bethune, on the other hand, wanted the NACW to act as a political lobby, taking the initiative in addressing *all* public issues, and empowering women as independent leaders. Despite such disagreements, however, the bottom line was one of loyalty; publicly Bethune and Terrell supported one another. In August 1928, Bethune wrote thanking Terrell for standing by her throughout the NACW convention and her tenure as president.[45]

Bethune also had differences of opinion with her successors as well as her predecessors. Sallie W. Stewart, who held the NACW presidency from 1928 to 1932, often clashed with Bethune, who was then chairman of Headquarters. In 1929, Stewart advised her executive secretary, Minnie Scott, that she

42. Mary Church Terrell to Mary McLeod Bethune, February 16, 1926, MCT.
43. Ibid.
44. Mary McLeod Bethune to Mary Church Terrell, March 30, 1926, MCT.
45. Mary McLeod Bethune to Mary Church Terrell, August 22, 1928, MCT.

was to "take no orders" from Bethune during an upcoming visit. Further-more, Bethune was not to have access to the books, reports, and intimate office affairs. Minnie was to "keep her own council" and keep her eyes and ears open during Bethune's visit. She closed by wishing Scott "a fine visit with Lady Bethune."[46] Clearly, Stewart resented what she perceived as Bethune's overstepping her boundaries as chairman of Headquarters and interfering in the affairs of the president.

Bethune could be as just as temperamental in dealing with Stewart. In June 1929, Bethune sent a rather lengthy, detailed letter to Stewart outlining the procedures for the disbursement of collected funds as well as the duties of the president, trustees, and executive secretary. When Bethune heard that Stewart had "plans for National Headquarters," she caustically quoted the NACW constitution regarding the obligation of the president to inform the board of trustees before the president could put any such "plans" into operation.[47] Bethune, of course, feared that Stewart was going to close the national head-quarters and justify the closure through funding deficits. Since Bethune con-sidered the opening of the National Headquarters as her greatest achievement as president of the NACW, she naturally saw this as a threat to her legacy as well as to any political clout that the NACW had gained through its presence in Washington.

It may have been these confrontations over ideological, philosophical, and substantial issues that prompted Bethune to begin thinking about the devel-opment of a new national organization of black women's organizations. This concept became a point of contention between Bethune and many women who were a part of the NACW leadership. Terrell, Stewart, Mary F. Waring, and others strongly opposed the organization of a new national organiza-tion because they feared a new national group would undermine the NACW. These women argued that the NACW had a place on the National Coun-cil of Women of America (NCWA) and this place gave them enough na-tional exposure for issues confronting the race.[48] Bethune disagreed. In Jan-uary 1930, Bethune wrote to at least thirty influential black women, telling them that "for the past three years" she had been considering organizing a "National Council of Colored Women of America." The purpose of the asso-ciation was

46. Sallie W. Stewart to Minnie Scott, n.d., NACW.
47. Mary McLeod Bethune to Sallie W. Stewart, June 10, 1929, NACW.
48. "Ex-President N.A.C.W. Enters Controversy on Forming New National Council of Women," n.d., BFC I.

to give opportunity to those who are interested in the many phases of work among our women in this country to cope with the problems affecting our status in America and to cement a spirit of cooperation and unified effort in the shaping of our destiny . . . I am concerned about the central Wheel, composed of the many spokes of religious, educational, fraternal, political, economic, welfare and business organizations of Negro women—developing the ideals of our several groups.[49]

Bethune's plan was born of frustration and passion. She believed the NACW's place on the NCWA was insufficient. She argued that the NCWA had thirty-eight member organizations, only one of which represented African American interests. Moreover, membership in the NCWA did not give other black women's organizations the opportunity to work together to address the problems facing African Americans as a group. During her tenure as president, Bethune tried to mold the NACW into a cohesive body that could speak on various public issues as the official voice of black women. She met constant resistance from individual members who saw this as an infringement on their individual power.[50] So, in 1930, Bethune began lobbying her fellow clubwomen to meet with her and develop plans for a new organization that would unite black women's groups, encourage black women's leadership, and speak with one voice for African American women's interests. In March, Bethune organized a conference of leading black women, but only twelve, including bank president Maggie Lena Walker, Republican national committeewoman Mrs. George Williams, and Mrs. Robert Moton, wife of Booker T. Washington's successor at Tuskegee Institute, attended.[51] Moreover, the leading women of the NACW were conspicuously absent. Bethune knew she needed more followers and she needed the cooperation of at least a few key women in the NACW. It took her five years of lobbying to gain enough support for her plan, but at no time did Bethune abandon her idea. She forcefully argued that black women's groups had to unite and was passionate in her belief that black women should now play a substantive role in mainstream politics. She was convinced a united effort for direct action and political mobilization among black clubwomen would win them recognition and a place they deserved in the body politic.

49. Mary McLeod Bethune to Mary Church Terrell, January 29, 1930, MCT.
50. Records of the NACW. Throughout her tenure as president of the NACW, Bethune's messages in the *National Notes* continually call on members for unity and stresses that whatever comes will come through united efforts.
51. Giddings, *When and Where I Enter*, 202–3.

Indeed, her personal experiences bore this out. By the later part of the 1920s, Bethune's educational and organizational work attracted the attention of many leaders in the political sphere. Senator Frederic C. Walcott of Connecticut and J. S. Peabody introduced Bethune to Washington politics during World War I when she spoke to Vice President Thomas R. Marshall about black participation in the Red Cross. In 1927, while Bethune was president of the NACW, Eleanor Roosevelt invited her to attend a luncheon for the presidents of women's organizations under the auspices of the National Council of Women of the United States. Then in 1928, Bethune's benefactors at Bethune-Cookman introduced her to Washington politics through her appointment to a variety of committees as an expert on black education. President Calvin Coolidge named her as a delegate to a Child Welfare Conference held in Washington, D.C., and later President Herbert Hoover named her as a member of his National Committee on Child Welfare. In 1933, she received an appointment to a planning commission established by the Federal Office of Education for Negroes.[52] Although Bethune was an active Republican, both political parties recognized her as an expert on black children and education. Inevitably, Bethune's increasing public activities and federal appointments broadened her access to influential political figures. This widening circle of political contacts had far-reaching consequences and long-term repercussions for African American men and women in the coming decades.

Yet, it was her growing constituency among black women that assured a following for the National Council of Negro Women. In the post–World War I period, women's national organizations grew in size and number. These new associations and a new generation of black female activists pursued a wider variety of interests, and exhibited a pronounced tendency toward cooperation and a visible interest in international issues. Many leaders of these new and reorganized black national organizations, including Alpha Kappa Alpha and Iota Phi Lamda sororities, the National Association of College Women, the National Association of Graduate Nurses, National Business Women of America, National Health Care for Colored People, Women's Auxiliary of the National Baptist Convention, as well as innumerable lodges and fraternal organizations, understood the necessity of forming an umbrella organization and wholeheartedly supported Bethune's vision. Clara Burrell Bruce, representing the National Association for Housing, succinctly stated what many black women leaders had come to realize: "We have been thinking too long on

52. Holt, *Mary McLeod Bethune*, 148; Giddings, *When and Where I Enter*, 201–2; Fleming, *The Answered Prayer to a Dream*, 26–28.

individual problems instead of national ones. The League of Women Voters is well informed on International problems and National affairs. We need to corrall [sic] the forces of our group."[53]

∞

Bethune's work in the black women's club movement pushed her further away from a gradualist approach to race relations. This change became most evident after women achieved suffrage in 1920. As the forces of segregation and anti-black violence continued to gain momentum and conditions for African Americans continued to decline despite clear indications of progress, Bethune began to focus on making systemic changes to improve the status and conditions of the race. She became more vocal in her criticisms of American democracy and began to focus on ways to put African Americans, particularly African American women, in decision-making positions in government. She worked to encourage block voting among black women in Daytona Beach and as president of the NACW pushed the organization to take a more politically active role in the legislative process. She tried to make the NACW a clearinghouse for studying and advocating black women's political concerns as well as a bulwark for black women's participation in the formal political sphere as administrators and managers. Still, two important ingredients were missing that kept Bethune from reaching her goal: she needed access to political power at the highest level, and she had to develop a black political power base. Ironically, the Great Depression provided Bethune with the opportunity to obtain both.

53. "Minutes of the founding meeting held December 5, 1935," NCNW, Series 2, Box 1, Folder 1.

| 4 |

In the National Youth Administration

Mary McLeod Bethune's visibility in the New Deal as head of the Office of Minority Affairs in the National Youth Administration (NYA) illustrates both the continuity of black women's political activism and the changing opportunities for black women leaders. In 1927, Bethune met Eleanor Roosevelt at a luncheon for the presidents of women's organizations held under the auspices of the National Council of Women of the United States. As historian Paula Giddings has clearly established, this meeting marked the beginning of a friendship and an important alliance between Bethune and Roosevelt. Bethune was the only black woman to attend the luncheon. When seating began for lunch, many of the white women present hesitated to sit next to Bethune. To avoid an awkward incident, Sara Delano Roosevelt, Franklin Roosevelt's mother, asked Bethune to sit next to her. According to Giddings, this gesture began a friendship between the two women that eventually came to include the future president's wife. Bethune used her women's club affiliation to cultivate a close relationship with Eleanor Roosevelt, and this relationship would eventually lead to her selection for an administrative position within the New Deal administration.[1] Bethune's relationship with Eleanor Roosevelt greatly enhanced Bethune's status and gave her greater access to political leaders than other black advisers in the Roosevelt administration. More important, as a government administrator, Bethune learned about the inner workings of the American political process firsthand and gained knowledge she would use to bring African American men and women into the process

1. Giddings, *When and Where I Enter*, 201–2.

and to keep issues of concern to African Americans on the national political agenda.

Bethune expanded her political connections by serving as well on various nonpartisan committees dealing with black children and education between 1928 and 1933. In 1928, President Calvin Coolidge named her as a delegate to a child welfare conference held in Washington, D.C. President Herbert Hoover later named her as a member of his National Committee on Child Welfare, an extension of the American Child Health Association (ACHA). As a member of the ACHA committee, Bethune worked with other members to design national surveys on health conditions, infant mortality, and public health programs. The dismal results of these surveys led to the establishment of Child Health Day, a campaign to improve America's milk supply, institute training programs for midwives, and lobby for legislation to regulate child labor. Members publicized the findings through a published plan for community organization that became the basis for community programs by local mother's societies and later a popular radio talk show. Follow-up studies based on uniform standards determined whether children were "healthy" and measured community progress in promoting child health. The work of the committee resulted in better record-keeping, including birth registration; a 70 percent decline in the infant mortality rate; and vaccination programs to eliminate smallpox and diphtheria. Continuing expansion of state and local programs led the ACHA to turn over their work to state and local health officials. In 1935 the ACHA disbanded.[2] In 1933, Bethune accepted an appointment to a planning commission to study methods for improving black education established by the Federal Office of Education of Negroes. Although officially a Republican, Bethune assumed a nonpartisan position when dealing with issues that related to children and education. She worked with both Democrats and Republicans in Washington on these matters and increasingly members of both parties associated Bethune's name with children's and educational issues and recognized her as an expert in these fields.

In addition to Bethune's specific experiences, two events taking place in the early years of the twentieth century encouraged African American women to turn from protest to politics. The first was the massive migration of southern blacks, commonly known as the first Great Migration in the period around World War I. Told of the "Promised Land" by relatives, labor recruiters, and black newspaper editors, southern blacks went north with the expectation of

2. American Child Health Association Papers, "Scope and Content," *Hoover Papers*, URL: http://hoover.nara.gov/research/hooverpapers/hoover/commerce/acha5.htm, August 8, 2001.

freedom from racial oppression. Between 1910 and 1920 the black population increased in northern cities such as Chicago (from 44,103 to 109,458), Detroit (5,741 to 40,878), Cleveland (8,448 to 34,451), New York (91,709 to 152,467) and Philadelphia (84,459 to 134,229).[3] The reality was that the growing number of black migrants put African Americans in competition with poor whites for resources such as jobs, housing, and recreational facilities, leading to race riots across the nation in the years following the war. Rather than freedom, southern migrants found northern racial attitudes confined them to low-paying jobs and social and residential segregation. Yet, migrants used this segregation to their political advantage. Through the NAACP's official publication, the *Crisis*, leading African Americans appealed to blacks to vote independently and to use residential segregation to increase black political power. Their political advice was heeded. Machine politicians quickly recognized the importance of blacks as swing voters in closely contested elections, and black wards began electing black representatives to seats on city councils, state legislatures, and eventually the U.S. House of Representatives. Increased black voting strength also meant that white politicians had to pay attention to the issues important to black voters if they expected to win and hold political office.[4]

The second event was the passage of the Nineteenth Amendment. In 1920, woman suffrage persuaded black women to broaden their ideas about the value of formal political participation and to reevaluate their political place. African American women found that despite segregation and racial oppression, new opportunities for women's political involvement gave them hope

---

3. Evelyn Brooks Higginbotham, "Clubwomen and Electoral Politics," 134.

4. On migration to the North and its effects see Peter Gottlieb, *Making Their Own Way: Southern Blacks Migration to Pittsburgh, 1916–1930* (Urbana: University of Illinois Press, 1987); James R. Grossman, *Land of Hope: Chicago, Black Southerners, and the Great Migration* (Chicago: University of Chicago Press, 1989); Joe William Trotter, Jr., *Black Milwaukee: The Making of a Black Proletariat 1915–1945* (Urbana: University of Illinois Press, 1985); Nicholas Lemann, *The Promised Land: The Great Black Migration and How It Changed America* (New York: A. A. Knopf, 1991); Joe William Trotter, ed. *The Black Migration in Historical Perspective* (Bloomington: Indiana University Press, 1991). On racial conflict see Elliott M. Rudwick, *Race Riot at East St. Louis, July 2, 1917* (Cleveland: World Publishing, 1966); William Tuttle, *Chicago in the Red Summer of 1919* (New York: Atheneum, 1970); Lee E. Williams, *Anatomy of Four Race Riots: Racial Conflict in Knoxville, Elaine (Arkansas), Tulsa, and Chicago, 1919–1921* (Hattiesburg: University and College Press of Mississippi, 1972). On black politics and voting see Harold F. Gosnell, *Negro Politcians* (Chicago: University of Chicago Press, 1935), 13–92, 180–90; Morris, *The Politics of Black America*, 148–65; Walton, Jr., *Invisible Politics: Black Political Behavior*, 8, 29–31.

for a brighter future. As historian Glenda Gilmore found in her study of black women in North Carolina, prior to passage of the Nineteenth Amendment black women acted as ambassadors for the black community to the white political power structure, approaching white officials and negotiating for civic improvements in their communities. They learned to work with white women's groups, gain their support, and have them lobby state legislatures for funding for black projects. After suffrage, African American women began to concentrate on building black female voting blocks, mobilizing African American women voters who would use the power of the ballot to compel public officials to institute programs designed to improve society and pass legislation geared toward eliminating segregation.[5]

The black press reinforced the value of African American women's political work by featuring positive stories dealing with women's political activities. Well-known black newspapers such as the *Chicago Defender* and the *Afro-American* in Baltimore marked women's political appointments, highlighted their voter registration activities, and gave positive coverage to women's political rallies and meetings. Newspapers also carried weekly columns written by women that served to educate women voters.[6]

Moreover, as Bethune's tenure as president of the National Association of Colored Women illustrates, African American women increasingly used their ready-made national network in the black women's clubs to disseminate information and promote collective political action. Just as Bethune used the NACW's *National Notes*, other women's groups began to use their club publications to encourage political consciousness, share ideas and strategies, and follow the political progress of various members at the state level. Black clubwomen organized politically oriented meetings in halls, churches, lodges, schools, and homes. In urban areas, members set up districts with block captains to coordinate house-to-house canvassing, voter registration, and Get-Out-the-Vote campaigns. Women printed circular letters and pamphlets, and held meetings to teach others how to organize new neighborhoods and the most effective ways to poll, register, and get out the vote. In 1924, black women organized their first overtly partisan political organization—the National League of Republican Colored Women (NLRCW). African

5. Gilmore, *Gender and Jim Crow*, 147–50; Brooks Higginbotham, "Clubwomen and Electoral Politics," 137–38.
6. Evelyn Brooks Higginbotham, "In Politics to Stay: Black Women Leaders and Party Politics in the 1920s," 199–220.

American women founded the NLRCW to ensure that black women would
have a long-term political organization designed to advance a specific political
party.[7]

Unfortunately, the Coolidge and Hoover administration's unresponsiveness
to increasingly hard economic times for blacks in the mid-1920s began to
undermine widespread support for the Republican party just as the NLRCW
was organized. As economic hardships deepened and dragged on, each year
an increasing number of black political activists objected to President Herbert
Hoover's policies. With the coming of the Great Depression, their opposition
hardened. They condemned Hoover's capitulation to "lily-white" Republicans in the South, his segregation of black Gold Star Mothers, and his nomi-
nation of John J. Parker, an overt racist, for Supreme Court justice. Yet, some,
including Mary Church Terrell and Bethune, continued to support Hoover
throughout his 1932 reelection campaign. In October 1932, Terrell wrote
Bethune asking her to write a statement for publication endorsing Hoover's
candidacy. Bethune replied, "I want you to know that I am doing all that I
possibly can for our party. I am using my influence in every section I touch.
I feel confident that the best efforts will bring forth the best result."[8] Like
other southern blacks, Bethune could not yet turn to the Democratic party,
the party of white supremacy in the South, despite the growing frustration
with Hoover and the Republicans among African Americans. With the election of Franklin D. Roosevelt and the implementation of the New Deal, new
political leaders with distinct political strategies emerged. The Roosevelt administration's willingness to appoint racial liberals to key government posts
encouraged African Americans. Bethune's transition from Hoover supporter
and member of the Board of Counselors to the Women's Division of the
Republican National Party in 1932 to her role as director of the Office of
Minority Affairs and organizer of the Black Cabinet under the Roosevelt
administration is symbolic of the shifting loyalties of the black electorate.[9]

After Roosevelt took office in 1933, Bethune politically aligned herself
with the new administration, classifying herself as a "New Dealer" and "making no apologies for that." She openly and resolutely believed "in the democratic and humane program" of FDR.[10] Behind the scenes, Bethune became
an adviser on black politics to Democratic party officials, New Deal administrators, and FDR himself. Yet, she was quite candid in assessing the New

7. Ibid.
8. Mary McLeod Bethune to Mary Church Terrell, October 24, 1932, MCT.
9. Brooks Higginbotham, "In Politics to Stay," 199–220.
10. Mary McLeod Bethune to Dr. Gordon B. Hancock, October 12, 1942, BFC I.

Deal's strengths and weaknesses concerning African Americans. As a political insider, she was well aware of the shortcomings within the New Deal programs and FDR's civil rights policies. At conferences, state meetings, and conventions, she reminded African Americans that even though federal programs sought to include them, they should not be satisfied with how New Deal officials implemented these programs at the state and local level. Moreover, blacks could not afford to become complacent about FDR's decidedly unsupportive position on civil rights legislation. She encouraged African Americans to take an active part in protesting FDR's meager civil rights initiatives. She encouraged them to fight against discrimination and segregation and for better housing, educational, and employment opportunities whenever possible. At the same time, however, Bethune advocated loyalty to the administration and support for FDR's efforts for relief, economic recovery, and reform by implying that Republicans offered much less to America's black citizens. Within four years of Roosevelt's election a political realignment among African Americans was well underway.

By the 1930s, African Americans were in dire need of a "New Deal," and many black leaders eagerly looked to the Roosevelt administration for the support they needed to achieve economic, political, and social equality. Roosevelt inspired many blacks when he appointed a number of men as agency heads who openly and aggressively committed themselves to the cause of social justice and civil rights for black Americans. They included Harold Ickes, secretary of the Interior and director of the Public Works Administration (PWA); Clark Forman, special adviser on the Economic Status of Negroes; Daniel C. Roper, secretary of Commerce; Harry Hopkins, head of the Civil Works Administration (CWA); Henry Wallace, secretary of Agriculture; and Aubrey Williams, executive director of the National Youth Administration (NYA). Other young policymakers, lawyers, and social workers streamed into Washington to "help right the wrongs that had befallen our country." Despite the fact that Roosevelt never initiated or passed civil rights legislation, did not offer executive support for any antilynching bill, and never publicly associated himself with African American issues before 1935, many black leaders had already worked with several of these appointees in southern interracial organizations and knew of their commitment to equality. Many of these appointees began hiring blacks as assistants. For example, Clark Forman hired Robert C. Weaver, a black economist and doctoral candidate at

Harvard, as his assistant and likely successor. These actions, in concert with FDR's campaign for using the resources of the federal government as a tool for achieving human betterment, prompted Robert Vann, editor of the black weekly *Pittsburgh Courier,* to advise blacks to "go home and turn Lincoln's picture to the wall. The debt has been paid in full."[11] African Americans expected the Roosevelt administration to support their continuing struggle for increased employment opportunities, economic security, and the protection of civil rights; however, the implementation and effects of many early New Deal programs did not always reassure them.

Black leaders such as John P. Davis and Walter White were openly critical of the early New Deal programs, calling the New Deal "slogans for the same raw deal" for African Americans. In fact, before 1935 many of the benefits of the New Deal programs rarely reached African Americans. An assessment of two years of relief programs under the Federal Emergency Relief Act (FERA) clearly shows that the number of black Americans on relief rolls increased from 17.8 percent in 1933 to 29 percent in 1935, or from 2,117,000 persons to 3,500,000 persons. Rather than indicating that relief measures were becoming more humane, according to Davis, these figures clearly show that African Americans were rapidly losing ground. Black workers did not have access to the small number of available jobs. Instead, employers gave unemployed white workers the first opportunity to fill available positions, and white workers even began taking the menial jobs normally reserved for black workers.[12] National Recovery Administration (NRA) programs excluded black industrial workers from minimum wage and maximum hour benefits through exemptions. For example, in the cotton textile industry, the minimum wage was set at twelve dollars a week in the South and the maximum number of hours was set at forty. On the surface, this code did not seem to treat black workers any differently from white workers. Yet, by exempting ten thousand cleaners, outside crews, and yardmen, the code actually discriminated against the black textile workers who filled the greatest number of these positions. At the same time, provisions that allowed manufacturers to set prices served to increase prices for finished goods from 10 to 40 percent with no corresponding increase in wages for blacks. Similar practices affected the lumber and steel industries.

11. Leslie H. Fishel, Jr., "A Case Study: The Negro in the New Deal," in *The New Deal: Analysis and Interpretation,* ed. Alonzo L. Hamby, 218–31; Patricia Sullivan, *Days of Hope: Race and Democracy in the New Deal Era,* 4, 24–25; Fishel, 220.

12. T. Arnold Hill, "The Negro Worker in the Nineteen-Thirties," reprinted in Herbert Aptheker, ed., *A Documentary History of the Negro People in the United States,* vol. 4, 268–79.

The complete exclusion of household workers under the NRA codes led to increased discrimination against black women workers and lower standards of living for thousands of black families. For many black Americans the NRA acronym meant "Negroes Ruined Again," and the NRA Blue Eagle was a "predatory bird."[13]

African Americans fared no better under the relief efforts of the Civil Works Administration (CWA) and the Public Works Administration (PWA). Complaints about these agencies were not without merit. In 1933, Harry Hopkins, head of the Federal Emergency Relief Administration (FERA), sent investigators into the field to report directly to him on the human dimension of the economic situation and the impact of relief programs on individuals. Lorena A. Hickok, an experienced newspaperwoman and close friend of Eleanor Roosevelt, provided Hopkins with reports from twenty-eight states and Puerto Rico. In Augusta, Georgia, Hickok spoke to a black preacher who told her another story about the effects of the NRA:

> . . . one of his parishioners had been employed at Western Union for five years at $6.25 a week. Under the code, for the work he is doing, he should be getting $13. He (the preacher) took the matter up with the compliance board, and Western Union promised to pay the Negro the code wage. Sometime later, he told me, the parishioner told him they'd raise his wage to $10 a week, $3 under the code rate, and told him not to tell the preacher or they'd fire him.
>
> "I could make an issue of this case, perhaps," the preacher said, "but I know that, if I did, sooner or later the boy would be fired. So we're not doing anything about it."[14]

The CWA ignored black skilled laborers in allocating CWA jobs. Contractors often forced skilled black workers to work at unskilled rates:

> Wherever the higher wage scale is adhered to, they say, the tendency is to throw out Negroes and hire whites. Negro workmen are uniformly lazy and shiftless, they say—and judging from the color of the bathtubs

13. John P. Davis, "What Price National Recovery," reprinted in Aptheker, ed., *A Documentary History of the Negro People in the United States*, vol. 4, 49–52; Fishel, Jr., "A Case Study: The Negro in the New Deal," 218–31; John P. Davis, "A Black Inventory of the New Deal," reprinted in Howard Zinn, ed., *New Deal Thought*, 316–24; William E. Leuchtenburg, *Franklin D. Roosevelt and the New Deal*, 185–87.

14. Richard Lowitt and Maurine Beasley, eds., *One Third of a Nation: Lorena Hickok Reports on the Great Depression*, 149.

in some of these Southern hotels I'll say they are—but heretofore have been tolerated because they were cheap. Now that they have got to pay higher wages—when they do—employers are going to hire whites, who do the work better.[15]

Civic improvement projects financed with CWA funds routinely overlooked necessary improvements in segregated black neighborhoods. Many cities denied African Americans access to public facilities funded by the CWA such as playgrounds, parks, hospitals, and libraries. When the PWA replaced the CWA, the same discriminatory practices continued. Hickok found dissatisfaction among white employers as well. In Charleston, South Carolina, farm owners complained that the Civil Works Administration (CWA) was creating a labor shortage. Farmers who used to pay their wage laborers about 75 cents a day now had to compete with the CWA, which offered African Americans 30 and 40 cents an hour.[16] This resentment was not confined to farm owners, but applied also to businessmen who employed black women as domestic servants. In a meeting with businessmen in Baltimore, Maryland, Hickok reported,

> The gentleman who presided—he says he pays his own servants $12 a week—thought that all women who refused to take live-in housemaid jobs at $3 a week should be cut off relief. Someone suggested that many of these women couldn't live-in because they had small children to look after at home nights.
> "We-e-ell," he said, "I don't believe ordinarily in separating mothers from children, but we've GOT to think of taxpayers money. And if we can institutionalize these children—for the time being, anyway—take care of them cheaper than we're doing it now and put their mothers to work, I think we owe it to the taxpayers, etc."[17]

Although Hickok's biases are apparent in her reports, these reports are invaluable for the firsthand accounts of how these programs were implemented. Surprisingly, they also highlight the fact that both blacks and whites were discontented and disillusioned with federal efforts toward relief. Whites believed

15. Ibid., 149–50.
16. Guy B. Johnson, "Does the South Owe the Negro a New Deal?" reprinted in Zinn, ed., *New Deal Thought*, 309–16; Davis, "A Black Inventory of the New Deal," 316–24; Lowitt and Beasley, eds., *One Third of a Nation*, 181.
17. Lowitt and Beasley, eds., *One Third of a Nation*, 350.

the federal government was "ruining" black labor by paying relatively high wages, causing a labor shortage in the farm districts by distributing CWA jobs to blacks, and encouraging domestic workers to demand better wages and working conditions. Disheartened African Americans saw whites taking jobs normally filled by blacks, skilled black workers being forced to accept unskilled, lower-paid positions, and threats of being fired if they went to compliance boards to force employers to pay NRA wages. As far as relief efforts were concerned, the federal government pleased neither whites nor blacks.

African Americans fared no better under the Agricultural Adjustment Act (AAA), the Civilian Conservation Corp (CCC), or the Social Security Act (SSA). Acreage reduction provisions of the AAA allowed white landowners to put black tenant farmers and sharecroppers off the land by excluding the land they farmed from production. Landowners often cheated those that remained on the land out of their federal parity checks, applying the sharecropper and tenant portion of the payments to "back debts." The AAA referred complaints made by black farmers back to local boards that favored white landowners. Local AAA boards often required black landowners to reduce acreage, thereby reducing their income and forcing them into foreclosure.[18] The CCC established segregated camps for young men who worked at conservation and reforestation projects across the country. Moreover, only about 10 percent of the young men who participated in the program were black. Provisions of the SSA gave retired workers government pensions and protected workers in cases of unemployment, but the act contained exclusions for agricultural workers and domestic service employees, most of whom were black.[19]

Despite its shortcomings, black appointees such as Bethune, Robert Weaver, and Ira DeA. Reid praised the New Deal and the Roosevelt administration.[20] Weaver agreed that some New Deal economic programs fell short as far as immediate benefits to African Americans were concerned, but pointed out that other programs such as housing and emergency education were highly successful. The Housing Division of FERA had sixty federal housing projects in construction by December 31, 1935. Twenty-eight of these projects were entirely for black families, and the FERA designated eight others mainly

18. Davis, "A Black Inventory of the New Deal," 316–24; Davis, "What Price National Recovery," 49–54.

19. Johnson, "Does the South Owe the Negro a New Deal?" 309–16; Davis, "A Black Inventory of the New Deal," 316–24.

20. James A. Harrell, "Negro Leadership in the Election Year 1936," 554.

for African Americans. Overall, the housing projects would provide 74,664 rooms and accommodations for about 23,000 low-income black families. FERA allocated approximately $64 million for the housing project, of which about $19 million (or 29 percent) was devoted to slum clearance. FERA also initiated housing projects for African Americans in Atlanta, Cleveland, Indianapolis, Detroit, Chicago, Nashville, and Montgomery, Alabama. Moreover, blacks benefited not only from having access to decent housing but also from housing construction contracts with specific provisions requiring a percentage of the payroll be allotted for skilled African American workers.[21] While these housing programs did not challenge racial segregation, they greatly improved the conditions under which many African Americans lived.

Emergency education programs under FERA were also benefiting African Americans, according to Weaver. Out of 17,879 teachers in the thirteen southern states, 5,476 (30.6 percent) were black, and out of 570,794 students enrolled in emergency classes, 217,000 (38 percent) were black. Moreover, African Americans received 26.1 percent of the monthly education expenditures. Weaver reported that approximately half of the southern states spent percentages of their emergency education funds on blacks that were larger than the percentage of blacks in those states' populations. Overall, the South spent slightly more for African American teacher salaries in relation to the percentage of blacks in the population. According to Weaver, FERA gave college and university scholarships equitably. Each college or university operated for profit received twenty dollars monthly per student as aid for 12 percent of its enrollment.[22]

The fundamental problem for African Americans with New Deal programs was implementation. Despite FDR's professed commitment to making government an active agent for change, his advisers' strong recommendations, and Eleanor Roosevelt's activism on racial matters, administration of these programs was highly decentralized. Because FDR was politically reluctant to ostracize southern Democrats, federal administrators developed programs at the national level, then handed them over to state and local officials to implement. In this way, benefits were distributed based on state and local customs. The administration did not interfere and so racial prejudice, discrimination, and segregation were endorsed, practiced, and sustained within these programs. Qualified African American leaders who would oversee program im-

21. Robert C. Weaver, "The New Deal Is for the Negro," reprinted in Zinn, ed., *New Deal Thought,* 324–31.
22. Ibid., 328–30.

plementation at the state or local level and appoint black representatives to local boards remained underrepresented at the federal level until 1935. There were very few New Deal programs that successful alleviated the worst effects of the depression for African Americans before 1935, even those headed by strongly committed white racial liberals.

Discriminatory implementation of many programs circumscribed material progress, but the psychological benefits that accrued to the black community as a whole were extensive. Blacks at the local level may not have shared equally in individual program benefits, but for the first time they saw the federal government hiring African Americans for a number of important positions. The Roosevelt administration hired black professionals as architects, lawyers, statisticians, economists, and engineers within the federal government. Non-professionals filled positions as stenographers, secretaries, messengers, elevator operators, and clerks. FDR appointed more black leaders to important posts than ever. Eugene Kinckle Jones of the National Urban League served in the Department of Commerce. William H. Hastie and Robert C. Weaver served in the Department of the Interior. The Social Security Board had Ira DeA. Reid, while Lawrence W. Oxley served in the Department of Labor and Ambrose Caliver worked in the Office of Education.[23]

On June 28, 1935, Bethune came to the attention of the Roosevelt administration when she accepted the Spingarn Medal, the highest honor bestowed by the NAACP for her race work and her unwavering commitment to social justice and human welfare. Josephine Roche, assistant secretary of the Treasury and chairperson of the NYA's executive committee, presented Bethune with the award. Bethune's acceptance speech was relatively short, slightly longer than five typewritten pages, but it illuminates her complex, and often conflicting, ideas about race and gender. First, although her audience was interracial, Bethune's address, like Booker T. Washington's Atlanta Compromise address, paid only lip service to the role of whites in achieving the brotherhood she sought. She acknowledged her regard for white liberals who "have been big enough, courageous enough, to stand for social justice and equality of opportunity."[24] Yet, she did not question white racial attitudes nor did she imply that white liberals bore any burden of responsibility for working to change those attitudes. Instead, Bethune endorsed self-help and

23. Fishel, Jr., "A Case Study: The Negro in the New Deal," 224.

24. "Response of Mrs. Mary McLeod Bethune, Twenty-first Spingarn Medalist at the Twenty-sixth Annual Conference of the National Association of Colored People, St. Louis, Missouri, June 18, 1935," MMB, 4.

placed the responsibility for overcoming obstacles squarely on the shoulders of African Americans. She maintained that whites harbored prejudices about blacks because of "misunderstandings" and that it was up to *all* African Americans to work together harmoniously to clear the interracial misunderstandings that "clutter up the highway of life" to achieve "true harmonious relations." Bethune was inherently a negotiator who abhorred interracial conflict; she believed that without collaboration and consensus, African Americans would not move forward as a race.

However, Bethune's remarks also reflected Du Bois's vision of the Talented Tenth as well as her personal preparation as a socially responsible black woman. She said, "Brotherhood is not an ideal. It is but a state or a condition attendant upon achievement of an ideal. It is one of the components of an ideal. I believe that brotherhood depends upon and follows achievement." She called on African Americans of vision and "educational advantages" to continue working until they reached "the lowest strata of the masses; that mass that is standing so helplessly waiting for you and me to administer the human touch." Race leaders must use their "broad vision, zeal, and preparedness" to lift the "veil of ignorance and superstition" so that misunderstandings about blacks which caused prejudice to continue would be swept aside. Educated black leaders must work to develop more than their "narrow selves."[25]

Perhaps the most intriguing part of this speech is in Bethune's use of gender-specific terms. Following the conventions of the day, she used generic terms such as "brotherhood," and spoke of the "black man," the "lowest man," "men of vision," "every man," "our brothers," and "free men." Yet, when she spoke of "humanity" Bethune reverts to the use of "her": "The creed of freedom has not yet been written. Humanity is yet a slave to her desires, her fears, her intelligence, her social standing, her craving for power."

When confronted with such suggestive linguistic evidence, historians are often tempted to read more than what was intended by the usage. It might be said that Bethune referred to humanity as feminine as a device to legitimate a public role for women. Who better to help a "female" humanity overcome these negatives and write the "creed of freedom" than other women? In the nineteenth century, women were stereotypically thought to be more moral and nurturing; therefore improving conditions for women and children was woman's "natural" charge. And it must be recalled that Bethune had been raised in that ethos. Combining this factor with the fact that during the New

25. Ibid., 2–3.

Deal black and white women were being condemned for working outside the home, taking jobs away from male heads of household, and an additional reason for feminizing her image arises. Women in the 1930s were being encouraged not to take jobs from men, to rely on their husbands as breadwinners. By 1937 FDR pushed for the passage of the Economy Act, which forced married women out of government jobs and married female teachers out of their positions. Women were being pushed from the stage only a few years after being welcomed into the body politic. These facts must have goaded Bethune, who had sacrificed so much for women's advancement. She continued, "Let us as workers under this banner spread truth and make men free—spread truth about economic adjustment; truth about moral obligation; truth about segregation; truth about citizenship; truth about abilities, achievements and accomplishments; . . . yes, truth wherever truth is needed. Then our lives may be lived with freedom." As for herself, she would not be silenced by the socioeconomic fashions of her day. She would tell the truth. She would speak her creed of freedom. She would not deny her craving for power. After hearing Bethune's acceptance speech, Roche became convinced that Bethune warranted a place on the National Advisory Committee of the NYA.[26]

After the Spingarn Medal presentation, Roche met with Eleanor Roosevelt and recommended Bethune for a position on the NYA committee. Previously acquainted with Bethune, and aware of her achievements, Roosevelt agreed with Roche's recommendation. Consequently, it was not surprising that within six weeks of receiving the Spingarn Medal, Roosevelt personally met with Bethune and asked her to become a member of the NYA advisory committee as a special consultant for education in the South.[27]

The National Advisory Committee of the NYA was composed of thirty-five representatives of business, agriculture, education, and youth, including Charles Taussig, president of the American Molasses Company; George W. Johnson, director of the Department of Education, National Catholic Welfare Association; Clarence Poe, editor of the *Progressive Farmer;* Adolf Augustus Berle, Jr., assistant secretary of state; Charles H. Judd, chairman, Department of Education, University of Chicago; Selma Borchardt, vice-president, American Federation of Teachers; Francis J. McConnell, bishop, Methodist Episcopal Church; Florence Thorne, American Federation of Labor; Owen D. Young, chairman of the board, General Electric Company;

26. Ibid., 5.
27. Giddings, *When and Where I Enter,* 201–2; Fleming, *The Answered Prayer to a Dream,* 25–28.

William Green, president, American Federation of Labor; Elizabeth Morrissey, professor of economics, College of Notre Dame of Maryland; George Zook, president, American Council on Education; George Harrison, grand president, Brotherhood of Railway and Steamship Clerks; Thomas Neblett, National Labor Relations Board; and Sidney Hillman, president, Amalgamated Clothing Workers.

Aubrey Williams, head of the agency, was a southern racial liberal. Williams was born in Springville, Alabama, in 1890. He attended Maryville College in Tennessee and the University of Cincinnati from 1911 to 1916. During World War I, Williams went to France with the YWCA, entered the Foreign Legion Services before America's entry to the war, and then served in the U.S. Army in France. At the end of the war, Williams remained in France to attend the University of Bordeaux, receiving a degree in philosophy in 1919. He then returned to the United States, where he attended the University of Cincinnati and received a degree in sociology. From 1922 to 1931, Williams was the director of the Wisconsin Conference on Social Work and taught at the University of Wisconsin. He then entered public service as a representative for FERA and served as an assistant to Harry Hopkins until 1933. In January 1934, Williams was appointed deputy administrator of the WPA and simultaneously served as the Executive Director of the NYA from July 1935 through September 1943.[28]

Williams insisted that the NYA committee have two black representatives at a time when African Americans held only one position on most other agency committees. The first appointment went to Mordecai Johnson. Many committee members knew Johnson because as president of Howard University he was involved with obtaining federal funds for the university.[29] On August 1, 1935, Williams officially appointed Bethune as the second black member of the Advisory Committee. Bethune accepted the position, although she realized the committee played only a limited role in the administration of the NYA. Officially, advisory committee members met only once or twice a year. Nevertheless, Bethune recognized her appointment as an opportunity, albeit a small one, for African American women to gain a foothold within the New Deal bureaucracy.

The NYA was one of the more racially progressive New Deal agencies. In 1935, the administration created the agency under the Emergency Relief Appropriations Act within the WPA by Executive Order 7034. Under

28. AW, General Files, Box 36.
29. Smith, "Mary McLeod Bethune and the National Youth Administration," 151.

the administration of Williams and Bethune's tenacious, watchful eye, the NYA became the basis for alleviating many problems faced by young African Americans during the depression era. The NYA's primary function and duty was "To initiate and administer a program of approved projects which shall provide relief, work relief, and employment for persons between the ages of sixteen and twenty-five years who are no longer in regular attendance at a school requiring full time, and who are not regularly engaged in remunerative employment."[30]

The NYA had two objectives. The first, called "work relief," was to provide for the part-time employment of youth from relief families on work projects designed to give them valuable work experience and benefit their communities. The program focused its efforts toward initiating projects such as the construction of recreational and community centers that would eventually become "self-liquidating." Those youths receiving work relief had to come from families certified as eligible for relief services. The program paid approximately fifteen dollars per month for about forty-four hours of work. Projects included work as professional, technical, clerical, and service assistants on residential projects, on construction and improvements of public buildings, recreational facilities, conservation projects, museum work, highway construction and beautification, and agricultural training. The NYA also provided placement services and vocational training projects. The NYA designed work relief and job training to provide aid to about 150,000 eligible young people.[31]

The second NYA objective, termed "student aid," was to provide funds for the part-time employment of needy secondary school, college, and graduate students sixteen to twenty-five years of age to enable them to continue their education. The program required students receiving aid to work a certain number of hours per week based on their grade level. Secondary level students received six dollars per month on average. Students used this money for transportation, lunch, and other incidental expenses necessary for continued

30. "The Establishment of the National Youth Administration within the Works Progress Administration," FDR.

31. "The Objectives of the Youth Administration," FDR; Palmer O. Johnson and Oswald L. Harvey, *The National Youth Administration, Staff Study Number 13,* 7, 48–77; Betty and Ernest K. Lindley, *A New Deal for Youth: The Story of the National Youth Administration,* 17–67, 156–91; Walter G. Daniel and Carroll L. Miller, "The Participation of the Negro in the National Youth Administration Program," 357–65; "The Establishment of the National Youth Administration within the Works Progress Administration," 1935, FDR; "Notes for Aubrey William," NYA, Record Group 119.

school attendance. Projects at the secondary school level included grounds and building maintenance and helped about two hundred thousand students. College level aid was an extension of high school aid for those students unable to attend college unless they earned money from part-time work. College students received an average of fifteen dollars per month. Students worked as professional and semiprofessional assistants, clerical and service assistants, construction and maintenance workers, home economics assistants, laboratory assistants, on library projects, and provided extracurricular recreational and educational activities. Student aid at the college level targeted approximately two hundred thousand students. Postgraduate aid was available to college graduates unable to find employment or to continue graduate studies unless given part-time work. Qualified students received thirty dollars per month on average and performed virtually the same work as college students. About thirty thousand postgraduate students were to receive funding from the NYA.[32]

The NYA student aid program was one that looked to America's future. Without this program during the darkest days of the depression, many young people would have had to leave school and most would never have returned to complete their education. Without NYA funding an entire generation of Americans would have been denied their education, and what is more important, America would have lost a valuable resource—the next generation of educators, journalists, scientists, artists, writers, and other professionals. The NYA funds were also important to traditionally black colleges and universities. The Agricultural Research and Experiment Station run by Dr. George Washington Carver at Tuskegee Institute operated entirely on NYA funds for student labor.[33] At Bethune-Cookman College, federal money was often the lifeline that kept students in the classroom and the college operating.

After her appointment to the NYA advisory committee, Bethune began to work immediately and aggressively to move beyond the limited role offered by her committee membership. In January 1936, Bethune delivered a report on the results of the NYA's first-year activities for minority groups to the Executive Committee and FDR. She explained what the NYA meant to

32. "The Establishment of the National Youth Administration within the Works Progress Administration," FDR; Lindley, *A New Deal for Youth*, 156–91; "Notes for Aubrey Williams from Mary McLeod Bethune on facts about African Americans in the NYA program," NYA, Record Group 119; Lindley and Lindley, *A New Deal for Youth*, 156–91; Johnson and Harvey, *The National Youth Administration*, 23–47.

33. Lindley and Lindley, *A New Deal for Youth*, 179.

minority groups and why the program was so important to black families in the impoverished South:

> The Negro views with deep interest the national program for all youth and approves most highly of its objectives. More particularly is the Negro interested in those phases of the program, which for the first time in the history of the nation, affords Negro youth through Federal benefits, larger opportunities for education, productive work and cultural and wholesome recreation. . . . Through the program of the National Youth movement touching the humblest black boy of the South has come to the realization on the part of thousands of untutored Negro parents that the government does care,—for "even the least of these."[34]

Bethune explained that the fifteen- to twenty-dollar checks impoverished African Americans received from the federal government were important. These funds allowed poor blacks to significantly improve their lives by gaining access to previously unavailable medical care, schoolbooks for black children, and the chance to take an occasional recreational break. Bethune's speech apparently impressed FDR. Shortly after this presentation, the president authorized the creation of an Office of Minority Affairs within the NYA and authorized Williams to appoint Bethune as head of the new division. This was the first federal post created for a black woman,[35] and made Bethune the highest placed African American woman in government. Bethune intended to make the most of her position.

Bethune effectively used her federal position to broaden and expand on the work she had begun as an educator and member of state, regional, and national women's clubs. She clearly took pleasure in her role as a leader, but she rationalized her desire for power. Bethune saw her attainment of power as beneficial to racial advancement. In keeping with her ideas of socially responsible individualism, Bethune did not view her public positions solely in terms of personal power. And to her credit, she used her federal appointment to open the doors of national politics to many other African Americans. She had three specific goals in mind. First, she planned to use her position to make sure African Americans received a fair share of benefits from New Deal programs. Second, she wanted to bring more blacks into the decision-making

34. "Minutes of the Executive Committee Meeting of the National Youth Administration," 1936, 135–36, FDR.
35. Rackham Holt, *Mary McLeod Bethune*, 191–94; Mary McLeod Bethune, "My Secret Talks with FDR," reprinted in Bernard Sternsher, ed., *The Negro in Depression and War*, 59.

process. Third, she intended to act as an advocate on black women's behalf. Bethune used her federal position and her friendship with Eleanor Roosevelt to push the administration into appointing qualified black women to positions of strategic importance in the federal government and to get as many women as possible named to at least honorary positions so that their names and qualifications would be recognized by the administration.[36]

As historian Elaine Smith has argued, Bethune's appointment did not mark a turning point in racial attitudes in America. FDR's goal was not to bring African Americans into the mainstream of American life and institutions. Rather, Bethune's appointment to a separate office set up exclusively to deal with minority affairs shows that the president was simply willing to provide blacks with a "separate equality." This policy angered African American leaders such as Walter White and John P. Davis who believed blacks should not accept any program that did not include full integration for African Americans. Bethune did not agree. As a federal official, Bethune did not publicly challenge state segregation laws. Her goal as director of minority affairs was to increase opportunities for blacks, even if achieving this did not necessarily result in integration into white institutions. She took a pragmatic approach and adapted her public objectives to the predominant goals of the administration, an approach that was in line with other black leaders of the time. W. E. B. Du Bois and James Weldon Johnson made the same argument in 1934. Both Du Bois and Johnson believed refusing to accept government aid simply because it was distributed through separate programs was impractical given the severity of the economic crisis. Du Bois asked, "The question is then, are we going to stand out and refuse the inevitable and inescapable government aid because we wish first to abolish the Color Line? This is not simply tilting at windmills; it is, if we are not careful, committing race suicide." Johnson concurred with Du Bois's opinion and wrote, "common sense compels us to get whatever and all the good we can out of the system of imposed segregation."[37]

Bethune publicly declared she "very definitely" believed in FDR's New Deal program. She saw the New Deal, with all of its limitations, as "helpful to the masses," and she believed it was her job to "integrate my people in the

36. Mary McLeod Bethune to Eleanor Roosevelt, January 27, 1941, Box 797, ER.
37. Smith, "Mary McLeod Bethune and the National Youth Administration"; B. Joyce Ross, "Mary McLeod Bethune and the National Youth Administration: A Case Study of Power Relationships in the Black Cabinet of Franklin D. Roosevelt," 12–14; Harrell, "Negro Leadership in the Election Year 1936," 546–64; Du Bois, *Crisis* (April 1934): 115–16; James Weldon Johnson, *Negro Americans, What Now?* 98–103.

set-up." Bethune often publicly applauded NYA programs despite their segregated nature. In a 1936 radio address, Bethune commended the NYA program for the construction of 213 separate black elementary and high school buildings at a cost of approximately $6 million in fifteen southern states. However, she also prodded the NYA executive committee to eliminate segregated programs outside the South. At an Executive Committee meeting in 1936, she cautioned the committee, "In places where there is no need for a separate program, for Negro and white groups, we most heartily recommend the one program. And in fields where it is necessary for us to have a separate program, we most heartily recommend a separate [sic] program, taking, of course, under advisement the necessity of proper leadership and guidance that we might be able to do the most effective work."[38]

Of course, to Bethune "proper leadership and guidance" meant black leaders for black programs, a conviction she applied whenever African Americans found themselves relegated to separate programs. She outwardly accepted the inevitability of racial separation in the 1930s, as long as African Americans had power over these separate programs. In order for this to happen, it was necessary to appoint African Americans to policy-making positions. Bethune believed only blacks in power positions could be sensitive to black needs.[39] The failure of many New Deal programs such as the CWA, CCC, and AAA for blacks confirmed Bethune's point of view and bolstered her argument in favor of black administrators and supervisors in New Deal programs:

> May I advise the committee that it does not matter how equipped your white supervision might be, or your white leadership, it is impossible for you to enter as sympathetically and understandingly, into the program of the Negro, as the Negro can do. Then it will give, also, the thing that we very much need nowadays, that opportunity for the development of leadership among the Negro people themselves, and it is becoming more important that the right type of leadership be produced. They can only become efficient by having the opportunity to develop and grow in participation in these programs.[40]

38. "Mrs. Bethune Won't Quit NYA Post; Seeks Security for Her School; Denies Rumors She May Become National Organizer for Democrats," Associated Negro Press, n.d., BFC I; Mary McLeod Bethune, "A Tribute to President Franklin D. Roosevelt," Transcript of radio address given on WJSV, Washington, D.C., October 26, 1936, FDR; "Minutes of the Executive Committee Meeting of the National Youth Administration," 1936, 135–38, FDR.

39. Statement of Mary McLeod Bethune to the NYA Executive Committee, 1937, FDR; Mary McLeod Bethune to Eleanor Roosevelt, January 27, 1941, Box 797, ER.

40. "Minutes of the Executive Committee Meeting of the National Youth Administration," 1936, 135–36, FDR.

Bethune firmly believed that "the white people have had to do our thinking long enough. We no longer want them to think for us but with us." America, she also asserted, must become "accustomed to seeing Negroes in high places."[41]

By the time of Bethune's appointment as director of Minority Affairs in 1936, she had named fourteen blacks to policy-making positions on state NYA committees. She was instrumental in getting two blacks appointed to the Florida state NYA advisory committee when most southern states had only one black appointee. By October 1938, twenty-one African Americans served as state administrative assistants or project supervisors for the NYA. By May 1939, Bethune had increased the number of black state administrators to twenty-three full-time administrators, three part-time administrators, and necessary office support and clerical staff positions, and she worked to ensure that local communities used these black administrators to dispense funds to black people.[42]

Of these black administrators, six were women. Some of these women had achieved recognition in the women's club movement, but others came to Bethune's attention through her expanding affiliations with groups such as the NAACP, Urban League, YWCA, settlement house movement, national health organizations, and education, business, fraternal, and religious organizations. They included Venice Spragg (Alabama); Vivian Osborne Marsh (California); Sadie C. Mays (District of Columbia); Anne Caution (Oklahoma); Josie C. Hazel (South Carolina); and Roberta Dunbar (Rhode Island). Women also occupied twelve clerical positions at the state level.[43] While Bethune could look with pride on her NYA appointments at the state level, she also knew she had had only limited success at the federal level.

Bethune took an active role as director of Minority Affairs, acting as a liaison between black youth and the administration in the implementation of the NYA program. Bethune's activities as director were unequivocally responsible for the increasing level of participation of African American youth in the

41. "Dr. Bethune in Opening Talk," n.d., BFC I.
42. "Director's Annual Report, July 1, 1936–June 30, 1937," NYA, Record Group 119; "State Supervisors of Negro Work, October 18, 1938," BFC I; "Analysis of the Positions of Negro State Supervisors," May 25, 1939, BFC I; "List of Negro Personnel on State Staffs," as of July 31, 1939, BFC I.
43. "State Supervisors of Negro Work," BFC I; "List of Negro Personnel on State Staffs (Information taken from July 31, '39 Reports," BFC I; "Analysis of the Positions of Negro State Supervisors," MMB.

NYA program. Immediately after her appointment, Bethune began publicizing the NYA program to African Americans nationwide. She oversaw the writing and distribution of more than twenty-five hundred circulars entitled "New Opportunities for Negro Youth" that explained the benefits available to young black people, and worked closely with state officials to secure a fair share of benefits for black youth. In her first year as administrator, she traveled forty thousand miles and visited sixty-nine NYA centers in twenty-nine states, promoting the NYA program and documenting the impoverished conditions of black youth.[44]

On a strictly political level, her appointments of black state administrators became one factor in the development of a national black political power base. Black state administrators distributed throughout the country effectively gave Bethune a national field staff that reported directly to her, although initially these reports were "off the record." The reports kept her up to date on the flow of NYA funds to black high school and college work-study programs, vocational training, and NYA job placement agencies in almost every state. In April 1936, the Office of Minority Affairs issued a confidential report based on the reports of black state administrators about the activities of the NYA offices in states having the largest black populations. The report gave a short overview of each state program including its vocational guidance program and summarized the difficulties facing African Americans within the NYA program in each state. For example, the report found that there was an excellent vocational guidance plan in operation in Georgia and that Illinois had a "fairly well developed" program, while in Indiana blacks had "no knowledge of NYA program."[45] In large measure, Bethune drew her conclusions about the effectiveness of the NYA program at the state level from these reports. In her summary, she noted six problems in the NYA program as it applied to young African Americans:

1. The program overlooked many young black people who were eligible for relief benefits because of eligibility rules. State administrators were automatically classifying many black youths as "unskilled" workers despite previous training and experience.
2. The majority of states had no black supervisors on NYA projects.

44. "Director's Annual Report, July 1, 1936–June 30, 1937," NYA, Record Group 119; Smith, "Mary McLeod Bethune and the National Youth Administration," 151–52.

45. "Confidential Report Re. Negro Activities in States Having Largest Negro Population," April 22, 1936, BFC I.

3. Those blacks holding supervisory positions, and black workers in general under the NYA program, received lower salaries than whites doing the same kind of work.

4. In communities where the black population was scattered, administrators were not making black youth aware of the program or available NYA benefits. The NYA needed to make special provisions to address the young people in these communities.

5. Black youth lacked adequate representation on State Committees.

6. Vocational guidance for blacks was weak. Additional trained black counselors were necessary and administrators needed to increase the number of occupational classes.[46]

Bethune arranged a series of State Youth Meetings based on the findings in these reports and targeted states where African Americans held positions as state administrative assistants and supervisors. These meetings focused attention on the NYA program and its goals for black youth in each state and gave young black people a forum for discussing the problems they faced. Moreover, the State Youth Meetings also gave black federal and state administrators the opportunity to candidly discuss governmental efforts to address problems of unemployment, health, housing, farm tenancy, and the special problems of black youth. The state meetings resulted in new recommendations by black state administrators for strengthening the NYA program for African Americans, particularly in the process of reporting on the operation of the program in the various states. Bethune returned to Washington determined to ensure that the Division of Minority Affairs have "free access to the viewpoint of Negro assistants in the field."[47] Before the state meetings, black assistants had to report to white administrators who summarized the reports to the NYA. Because of prevailing white racial attitudes, many black assistants in the South could not be blunt about the shortcomings and effectiveness of the program in their state. After the state meetings, Bethune lobbied Williams to change the reporting process. Black state administrative assistants stopped filtering their reports through white state directors and began reporting their observations and experiences on the program and its operation at the local level directly to Bethune.

Bethune's insistence on this change in reporting procedures marked an important departure in the operating procedure of New Deal agencies. All other

46. Ibid.
47. Mary McLeod Bethune to Tom L. Popejoy, September 16, 1936, BFC I.

programs, including NYA programs aimed at white youth, embraced a decentralized operating structure. That is, federal administrators gave control over nationally devised projects directly to the state and local authorities in order to keep federal intervention in state affairs to a minimum. Federal agencies refused to interfere with state and local customs, allowing local administrators to distribute program benefits as they deemed appropriate. In altering this process, Bethune essentially began the process of redefining the relationship between federal, state, and local authority.

Reflecting her belief in the value of American democracy and her faith in the political process, Bethune also used NYA state youth meetings to promote citizenship training and civic participation among young black people. She took these opportunities to explain the social legislation enacted under the New Deal, particularly in the work of the CCC, NYA, and employment offices. More important, she advocated voter registration, encouraged young African Americans to use the ballot wherever possible, and discussed national issues and party platforms.[48] For Bethune, the ballot was the most effective weapon African Americans had against discrimination and segregation, and she continually encouraged its use in places where blacks retained the vote. In areas where legal or customary disfranchisement prohibited black voting, Bethune advocated citizenship training so that African Americans would be ready to exercise their voting rights as soon as they had successfully dismantled Jim Crow segregation.

Bethune worked continually and consistently to ensure black youth their fair share of all NYA benefits. During the first year of her directorship, 28,335 black elementary and secondary school children, 6,983 black college students, and 369 black graduate students received student aid while approximately 18,000 black youths received work relief benefits totaling $441,260. Moreover, she also used her access to the White House to ensure blacks had access to nonstudent-oriented programs. Resident camp programs were a case in point. As early as 1933, Hilda Worthington Smith proposed a resident camp program for unemployed white women and used her friendship with Eleanor Roosevelt to bring her plan to the attention of the Roosevelt administration through a White House conference. The FERA inaugurated the camp program for white women in 1934. The number of resident camps expanded in late 1935 when the NYA took over their administration. By March 1936, ninety camps served about five thousand unemployed white women. In 1937,

48. Bethune to Popejoy, September 16, 1936.

Bethune used Smith's strategy and her connection with Eleanor Roosevelt to promote resident training centers for black youth in twenty-five southern communities. After the First Lady entertained Bethune over tea, Bethune spent an hour with FDR discussing the future of the NYA and the possibility of a camp program for young black people. By 1937, black NYA administrators were publicizing the program as an "opportunity for girls to develop self-confidence and learn a number of things that will be useful to them in obtaining private employment." During the same year, eleven hundred young men and women took part in camp resident training programs. The young men's program emphasized instruction in new farming techniques, soil conservation, crop rotation, animal husbandry, auto mechanics, machine shop work, brick masonry, printing, painting, building and construction, and industrial methods. The young men also worked at plastering, painting, repairing school buildings, and constructing new dormitories and recreation centers. Young women's programs focused on health education, home management, social sciences, sewing, food preparation, marketing, gardening, canning, personal hygiene, and laundry work. Trained women worked in school cafeterias and kitchens, decorated school dormitories, and planted gardens. By 1940, the program served 3,836 young people. Part-time work projects allowed participants to earn about five dollars per month in addition to paying for their training and support. Bethune also oversaw the founding of five special camps for 300 unemployed black women between July 1936 and June 1937. These camps were experimental and offered "cultural guidance," recreational activities, instruction in health and nutrition, training in homemaking and citizenship, and some vocational guidance.[49]

Bethune also worked to address the needs of young people in rural areas. When the NYA established practical farm-and-home training programs for the sons and daughters of tenant and needy farm families, Bethune was there to ensure that black youth had access to the training and work opportunities offered at resident vocational training centers operating at a number of agri-

49. These numbers represent 11.8 percent, 5.4 percent, and 7.4 percent of the total number of students aided in each group respectively. "Director's Annual Report, July 1, 1936–June 30, 1937," NYA, Record Group 119; Mary McLeod Bethune to Bishop R. R. Wright, September 19, 1940, NYA, Record Group 119; Susan Ware, *Beyond Suffrage: Women in the New Deal*, 111–13; "Opportunity for Girls at St. Augustine," *Tampa Bulletin*, March 20, 1937; "NYA Girls Training Camp, St. Augustine," *Tampa Bulletin*, March 20, 1937; "NYA Projects Aiding Negro Youth, Mrs. Bethune Tells President," press release, February 14, 1938, BFC I; "The National Youth Administration Serves Negro Youth," n.d., BFC I; "Relation of the National Youth Administration to Negro Youth," n.d., BFC I.

cultural training schools throughout the South. The centers focused primarily on training young men in modern farming techniques and offered young women instruction in dairying, raising poultry, and food preservation as well as the inevitable focus on proper home management, family recreation, and use of leisure time. Work projects included dormitory and farm shop building construction and employment in the cafeteria, sewing rooms, and on the school farm. As with the camp program, students earned about five dollars in cash per month from the work projects plus the costs of their food, lodging, and training.[50]

Despite all Bethune's efforts, the camp and farm training programs for young black men and women were not a stunning success. Like most New Deal efforts, the programs remained racially segregated, and training programs largely reflected the discriminatory nature of black employment, relegating blacks to the lowest rung of the employment ladder. Yet, thousands of black youth participated in the program and earned some income through their work in the camps. It is unlikely that these young people would have had even that opportunity if Bethune had not succeeded in forcing the Roosevelt administration to make at least this token effort to meet the needs of young, unemployed black men and women.

Through reports, studies, and personal involvement in the NYA program, Bethune found that while blacks constituted 13 percent of the youth population, they represented 15 percent of all youth on relief. She believed this was a result of the inferior education given to blacks in the South. A primary goal for her was to "erase the race differentials operating in the NYA and to extend training and educational opportunities for Negroes." This was important because, "If the children of Negro people must adjust themselves to the White man's civilization, fit themselves into the White man's industrial scheme, be measured by the White man's standards of intelligence and answer to the White man's law then they must have an equal measure with the White man's children in thoroughness of preparation."[51]

At Bethune's insistence, the NYA created a Special Negro Higher Education Fund that distributed $609,930 in student aid for black college students. This funding was in addition to $2,271,336 granted from the regular student aid fund. The special fund allowed graduate students to attend traditionally black universities in the South or northern colleges when white

50. "NYA Trains Negro Farm Youth," *Tampa Bulletin,* September 11, 1937.
51. Giddings, *When and Where I Enter,* 222–24; Mary McLeod Bethune, "What the Negro Wants," MMB papers.

southern school administrators denied them admission to graduate programs in their own states. In the seven years of its existence, the Office of Minority Affairs helped 180,000 black children nationwide to attend high school. It arranged employment and work training on NYA projects to more than 300,000 black youths and provided health exams and health counseling to 26,000 black children. Bethune was also instrumental in establishing training for librarians and high school teachers in rural Mississippi. She involved black universities in training projects sponsored by the NYA, including industrial training and manpower training for war industries and construction, and played a part in establishing the Civilian Pilot Training Program that paved the way for black pilots in World War II.[52]

Bethune's efforts on behalf of African American youth were impressive. She effectively used her position as director of Minority Affairs to ensure expanding educational and work opportunities for young black people, and she took pride in her accomplishments. However, her work on behalf of African American youth was only one of her goals. Bethune wanted to use her federal position to pave the way for the appointment of other African American women to prominent leadership positions within the government, although she knew that prevailing racial and gender attitudes would limit the number of appointments African American women received to key federal positions. Rather than settle for a reduced number of women's appointments, Bethune used her favored status to lobby for government positions for all well-qualified African Americans.

The president and First Lady extended regular invitations to Bethune and relied on her for recommendations, as did Aubrey Williams and other white administrators. On June 29, 1939, Bethune replied to Williams's request for the names of educators who could be "consulted in conference concerning the NYA relationship to Negro education and the best possible use of special funds." On January 18, 1940, Bethune met with FDR for a conference she called "merely routine." Her official statement to the press was that FDR was anxious to discuss the work of the NYA and "particularly interested in how the Negro is faring under the various federal programs." An unofficial source reported that Bethune had also discussed the "advisability of appointing more federal judges; elimination of the photograph from the civil service

---

52. "Director's Final Report," NYA, Record Group 119; Giddings, *When and Where I Enter*, 224–30; Smith, "Mary McLeod Bethune," 125; Mary McLeod Bethune to Bishop R. R. Wright, NYA, Group 119; "Notes for Aubrey Williams from Mary McLeod Bethune," NYA, Record Group 119; Bethune, "My Secret Talks with FDR," 59.

blanks; fuller representation in the agriculture department with Negroes on policy forming boards and in such positions; the appointment of Negroes to Annapolis and more cadets to West Point." Bethune followed up on this meeting with a memorandum to FDR summarizing what African Americans hoped to see the administration accomplish. In addition to the listed items, the memo included the appointment of African Americans to the Board of Appeals of the Civil Service Commission, the Council on Personnel Administration, special assistant to the secretary of war, administrative assistant in the Labor Department to oversee policies dealing with black labor, assistant to the administrator in the Federal Security Agency, administrative assistant to the Social Security Board, and the Federal Works Agency. She also requested that blacks be reappointed to the Register of the Treasury, as minister to Haiti, auditor to the Navy, and collectors of customs in New York, Charleston, and other cities. In addition to her personal efforts with FDR, Bethune often solicited Eleanor Roosevelt's help in securing federal positions for black leaders. In several letters written between October 1940 and January 1941, Bethune asked Mrs. Roosevelt to persuade FDR to appoint William Hastie and Hubert Delaney to federal judgeships and have Frank Horne appointed as an assistant to Robert Weaver in the Housing Department. On November 20, 1940, Mrs. Roosevelt sent a memo to FDR that said, "How about these requests? The young lawyer she [Bethune] wants as judge made a very good impression at the Urban League dinner." Both Hastie and Horne received these positions. At the request of administrative leaders, Bethune also recommended African Americans to fill positions in the Office of Policy and Management (OPM) and the Office of Price Administration (OPA).[53]

Bethune also endorsed increasing the number of qualified black women in government service through patronage appointments, supporting many of the nine women who received appointments to administrative posts in various government agencies: Frances Williams (Council of National Defense); Constance Daniel (Farm Security Administration); Venita Lewis (Children's Bureau of the Department of the Department of Labor); Corienne Robinson

53. Memo from Mary McLeod Bethune to Aubrey Williams, June 29, 1939, BFC I; "Mrs. Bethune Calls on President but Won't Tell What Was Discussed," BFC I; Memorandum to the President from Mary McLeod Bethune, n.d., BFC I; Mary McLeod Bethune to Eleanor Roosevelt, October 28, 1940; June 9, 1942, FDR; Bethune to Eleanor Roosevelt, May 30, November 20, 1940, Box 1537, ER; Bethune to Eleanor Roosevelt, January 27, 1941, Box 797, ER; Memo from Eleanor Roosevelt to Franklin D. Roosevelt, November 20, 1940, FDR; Memo from Mary McLeod Bethune to Richard W. Bunch, December 11, 1941, BFC I; Bethune to Eleanor Roosevelt, June 9, 1942, ER.

(United States Housing Authority); Jennie B. Moton (Farm Security Administration); and Ora Brown Stokes, Venice Spragg, Pauline Redmond, and Nell Hunter (National Youth Administration). Bethune also tried to open additional positions for black women through her affiliation with Eleanor Roosevelt. In October 1941, Bethune offered the names of twenty-five black women who she believed were qualified for employment or voluntary service in the federal government. Bethune knew that it was unlikely that the First Lady could find positions for many of those on the list, but she continued to recommend African American women for federal appointments. Despite their inability to meet many of Bethune's desires, both FDR and Mrs. Roosevelt valued her judgment and always took her suggestions seriously. Throughout her tenure in government service, they continued to solicit Bethune's opinions on how African Americans interpreted certain issues. FDR so trusted her opinions and insights that she was the only woman invited to attend meetings between Roosevelt, A. Philip Randolph, and Walter White regarding Randolph's proposed "March on Washington" in 1941.[54] The Roosevelts and other government officials seriously considered Bethune's informed opinions.

Bethune did use her position to open doors in Washington for other African Americans. She believed that once she succeeded in opening a door, she had the responsibility to hold it open so that others could rush in. Nevertheless, Bethune was not a saint. She was dominating, stubborn, and strong-willed. While she sincerely saw herself as a representative for her race, and as a means for others to gain the opportunity to come along and achieve as well, she also played a significant role in determining who would move ahead and by what means. The controlling aspect of her personality is readily apparent in the way she ran the Office of Minority Affairs.

As the director of her division, she insisted the staff follow her procedures and abide by her rules, and she brooked no deviation in this, as T. Arnold Hill, her assistant director of Negro Affairs, discovered in December 1940. Hill's primary duty was to serve "under the direction of the Director of Negro Affairs" in supervising the work of the Negro Relations and Administrative sections of the office as well as overseeing the secretarial employees. His job description clearly assigned him a secondary role to Bethune, confining him to "collaborating with" the director, "carrying through" her projects and programs, "participating in conferences with" her and "relieving her of as many

---

54. Memo from Eleanor Roosevelt to Franklin D. Roosevelt, November 20, 1940, FDR; Memo from Walter White to Franklin D. Roosevelt, March 13, 1941, FDR.

problems as possible arising from the internal administration of the NYA affecting the Negro." Hill's responsibilities also included traveling to address and participate in meetings and serving for the director in her absence.[55] During the latter part of November in his capacity as assistant director, Hill visited the Florida state NYA office and prepared a summary of recommendations for its operation. In Bethune's absence, Hill completed his report and forwarded it without her approval. This would seem to have been within the scope of his official activities. However, on December 14, Hill received a blunt memo from Bethune advising him to confer with her executive secretary, Arabella Denniston, about office procedure. She instructed another member of the staff to prepare a folder outlining office procedure for Hill to help him "understand our method of keeping our program harmoniously going." Then Bethune curtly reminded Hill again that office procedure required that *all* field reports "be made to my desk and together we will study them and send such part of them we deem wise to Mr. Lassiter over my signature."[56] Bethune had specific reasons for her tight control over the information that left the Office of Minority Affairs.

Bethune's notion of socially responsible individualism and her belief in women's special moral capacities strongly influenced her administrative style. Bethune believed she was better suited than Hill to represent African Americans and ensure continued progress. Media reports confirmed that others saw her in the same light. In 1937, the Washington, D.C., *Flash* reported, "When leaders of the male persuasion quibbled as to distinctive titles and full-fledged authority, Mrs. Bethune quietly assumed leadership in the national movements that represented constructive racial endeavor. Her unusual tact, her genius as a presiding officer, her rare histrionic powers, and her ability as an executive place her in the forefront where her poise and dignity have maintained her."[57]

Bethune was sure she was unconcerned with individual advancement, she was not so sure about Hill. She was careful to word her reports to superiors in such a way as to protect black state administrators and supervisors. She jealously guarded the positions she worked so hard to create and did not want to give whites any justification for eliminating those posts. Bethune steadfastly believed that having black administrators in place was critical to protecting

55. "HILL, T. ARNOLD—Assistant Director of Negro Affairs—P 5," BFC I.

56. Memo from Mary McLeod Bethune to T. Arnold Hill, December 14, 1940, BFC I. There is no record of Hill's response to Bethune's memo.

57. "Assumed Race Leadership," *Flash*, December 20, 1937, Washington, D.C.

the interests of African American children on a day-to-day basis. In short, Bethune mistrusted Hill's intentions. She worried that his primary aim was to further his own career without thought of his obligation to the race, and she most likely resented his assumption that he need not follow the office proce-dures she had established. After this incident, she monitored Hill's activities closely and his subsequent reports passed through her desk.

Although Bethune did not openly seek individual advancement, she was not above practicing what we have come to know as "pork-barrel politics." She openly lobbied New Deal agencies for hometown projects, including projects that benefited her own Bethune-Cookman College. In 1942, the college re-ceived financing for a Trades Building for National Defense to train young people in auto mechanics, masonry, electrical work, and tailoring. Bethune-Cookman also received its share of student aid. Moreover, Bethune used her position to ensure federal funding for other Florida projects such as a 167-unit housing project in Daytona Beach. Although Bethune did not always receive the funding for her special projects, she continued to work to increase the share of New Deal benefits African Americans received.

There is no question that Bethune did not publicly condemn the separate programs instituted by the NYA; nevertheless, she consciously, deliberately, and continuously worked behind the scenes to promote more inclusive pro-grams. Bethune forced the Roosevelt administration and NYA leadership to acknowledge and deal with the limitations of the separate programs they in-stituted. Bethune believed that African Americans would need to "take steps slowly but surely" to overturn segregation primarily through the development of a separate black power base. Yet, she also emphasized the responsibility of the administration to "stand by the policy of opening the doors as rapidly as possible, with sane, qualified leadership." In her first annual report to the executive director, Bethune detailed the weaknesses of the NYA program for African Americans. She drew attention to the fact that as of June 1937, 35,687 African American students had received student aid. At the same time, she also pointed out the proportion of available NYA student aid funding they received was only 11.8 percent of elementary and secondary aid, 5.4 percent of college aid, and 7.4 percent of graduate aid, although black youth made up about 13 percent of the population. Bethune called for the continuation and expansion of these student aid programs for black children. She called on the NYA to ensure the employment of young black people in work pro-grams in rural areas and improve the program of guidance and placement for African Americans. Bethune believed the best way to improve the programs and reach more black children was not to set aside separate funds for African

Americans, but rather to allocate a proportion of the funding for designated projects for expenditures among blacks.[58] Proportional funding would give African Americans their fair share of government monies, especially in agricultural areas with predominantly black populations. Moreover, it was more likely that the NYA would renew funding for the general educational program than special "set aside" programs for black children given the prevailing racial climate.

Internally, she demanded the expansion of competent black administrative and supervisory personnel in the division. She also called for implementing adequate provisions for black personnel filing field reports. She insisted that white officials not interpret these reports. Rather, reports were to come directly to her at the Office of Minority Affairs and she would then interpret those reports to the heads of the various divisions. She castigated various internal NYA divisions for not developing adequate procedures to inform the "Negro Division" of the specific projects, plans, and programs under consideration. She demanded that representatives of the "Negro Division" participate in any meeting or conference that could affect NYA policies. Bethune questioned NYA policy that did not require state officials to designate the racial composition of those employed on specific NYA projects. Specifically, she wanted statistics that indicated what kind of work black youths were involved in, how long they had been working on specific projects, and their placement rate into private and other industries. Her primary concern in seeking these statistics was to make sure state officials were not keeping blacks on NYA projects long-term while giving better-paying private sector jobs to whites.[59]

After traveling to every state in which blacks participated in the NYA program, Bethune wrote a memo to Williams in June of 1938, detailing the problems of implementation of the NYA program among African Americans. She found that general projects for African Americans were "far too meager" and the organization and supervision of existing projects was poor. Further, apprenticeship-training programs virtually excluded young black workers, there were problems in getting black youth certified as eligible to receive aid, and health programs were weak. On the management level, Bethune castigated state administrators for having an inadequate number of African

58. "Minutes of the Executive Committee Meeting of the National Youth Administration," 1936, 135–38, FDR; "Director's Annual Report, July 1, 1935–June 30, 1936," NYA, Record Group 119; "Relation of the Division of Negro Affairs to the General Program of the National Youth Administration," n.d., NYA, Record Group 119.
59. "Director's Annual Report, July 1, 1935–June 30, 1936," NYA, Record Group 119.

Americans in administrative, supervisory, and clerical positions as well as having too few black social workers. She also found that blacks had little part in the vocational guidance program, especially in counseling or placement. Bethune argued that an increased number of black administrators were necessary to alleviate these shortcomings.[60]

By 1939, Bethune's administrative role as director of Minority Affairs had made her an accomplished political negotiator, and the realignment of black voters from the Republican to the Democratic party in 1936 only served to strengthen her negotiating position. On the national level, African American votes were becoming increasingly important to the Democrats. Before the 1940 elections, Bethune met with James Farley of the Democratic National Committee (DNC) to discuss how the party could counteract the Republican party's courting of the black vote. She lobbied for an African American publicity agent, a black representative to the DNC, and a meeting of black democrats to help frame the policies of the committee. She also suggested that the DNC choose "key professors" at historically black colleges to make a "factual study of the New Deal" as it related to blacks to offset the negative report made by Dr. Ralph Bunche of Howard University. To reach the masses of black voters, Bethune suggested the DNC publish a four-page bimonthly newsletter detailing New Deal policies and benefits for African Americans. This would counteract the Republican-issued "Woman's Voice" designed to attract and solidify black women's votes for the Republicans in the 1940 election. She cautioned Farley to act quickly because "Seventy-five percent of the Negro Press and the Associated Negro Press have been purchased or bartered with to date by the opposition." Bethune also pushed the Democratic Women's Committee (DWC) to give African American women a larger and more prominent role in Democratic politics. She lobbied the DWC to appoint a black woman to organize and work with black women voters and black Democratic committees nationwide. She also stressed the necessity of a meeting of black Democratic women in Washington before 1940 to plan strategy as well as the DNC giving "ample space" in its publications to black women's activities. Bethune recognized the need for the DWC to cater to Democratic women, but she also understood the need for the DWC to "consolidate younger groups who are unattached."[61]

60. "Relation of the Division of Negro Affairs to the General Program of the National Youth Administration," n.d., NYA, Record Group 119; Memo from Mary McLeod Bethune to Aubrey Williams, June 10, 1938, NYA, Record Group 119.

61. James W. Ford, "The National Negro Congress," in Aptheker, ed., *A Documentary History of the Negro People in the United States*, vol. 4, 229; "To Talk Over with Mr. Farley," n.d.,

In October of 1939, Bethune wrote to Williams telling him of the "glaring difficulties" that continued to exist in the NYA program and gave her assessment of African American positions in the federal bureaucracy in general. She insisted that the number of black personnel in policy-making positions was insufficient in the Civil Service Commission, the Federal Loan Agency, the Federal Works Agency, the Federal Security Agency, the Home Owners Loan Corporation, the Departments of Justice, Labor, and Commerce, and the Women's Bureau of the Department of Labor. She castigated the administration for failing to appoint African American representatives to important emergency committees such as the National Emergency Council and the Federal Commission on Apprenticeship Training. Moreover, Bethune also monitored the "progress" of African Americans in other government departments not created under the New Deal policies of the Roosevelt administration. She made it clear she noticed a marked decrease in the number of black messengers and clerical workers in the Departments of State, Treasury, Justice, War, and Navy as well as other "old line" government agencies. She wrote Williams that while a growing number of African Americans were being placed in the "Negro Division Emergency Agencies and on relief rolls, there has been a steady decline in employment figures among Negroes in government agencies regarded as permanent."[62] This situation was untenable because once the national economic emergency was over and emergency agencies disbanded and relief discontinued, African Americans would once again find themselves without adequate government representation, especially at the higher levels. African Americans needed a sufficient number of representatives in "old line" agencies to safeguard their recent gains. Without adequate representation, black workers who were traditionally subject to high unemployment levels and the masses of black citizens would be subject to increasing levels of poverty. She concluded her report to Williams with an appraisal of the consequences for the Roosevelt administration in the 1940 elections if inadequate programs remained in place and the political "opposition" somehow made the deficiencies public—certainly black political support for Roosevelt would wane.[63] Bethune had become an astute politician. She understood the leverage the African American vote held in the 1940 election.

BFC I; "To Talk Over with Mrs. Evans—Chairman of Democratic Women's Committee," n.d., BFC I.

62. Memo from Mary McLeod Bethune to Aubrey Williams, June 10, 1938, NYA, Record Group 119.

63. Memo from Mary McLeod Bethune to Aubrey Williams, October 17, 1939, NYA, Record Group 119.

Bethune also wrote directly to President Roosevelt, baldly asserting that it would be a mistake to believe that the black vote was "irrevocably fixed in the Democratic ranks" or that black leaders and the rank-and-file were "satisfied with the deal the Negro has received even under your administration." Bethune stated very explicitly that African Americans were *very* disturbed by Roosevelt's silence during the filibuster waged by southern Democrats against the antilynching bill, the lack of black federal judges, and discrimination in the Federal Housing Authority, the Tennessee Valley Authority, and other federally financed projects. Bethune pointedly reminded Roosevelt that African American voters had become increasingly independent and cast a skeptical eye on white politicians in all parties who paid only lip service to their political demands. In short, she advised Roosevelt that unless he did something more substantial to meet African American needs he would not retain the support of "any considerable percentage of this group in 1940."[64]

In her self-appointed political role as race representative to the Roosevelt administration, Bethune kept track of federal programs, made recommendations for increased black participation, and maintained important contacts to promote the implementation of her recommendations. She also played a substantial part in allocating patronage appointments. By 1938, Bethune was brokering transfers and reassignments within the bureaucracy for appointees such as Frank Horne and Robert Weaver. She also had a direct role in securing a federal judgeship in New York for Hubert Delaney. Through her correspondence with Eleanor Roosevelt, she advised the administration on important matters such as the role of black workers in the Ford strike in 1941.[65] Moreover, through her management of the Special Negro Higher Education Fund she literally controlled the hundreds of thousands of dollars disbursed to black communities through the NYA. Bethune strengthened her effectiveness as a political leader through her expanding ties to national organizations such as the NAACP and Urban League, her access to the Roosevelts, and her ability to organize and gain a consensus among various black leaders. Bethune used her political position to serve African Americans, condemn discriminatory practices, and change discriminatory policies.

64. Mary McLeod Bethune to President Franklin D. Roosevelt, November 27, 1939, BFC I.

65. Mary McLeod Bethune to Eleanor Roosevelt, February 10, 1938; October 30, 1941, ER; Memo from Mary McLeod Bethune to Eleanor Roosevelt, April 4, 1941, ER.

Bethune never allowed the Roosevelt administration to use her as a puppet to "smooth things out," and she never blindly supported the administration. However, unlike African American leaders such as George Edmund Haynes, John P. Davis, and Walter White who were openly critical of New Deal programs, Bethune selectively chose times and places to criticize New Deal administrators and programs.[66] Soon after her appointment as director of minority affairs, Bethune enlarged the scope of her political activities, taking a more dynamic role in an ever-increasing number of black conferences and organizations. Through her position as a government appointee, she had an insider's view of the administration and implementation of New Deal programs. Her strategic position allowed her to become *the* key interpreter of those programs to other African American leaders and organizations. Moreover, through her various affiliations, both public and private, she influenced the African American vote. One public conference that Bethune was active in and one that received a significant amount of attention from the Roosevelt administration was the National Negro Congress (NNC).

The NNC was not the first organized black movement to put African Americans on the national political stage. Historical precedents for the NNC reach back at least to the 1830s and the formation of the Negro Convention Movement. Howard Bell has effectively shown that the earliest black political conventions were effective propaganda agencies that promoted black causes and educated the black masses. These early conventions used debate on the convention floor, resolutions, public addresses, and petitions to state legislatures and Congress to disseminate ideas and bring black issues onto the political agenda. Conventions of the 1830s employed moral persuasion techniques that placed the burden for improving racial conditions on African Americans. These early convention delegates advocated the mental, moral, and industrial improvement of African Americans as a means of destroying the color caste system in America. However, as conditions continued to worsen for blacks with the passage of the Fugitive Slave Law and the Dred Scott decision that struck down the concept of "once free always free," the movement became more radicalized, more self-contained, and more independent of white liberal support. Conventions became more widespread, although the movement began to fracture. Delegates such as Henry Highland Garnet and Martin R.

66. Memo from Franklin D. Roosevelt to Eleanor Roosevelt, November 1944, President's Personal Files, FDR. For views of these black leaders of the New Deal programs, see Aptheker, ed., *A Documentary History of the Negro People in the United States*, vol. 4, 164–80.

Delaney advocated emigration and Black Nationalism, while more conservative delegates such as Frederick Douglass advocated development of a more compact black organization to control the affairs of the race on a national basis but continue to work within the framework of the U.S. government. By mid-1861, staunch emigrationists and conservatives found a middle ground. Conservative leaders no longer championed a "stay at home at any cost" position, although they did not see emigration as the "true road to progress" for blacks. Rather, all factions agreed that emigration was a personal decision, and rather than divide over the question, leaders came together to advocate unrestricted suffrage and equality before the law.[67]

The NNC used many of the same strategies and faced many of the same problems encountered by the Negro Convention Movement. Founded in February 1936 and composed of 817 delegates representing 585 organizations from twenty-eight states, the first NNC met in Chicago. This group of black men and women represented a collective membership of 1.2 million African Americans. Its constituents belonged to church and religious, youth, farm, women's, educational, and business and professional groups, trade unions, and fraternal societies, as well as various political parties. Because of its diverse membership, the NNC had serious problems in fostering a sense of unity among its members; however, for a decade it led a serious attack on racism in America. Although nonpartisan, the NNC was not nonpolitical. It formulated a platform of minimum demands on "Negro issues" and measured the acceptability of every political party and every political candidate against these criteria. The NNC then advised its members if they should give their support to a party or candidate based on how well a particular party or candidate measured up to NNC standards.[68]

In November 1936, Bethune received a letter from John P. Davis, then president of the NNC. Davis called for unity of action among African Americans and the creation of a federation of local protest groups to work for black rights. This was apparently the first formal contact between the NNC and Bethune. Davis told Bethune that the NNC was organizing a National Negro Youth Week and holding a conference in Washington, D.C., in January 1937. Davis wished to have a delegation of black youth meet with Roosevelt during the conference and asked Bethune to endorse the event as an individual and as an official of the federal government. Moreover, Davis asked

67. See Howard Holman Bell, *A Survey of the Negro Convention Movement, 1830–1861*.
68. Aptheker, ed., *A Documentary History of the Negro People in the United States*, vol. 4, 211; Ford, "The National Negro Congress," 229.

for the cooperation of the NYA in planning and carrying out the conference. Bethune gave more than her cooperation. In her usual style, she took control of the conference and became the chairperson of what became the National Conference on the Problems of the Negro and Negro Youth held January 6–8, 1937. Bethune used her close relationship with Eleanor Roosevelt and her capacity as a federal official to make the conference a meaningful event. She ensured NYA sponsorship for the conference and arranged for meetings to take place at the Department of Labor. Speakers at the conference included Secretary of Agriculture Henry A. Wallace, Secretary of Commerce Daniel C. Roper, Aubrey Williams, and Eleanor Roosevelt, as well as four other cabinet members and six additional agency heads. Further, the First Lady interceded in support of Bethune and the conference and had President Roosevelt send a personal message to the conferees. Ultimately, Bethune was instrumental in producing a comprehensive report on the conference proceedings entitled "Recommendations of the National Conference on Problems of the Negro and Negro Youth."[69] She made sure that all members of the cabinet, the directors of various administrative agencies, all members of the seventy-fifth Congress, and President Roosevelt received a copy of the recommendations and understood their import.

The report detailed every problem of concern to black Americans and outlined specific recommendations for their amelioration. In the letter of transmittal, Bethune told Roosevelt, "The conference, speaking with one voice for twelve million American Negroes, offers these recommendations as the basic outline for a program as a challenge to the social consciousness of the present administration. We feel now that this is the one time in the history of our race that the Negroes of America have felt free to reduce to writing their problems and their plans for meeting them with the knowledge of sympathetic understanding and interpretation."[70]

Although African Americans were aware that through the Roosevelt administration they received many federal benefits previously denied to them, "still numerous instances of racial discrimination and inequality" remained. This was especially true in employment, economic security, educational and recreational opportunity, health, housing, and equal protection under the law.

69. John P. Davis to Mary McLeod Bethune, November 25, 1937, FDR; Mary McLeod Bethune to Steven Early, Assistant Secretary to Franklin D. Roosevelt, February 1, 1937, President's Personal File, FDR.
70. Letter of transmittal from Mary McLeod Bethune to Franklin D. Roosevelt, January 18, 1937, 2, FDR. There is no record of FDR's response to this letter or to the report.

The conferees pointed out that the federal government was the protector of all American people and as such was responsible for taking the lead and setting an example by abolishing segregation in all departments, divisions, and branches. Moreover, the federal government must withhold benefits to states and territories that practiced segregation.[71]

Throughout her years in government service, Bethune remained a strong advocate for the race and retained her ability to be frank when necessary. According to the NAACP's report on the conference,

> Of all the conferences on the race problem held, certainly in the last ten years, sponsored either openly or semi-officially by the government, this gathering on January 6–8 was the freest from those controls which have become familiar to Negro citizens. The recommendations adopted by the conference committees to be incorporated in a report to President Roosevelt are of a tone not usually found in government sponsored conventions. There was no mincing of words and no "pulling of punches" and no smoothing down of condemnation of present practices.[72]

After carrying out such a successful program, Bethune arranged for a follow-up conference of black leaders and representatives on January 12–14, 1939, also under the auspices of the NYA. The highlight of the second conference was a personal appearance by President Roosevelt that Bethune managed to orchestrate despite the opposition of FDR's advisers.[73] Throughout her lifetime, Bethune took part in or sent messages of support to most major conferences and protest meetings.

Bethune purposefully pursued a dual strategy to ameliorate racial discrimination that became a double-edged sword. She encouraged and assisted African Americans in building strong black political power bases while she unrelentingly sought to reshape white political agendas and influence white liberals. Clearly, black organizations of the time, as well as other black leaders, recognized Bethune as an important political leader and the highest-ranking black official in the New Deal—a status that was considerably enhanced by

71. "Recommendations of the National Conference on the Problems of the Negro and Negro Youth," President's Personal File, 2, FDR.

72. "Problems of Race before President," *Crisis* (February 1937): 46, 62.

73. Memo from Marvin McIntyre to Aubrey Williams, December 20, 1938, FDR. This memo has a penciled notation from McIntyre to Williams, "Do you think he has to see them? Frankly, I do *not*. MHM"; Memo from Franklin D. Roosevelt to Mary McLeod Bethune, January 14, 1939, President's Personal File, FDR.

her close relationship with the Roosevelts. Bethune was widely known as an advocate for black equality and civil rights, and other black leaders often characterized her as wielding an iron fist in a velvet glove.

Bethune's dual strategy was apparent in her choice of affiliations outside of government service. In 1938, Bethune joined the Southern Conference on Human Welfare (SCHW), an interracial coalition of southern liberals, intellectuals, labor leaders, and activists dedicated to improving civil liberties, justice, and equality. The SCHW fought for southern industrial development, minimum wage and maximum hours legislation, educational equality, voting rights, the abolition of the poll tax, abolition of tenant and sharecropper systems, and antilynching legislation. The SCHW also opposed segregation and tried to hold nonsegregated meetings in the South, although the race issue was always conspicuous, sometimes embarrassingly and regrettably so. When the first chairperson of SCHW, Judge Louise O. Charlton, addressed Bethune in the traditional southern manner by referring to her as "Mary," Bethune stopped the meeting and insisted that the secretary amend the record to show the chair had recognized her as "Mrs. Mary McLeod Bethune." This incident cost Judge Charlton her leadership role. Although the race issue was sometimes divisive, it did emphasize that addressing and overturning southern racial traditions was a challenge members of the interracial movement must overcome themselves if they hoped to achieve their broader goals.[74]

Bethune took part in boycotts, marched, picketed, and signed proclamations as a member of the New Negro Alliance. At the end of June 1938 she joined a picket line outside of two People's Drug Stores. People's Drugs was one of Washington's largest corporations, owning and operating forty-four stores that profited from a predominantly black clientele. When People's refused to hire black clerks, the alliance formed picket lines that operated for fifteen hours a day until the corporation capitulated to the alliances' demands. Bethune also took part in the protests against the Daughters of the American Revolution when they refused to allow Marian Anderson to sing at Constitution Hall, and she was instrumental in involving Eleanor Roosevelt in the dispute. She fought for the release of the Scottsboro Boys as well as for equal rights for sharecroppers and domestic workers. She supported A. Philip Randolph's march on Washington movement in 1941. She consistently demanded antilynching and anti–poll tax legislation. In addition, she served as

74. See Linda Reed, *Simple Decency and Common Sense: The Southern Conference Movement, 1938–1963*; "Mrs. Bethune, Not 'Mary,' Gets Into the Records," *Chicago Defender*, December 3, 1938, BFC I; Charles S. Johnson, "More Southerners Discover the South," in Aptheker, ed., *A Documentary History of the Negro People in the United States*, vol. 4, 347–52.

a member of the advisory committee of the Southern Negro Youth Confer-ence (SNYC), an interracial youth group and an outgrowth of the NNC that advocated citizenship, equal opportunity, and black culture.[75]

As clearly depicted by the National Conference on the Problems of the Negro and Negro Youth, Bethune took advantage of her access to govern-ment facilities, agencies, and officials to promote a series of conferences that brought issues of African American oppression into the public spotlight and onto the national political agenda. More important, the groundwork Bethune laid in the 1930s and 1940s framed an explicit agenda for the post–World War II black freedom movement.

By 1936, the number of black advisers in Washington had risen to about forty-five and included young African Americans directly out of college as well as seasoned veterans of the struggle for black freedom. Bethune took the initiative of organizing these advisers into a "Federal Council on Negro Af-fairs," commonly known as the "Black Cabinet." By 1939, this group included black representatives from every major department of the federal government, such as Dr. Ambrose Caliver, senior specialist in Negro Education; Con-stance Daniels, special assistant in the Farm Security Administration; James P. Davis, head officer, Department of Agriculture; Charles S. Duke, U.S. Housing Authority; Dr. Frank Horne, assistant consultant on Race Relations; William L. Houston, assistant to the Attorney General; Louis Lautier, De-partment of Justice; Venita Lewis, U.S. Children's Bureau; and Lt. Lawrence Oxley, supervisor, negro placement officer, Social Security Administration. Race leaders outside of government service included Federal Judge William Hastie and Charles H. Houston, vice dean of Howard Law School and spe-cial counsel for the NAACP. On Friday nights, the cabinet met at Bethune's apartment in Washington, D.C., to discuss problems faced by blacks in hous-ing, education, employment, health, and equal justice. They also discussed ways for African Americans to achieve full integration and participation in all national arenas. What is more important, they shared information and developed strategies for focusing government attention on these issues. Ac-cording to historian Harvard Sitkoff, civil rights leaders such as Walter White and A. Philip Randolph often joined these meetings. In doing so they kept informed of government policy-making developments and were able to ar-

75. John Lovell, Jr., "Washington Fights," in Aptheker, ed., *A Documentary History of the Negro People in the United States,* vol. 4, 367–72; Harvard Sitkoff, *A New Deal for Blacks: The Emergence of Civil Rights as a National Issue. The Depression Decade,* 58–83; Robin D. G. Kelley, *Hammer and Hoe: Alabama Communists during the Great Depression,* 200–203.

range joint protest actions aimed at biased New Deal officials.[76] For Bethune these meetings were also a way to keep up to date with the opinions of these prominent African American leaders and their constituencies. She used them as a means for testing her ideas and making sure that she represented the true interests of blacks in suggesting goals and implementing official government programs.

At first, Bethune was the sole woman in the Black Cabinet, but even after additional women joined the group she remained the only member to have a direct link to the Roosevelt administration. This unusual set of circumstances compelled her male counterparts to recognize her importance and gained respect for her. However, there were times when the men she led were not entirely comfortable with her plans. In December 1941, Bethune called for a meeting including Walter White, Carl Murphy, A. Philip Randolph, C. C. Spaulding, F. D. Patterson, Channing H. Tobias, Bishop R. R. Wright, and Reverend Marshall Shepard. She wanted to discuss the creation of a new government agency formed from a merger between the CCC and the NYA. Both White and Randolph were uncomfortable with the plan. In a letter to Randolph, White expressed his discomfort, writing, "I agree with you 100% about not being a part of any secret black cabinet." Nevertheless, Bethune was comfortable in her position as head of the Black Cabinet. Her political activity often crossed traditional male-female lines. Throughout her lifetime, she saw herself as a leader who was equal to any male in a leadership position. She was comfortable dealing with men, and never thought of herself as inferior simply because she was a woman. She once said she believed "I always had a mind."[77]

Bethune played a unique political role and occupied a position of great influence during her tenure in the National Youth Administration. She significantly increased the number of black NYA state and local administrators and worked closely with them to secure a fair share of benefits for black youth. A redesigned reporting process allowed Bethune to keep close watch over discriminatory practices and work quickly to overcome them. Moreover, through her role in changing this procedure Bethune began the process of redefining

76. For a complete roster of the Federal Council on Negro Affairs see memo from Dutton Ferguson to Mary McLeod Bethune (Attention Mr. R. O'Hara Lanier), September 23, 1939, BFC I. Holt, *Mary McLeod Bethune*, 196, 197; Height interview, 70; Sitkoff, *A New Deal for Blacks*, 79.

77. Walter White to A. Philip Randolph, December 31, 1941, NAACP; Untitled biographical interview of Mary McLeod Bethune, BFC I, 3.

the relationship between federal, state, and local government. Bethune's activities as director of Minority Affairs were directly responsible for increasing the level of participation of African American youth in the NYA program. Her work contributed to the continuing education of hundreds of thousands of black youth, assured employment and job training for countless others, and improved the living standards for all in numerous black communities.

Bethune was an accomplished coalition builder. She successfully organized a diverse group of African American leaders into a well-oiled deliberative body known as the Black Cabinet. She compelled men who might otherwise have sought individual power and recognition to employ a feminist political model, although no one in the group, including Bethune, would have recognized it as such. Bethune prodded the male members of the Black Cabinet to work together as a group for a common goal. She was the only person among the black leaders in Washington who worked assiduously to bring together advisers with different political affiliations and points of view. She pressured them to focus their attention on common objectives, and she held them together. She often told them, "We are here to think together. Let us not lose sight of our objective; what these committees are after is a larger participation of Negroes in the upper brackets of government."[78] Moreover, Bethune was the conduit by which the ideas and suggestions developed by the Black Cabinet gained a hearing by the Roosevelt administration.

Throughout the 1930s and 1940s, Bethune used her relationship with Eleanor Roosevelt in conjunction with her governmental position to penetrate the system, increase the racial consciousness of federal officials, press for the employment of qualified black Americans within the government bureaucracy, and open a greater variety of positions for black women in government service. Moreover, Bethune simultaneously used her position within the African American community to promote civil rights activism and define and advance a civil rights agenda in the New Deal years.

Bethune worked with many different people: black and white, male and female, who represented a seemingly endless array of viewpoints. She was often successful in gaining their approval and securing a following. She worked to connect with people, to shape the way they looked at the world and inspire them to cast off their doubts and follow her lead. She was a representative

---

78. Holt, *Mary McLeod Bethune,* 200.

of the race at large in the federal bureaucracy, and her efforts forced politicians to recognize the political importance of African Americans. Because of Bethune's work, the national political agenda began to reflect African American concerns, although the nation did not direct its full political attention to those issues until the black freedom movement of the 1960s.

Nevertheless, Bethune fell short of achieving her larger goals of inclusion for African Americans for several reasons. Bethune underestimated the strength and persistence of racism and racist attitudes. She tenaciously clung to her belief that placing qualified, well-educated, competent African Americans in visible positions would automatically open the doors of government for others. Despite the presence of racial liberals within the New Deal administration, this did not happen. For FDR, the necessity of placating southern Democrats took precedence over African American advancement. Bethune also misjudged the depth of commitment to collective advancement within her race. She believed that high-ranking black administrators could and would work unselfishly from inside their agencies to undermine discriminatory practices, achieve inclusion, and obtain greater benefits for the masses. However, those who did not share her background and experiences held different values—values grounded in the notion of "rugged individualism" and individual achievement. These were indeed foreign notions for Bethune.

Finally, Bethune failed to move a significant number of African American women forward to the policy-making level. Each time she approached agency administrators to secure patronage positions for African American women, they listened politely but did not act upon the recommendations. The first question administrators repeatedly asked was "What group do you represent?" Bethune soon learned that interest-group politics was the order of the day, and black women needed to form a powerful organization if they wanted recognition at the federal level. If African American women were ever going to have a role in shaping public policy, Bethune had to realize her dream of creating a national organization of women's organizations. This new organization would need to unite all existing black women's organizations into a working whole—to pool experiences, supplement programs, and call together all members when necessary for large and important endeavors. On December 5, 1935, Bethune called to order the first meeting of the National Council of Negro Women (NCNW)—the organization she believed would fulfill her vision of creating high-level positions for more black women in the federal government.[79]

79. Roane interview, 211; "The National Council of Negro Women, 1935–1949," Series 5, Box 16, Folder 262, NCNW; NCNW Series 2, Box 1, Folder 1.

The National Council of Negro Women

The Great Depression was a profound crisis for the nation, yet this national emergency presented an opportunity for Americans to redefine the meaning of community. Local, state, and regional attempts to stem the economic crisis were ineffective. Through New Deal programs, the federal government worked to coordinate, manage, and supplement the myriad relief efforts begun across the nation. The nation learned the value of a national effort in dealing with the economic crisis. Regionalism gave way to nationalism. As director of Negro Affairs in the National Youth Administration, Mary McLeod Bethune gained a government insider's perspective on the importance of coordinated national efforts to deal with national crises, discovered how to organize such programs, and learned new administrative skills necessary to accomplish specific goals. Bethune then applied those lessons to African American women's efforts for racial equality. Local, state, and regional black women's organizations' efforts proved ineffective in overcoming racial prejudice, segregation, and discrimination. The multitude of local, state, and regional programs women's organizations had put in place were designed to change the manners, morals, and behavior of the "lower classes." Bethune saw the futility of using these types of programs as a means of modifying white attitudes toward blacks. Moreover, she believed African American women were not using their resources wisely. Overlapping programs wasted both time and resources. She also rejected black separatism and emigration as a viable solution. African Americans needed to tap into the power and wealth dominated by whites, not opt for a black-controlled empty larder. Bethune saw racism as a national issue of the same magnitude as the Great Depression. She concluded that African Americans must join forces with people of color worldwide while fighting for integration within American society. In founding the National Council of Negro Women (NCNW), Bethune sought to apply the lessons of the Great Depression to black women's efforts for social justice and redefine the parameters of the African American community.

❧

The midst of a worldwide depression seemed an inauspicious time to establish a new black woman's organization. Yet, by 1935 several changes within the operating structure of the most prominent black women's association, the National Association of Colored Women (NACW), led Bethune to believe that the time was right to organize the NCNW. The NACW was supposed to be the official voice of black women, yet by 1935 Bethune believed the organization was not changing to keep pace with modern political realities. She saw the NACW maintaining its focus on a crusade to make poor and rural black women "better" wives, mothers, and workers. Its principal mission remained that of bringing the behavior of the masses of black women closer to that of middle-class women through an increased effort to improve individual habits and behaviors. According to Bethune, this concentration on reforming the habits and culture of a specific group of black women meant that the NACW leadership was creating "artificial" divisions among black women based on class status. Bethune argued that this approach undermined black women's collective power. As a womanist, she recognized the inherent link between race, class, and sexual oppression. Since whites routinely judged blacks by those in the lowest socioeconomic class, NACW programs that publicly denounced lower- and working-class habits merely legitimized negative white perceptions of all African Americans.[1] Moreover, Bethune's exposure to the inner workings of the federal government through the NYA allowed her to reshape her perspectives on what were appropriate means, objectives, and goals for African American race leaders. She now argued that conditions for African Americans would not improve simply because the personal habits of a certain group of individuals changed. She insisted instead that fundamental changes in the American social, economic, and political structure were necessary for racial progress. The NACW program was not addressing systemic change.

1. For a fuller discussion of this phenomenon, see Gaines, *Uplifting the Race.*

Bethune had other concerns about the efficacy of the NACW and its programs. First, she was concerned that the decentralized structure of the NACW was undermining its effectiveness as a vehicle for representing the concerns of black women. As she knew from her tenure as president of the association, individual African American women affiliated with the NACW were more concerned with their local and regional club activities than with national programs. Influential clubwomen gave local programs precedence over national programs and diverted increasingly scarce resources to their local affiliates. Moreover, in many instances, the objectives of the local, regional, and national programs overlapped. Bethune saw this duplication of programs and increasing competitiveness among the various groups as highly inefficient and effectively eroding the impact of the NACW.[2]

Bethune was also greatly concerned about programmatic changes in the NACW. Because of the declining financial position of African Americans throughout the 1920s, the NACW cut many of its programs, keeping only two major departments intact: "Mother, Home and Child" and "Negro Women in Industry." The Mother, Home and Child department focused on creating a better environment for black children by instituting adult education for parents and encouraging parents to create homes that gave children a "proper cultural background." The association designed the Department of Negro Women in Industry to instruct black women in proper work habits and organize them to take advantage of new opportunities and improve working conditions.[3] Neither program supported political action to institutionalize any gains that the NACW may have won for blacks. Instead, NACW leaders focused their efforts on program consolidation that fostered greater centralization and conserved the association's declining financial resources.

Bethune rejected the NACW's program. In January 1930, she wrote to at least thirty influential black women, telling them that for the past three years she had been considering organizing a "National Council of Colored Women of America." The purpose of the association was "to give opportunity to those who are interested in the many phases of work among our women in this country to cope with the problems affecting our status in America and to cement a spirit of cooperation and unified effort in the shaping of our destiny . . . I am concerned about the central Wheel, composed of the

2. Banks interview, 180.
3. Sallie W. Stewart, "President's Report," July 21–28, 1933, NACW; Dr. Mary F. Waring, "President's Address," July 21–26, 1935, NACW; Wesley, *The History of the National Association of Colored Women's Clubs,* 105–11.

many spokes of religious, educational, fraternal, political, economic, welfare
and business organizations of Negro women—developing the ideals of our
several groups."[4]

She envisioned her council as a vehicle for constructing a wider scope for
African American women's organizations and promoting black women's participation within the new political climate created by the New Deal. During her tenure in the Roosevelt administration, Bethune attempted to expand black women's roles in New Deal programs, yet whenever she tried to
get black women patronage positions, white administrators often wanted to
know what organization she represented.[5] Interest group politics was the order of the day, and Bethune found herself as a black leader without a formal
following. Without large numbers of interested voters behind her, she had
little leverage. Bethune was out of step with political realities. This realization pushed her to argue that African American women needed to build a
separate association where they could articulate an independent worldview,
build political strength and solidarity, and prepare to take public offices. Although she understood her role as representative-at-large for the race, she
needed a formal organization with large numbers of black women members
to pressure the federal government to recognize the importance of African
American issues and place them on the national political agenda. Only then
would African Americans have any hope of achieving social, economic, and
political justice. From the beginning, Bethune worked to make her organization a conduit for giving black women visibility and power on a national scale
by forcing the government to recognize their collective power. She envisioned
it as the authoritative voice of African American womanhood so that "when
the council speaks its power will be felt."[6]

The immediate purpose of this new group, then, was to operate as an
African American women's lobby in Washington, D.C. Bethune envisioned
this council as the hub of a wheel and the various national women's associations as the spokes.[7] It would unite national educational, business, religious,
fraternal, labor, and welfare associations under one umbrella association. This
structure would make African American women's civic, educational, cultural,

4. Mary McLeod Bethune to Mary Church Terrell, January 29, 1930, MCT.
5. Roane interview, 211–16.
6. NCNW, Series 5, Box 16, Folder 262; "Minutes of the founding meeting held December
5, 1935," NCNW, Series 2, Box 1, Folder 1; Mary McLeod Bethune to Program Committee,
December 1936, NCNW, Series 2, Box 1, Folder 2.
7. "Minutes of the founding meeting held December 5, 1935," 3.

social, economic, and political programs more efficient by coordinating local, state, and regional programs. The organization would collect, interpret, and disseminate information about the activities of all the member associations as well as encourage political action, teach self-reliance, and hone women's leadership skills through its programs. Within its separate spaces women would form groups to investigate problems, analyze political campaigns, and become familiar with state constitutions and voting laws. They would study and publicize voting records, organize voter registration campaigns, and mobilize voters. They would learn to draw up and present petitions on behalf of African Americans. Bethune saw local, state, and regional women's groups coordinating their activities and significantly increasing their political impact through the group. She also saw the organization working to place competent black women leaders in decision-making positions who would in turn open additional positions to as many other black women as possible.[8] Bethune's vision was to create a mechanism that would train African American women to be insightful political activists and lobbyists, increase black women's collective political power, and give them greater representation at the highest levels of government.

Bethune's focus on advancing black *women* to places of political decision-making and power has led various observers to hail her as "one of the chief exponents of feminism"[9] in the modern sense of the term. In one respect, this was feminism. Bethune certainly did seek high-level political positions for women, encourage women's economic autonomy, and support women's independent action. However, Bethune was a womanist. Promoting women for decision-making public positions was the means to an end—the advancement of the *race*. Bethune continued to believe in the moral superiority of women and their primary responsibility for sustaining the ethical strength of the race. She continued to believe in the principle of socially responsible individualism, trusting that women would use public positions for group advancement, so she steadfastly fought for women's right to hold key public posts. Bethune envisioned this new organization as a vehicle for realizing equality for *all* African Americans.

On December 5, 1935, Bethune called together thirty women, including Charlotte Hawkins Brown (principal, Palmer Memorial Institute, Sedalia,

---

8. "Tentative by-laws of the NCNW," April 1936, NCNW, Series 1, Box 1, Folder 1; Executive Secretary Report, 1938, NCNW, Series 2, Box 1, Folder 4; NCNW, Series 5, Box 16, Folder 262.

9. Radio station KFOX, "National Council of Negro Women," July 14, 1946, Interview of Mary McLeod Bethune by Fay M. Jackson.

North Carolina); Addie W. Hunton (National Alpha Kappa Alpha Sorority, New York City); Irene E. Maxwell (Women's Auxiliary of the National Baptist Convention); Mary Church Terrell (NACW, Washington, D.C.); Mabel Keaton Staupers (National Association of Graduate Nurses, New York City); Carita V. Roane (Social Workers of Greater New York, New York City); Daisy Lampkin (NAACP, Pittsburgh); Addie W. Dickerson (National Business and Professional Women's Club, Philadelphia); and Florence K. Williamson (National Iota Phi Lambda Sorority, New York City). Meeting at the 137th Street branch of the YWCA in New York City, these women were the leading representatives of national education, health, nursing, religious, fraternal, and business associations as well as community, women's, and racial organizations. Bethune's goal was to win their support for the NCNW. The female "Talented-Tenth" who attended this gathering discussed the possibility of forming a permanent council, and Bethune began the process of defining her vision of a new African American community. Bethune saw the NCNW as the genesis of this new community; a community of women that would unite divergent national groups into a working whole to pool experiences, supplement individual programs, and bring their total memberships together whenever necessary to advance issues of importance to African Americans. Bethune appealed to the women to expand their racial and gender interests by thinking "of the big things done by past leadership who dared to stand for right and let us fight today with Negro womanhood in mind."[10] She believed women's groups needed the vision to address issues of national and international concern through one national organization that could make a strong appeal to advance African American interests. Bethune summarized her vision of this community, saying, "The National Council of Negro Women has as its aim the bringing together of the Negro race for the united effort, in the things where we need to be united. It does not aim to stand in the way of the program of any individual organization, but to pool our interests, in order to be able to show the activities of Negro women in this country wherever pressure is needed, on whatever needs to come together for the opening of doors for our group."[11]

The majority of women at the NCNW's founding meeting were enthusiastic and supported Bethune's proposal wholeheartedly; however, several of

10. "Minutes of the founding meeting held December 5, 1935," NCNW, Series 2, Box 1, Folder 1.

11. Mary McLeod Bethune to Halena Wilson, October 4, 1942, NCNW, Series 18, Box 1, Folder 12.

Bethune's closest colleagues did not see the necessity of establishing yet another black women's organization. Charlotte Hawkins Brown, founder and principal of Palmer Memorial Institute, called the idea "air castle building and dreaming." Mary Church Terrell "did not see how the mistakes made by other groups will not be made by this one." Still, in a show of unity, the women voted unanimously to establish the NCNW, and Terrell insisted that the women cast a unanimous ballot for Bethune as first president of the council.[12]

Bethune knew that the best way to secure wider support for the NCNW program from those opposed to it was to incorporate them into the upper ranks of the association. She often said that if a woman had time to criticize and complain she obviously did not have enough to do. Bethune's avid supporters elected the two most vocal opponents at the founding meeting—Brown and Terrell—as first and fourth vice presidents respectively. Although this was an obvious attempt to quiet her opposition, Bethune also believed that it was time for these women to push themselves to be something greater than they thought they were.[13] Bethune often saw expressions of opposition as an opportunity for her to compel women to move forward and do more. However, as an astute politician, Bethune also recognized the need to keep her opposition close to her—they were easier to monitor that way.

Originally, Bethune built the internal structure of the organization around national women's organizations and a small group of individual life and associate members. Within a year, however, it became obvious that this organizational structure did not allow African American women in smaller cities, towns, and rural areas representation on the council program. To remedy this situation, the council authorized the development of Metropolitan Councils and Junior and Registered Councils in rural areas to increase the scope and base of the national program. Rural women organized through local networks of Jeannes Teacher Supervisors.[14] Local organizations worked with the Metropolitan Councils on local problems and issues. The Metropolitan Councils worked with the standing committees of the NCNW and informed

12. "Minutes of the founding meeting held December 5, 1935," 4.
13. "The National Council of Negro Women 1935–1949," NCNW, Series 5, Box 16, Folder 262, 2; Height interview, 28.
14. The Negro Rural School (Jeannes) Fund was established in 1907 by Quaker heiress Anna Jeannes to improve small, rural black schools in the South. Many African Americans became teachers in the first part of the twentieth century because of the financial support offered by the Jeannes Fund. By 1945, there were approximately 475 Jeannes Teacher Supervisors throughout the South. Maynce L. Copeland to Mary McLeod Bethune, December 21, 1945, NCNW, Series 18, Box 6, Folder 8.

them about local issues and the activities of local affiliates. Each committee explored the major issues in their field and reported their findings to the
national office. At annual meetings, the Executive Committee studied the
reports and developed an agenda for national action. The national office then
sent material to member organizations and life members to use in local programs and represented local and regional interests at the national level.[15] The
NCNW and its member organizations, Metropolitan, Junior, and Registered
Councils, maintained a symbiotic relationship. Within this structure, member groups could retain their highly individual character, and the council could
speak as one voice for all member associations on critical local issues and in
matters of national importance.

The responsibility for the general administration of the council was in the
hands of the board of directors. The board consisted of the council officers,
four members at large, and the chairs of the thirteen standing committees.
Voting membership in the NCNW was limited to national organizations
with active branches in at least five states and national organizations with
specialized constituencies who paid annual membership dues of fifty dollars.
In 1944, the council members voted to increase the annual membership fee
to one hundred dollars. Individuals could join the council as life members if
they paid a fifty-dollar membership fee or as associate members if they paid
$2.50 annually. The NCNW allowed life and individual members to attend
annual meetings and receive official publications, but not to vote.[16] Bethune
hoped that this structure would minimize the impact of individual interests
and undercut any power struggles that might have undermined the councils'
larger goals.

The organizational structure of the NCNW also reflected a significant
change in the relationship between black women activists and the communities they served. During the late nineteenth and early twentieth centuries,
parents, teachers, and mentors taught educated black women that they had
an obligation to use their education to help those who were less fortunate.
This emphasis on mutual obligation meant that these women must serve their
communities by assuming a wide variety of community roles while acting as
diplomats to the white community on behalf of the masses.[17] During the
twentieth century, wider access to education, declining illiteracy rates, and
demographic change led to increased political influence and forced educated

15. NCNW, Series 5, Box 16, Folder 262.
16. "Tentative by-laws of the NCNW," April 1936, NCNW.
17. See Gilmore, *Gender and Jim Crow*, especially chapter 2.

black women instilled with a commitment to socially responsible individualism to redefine their roles. Women in many communities were capable of organizing grassroots movements in defense of their community. For example, the Housewives' League of Detroit mobilized in 1930 to strengthen the black economy and minimize the economic devastation brought on by the depression. Throughout the 1930s, Housewive's Leagues in Chicago, Baltimore, Washington, Cleveland, and Harlem organized boycotts to secure new jobs for African Americans, and urban residents launched "Don't Buy Where You Can't Work" campaigns.[18] The NCNW did not help coordinate any of these activities, and that was the point. Local activists were capable of organizing individual actions; the organizational structure of the NCNW was designed to incorporate community activists into a wider program focused on national legislative reform. Under Bethune's leadership, the NCNW concentrated on empowering women by helping them find ways to achieve economic independence, teaching lessons in citizenship training, and instructing them in techniques for bringing about long-term political change.

The council was a voluntary female association where politically inclined women could cultivate a female-centered ethos of resistance, encourage female autonomy, create a supportive environment, and promote a female sphere of influence, authority, and power in their efforts to enhance African Americans' political status. The NCNW did not focus on changing individual attitudes and behaviors, but rather on changing social, economic, and political institutions that shaped Americans' collective ideas. The council created programs designed to teach political skills that would build black political power bases. It lobbied political representatives to open new places for black women on policy-making boards and committees. It reflected Bethune's political education in the New Deal by focusing on interest group methods, such as lobbying, to eliminate discrimination in housing, health, education, employment, public accommodations, and political representation. The council was to be the organizational heart of a wider African American women's community.

Bethune had become an outspoken advocate for systemic change and redirected her energies in that direction. She intensified her efforts to compel the federal government to remove every hindrance to black equality. As early as 1926, Bethune had castigated the U.S. government for disregarding its moral, social, economic, political, and spiritual obligations to more than twelve million blacks simply because of the color of their skin. "America," she said,

18. See Jones, *Labor of Love, Labor of Sorrow*, 215; Darlene Clark Hine, "Housewives' League of Detroit," 584–86.

" . . . belongs to Negroes as much as it does to those of any other race. Our forebears and those of us living in this time have suffered, agonized, bled for this—our land. We have helped make it what it is today. Denied equal share in the fruits of our sacrificing and suffering, we have protested. We shall protest, and protest again." She encouraged African Americans to protest openly against discrimination and unequal treatment. In an obvious reference to Marcus Garvey and the UNIA's call for black separatism, she encouraged blacks to "resist the implication that we constitute a separate part of this nation." Bethune believed African Americans had every right to participate in American institutions and should "invade every field of activity in America," especially public offices in city, state, and national government.[19]

Bethune's desire to organize an African American women's group may appear out of step with her larger integrationist goals, but she saw it as a necessity given the reality of the racial attitudes of the time. Mary Church Terrell, Sallie Stewart, Mary F. Waring, and others opposed her. They argued that the National Association of Colored Women (NACW) had a place on the National Council of Women of America (NCWA) and this place gave them enough national exposure for issues confronting the race.[20] Bethune disagreed. She believed the NACW's place on the NCWA was insufficient. She argued that the NCWA had thirty-eight member organizations, only one of which represented African American interests. Moreover, membership in the NCWA did not give other black women's organizations the opportunity to work together to address the problems facing African Americans as a group. Of course it is also likely that Bethune was motivated to build new, rival power bases to those dominated by the likes of Mary Church Terrell. Because Bethune held a relatively high position in the New Deal administration and a prominent place in the Black Cabinet, she had come to see herself as the spokesperson for black America. Bethune's ego was certainly a factor in her insistence on organizing the NCNW.

The NCNW struggled to become a permanent, financially stable, and respected African American women's political organization. Its first few years were precarious. The council conducted business from Bethune's living room with very little money and no permanent office help. Volunteer executive secretaries Lucy Stowe, Clara Bruce, Carita Roane, Dorothy Height, and Florence Norman laid much of the groundwork for the council despite being

19. Mary McLeod Bethune, "President's Address to the 15th Biennial Convention of the National Association of Colored Women," MMB, 19–22.

20. "Ex-President N.A.C.W. Enters Controversy on Forming New National Council of Women," n.d., BFC I.

handicapped by lack of funds and only periodic office help. In 1942, Bethune finally managed to raise sufficient monies to establish a national office, employ Jeanetta Welch Brown as the first paid executive secretary, and hire a stenographer and clerk.[21] (Still, the council's agenda was always ambitious because it reflected Bethune's personal belief that there were no limits to what organized women could accomplish.) Throughout the 1930s and 1940s, the council addressed all major issues of the time, including racism, segregation, race relations, lynching, voter education, public housing, education and job training, civil service reform, consumer rights, day care, public health, expansion of social security benefits, equity in social welfare programs, and international relations.

In April 1936, the NCNW held its first conference to adopt a constitution and elect permanent officers. This first NCNW convention was composed entirely of "high society ladies" who seemed to be more concerned with how they looked than with what Bethune wanted to accomplish. The women were fashionably dressed in their "hats and mink coats and fancy dresses" and spent more time in the first few days running back and forth to change clothes than attending program meetings. Bethune's vision of the NCNW was one of a hard-working, forceful, inclusive group with solid roots, and she quickly tired of the country club atmosphere at the conference. She faced the women and in her strong voice said, as Henrine Ward Banks recalled, "Ladies, I am going to tell you something. Take off your hats. Let's leave the mink coats in the back. Let's roll up our sleeves and get ready to go to work. I am putting someone on the doors. And you are not to leave the building. We will go downstairs to lunch—we will not leave the building for lunch. We will close our meeting at five. You will have plenty of time to go back and put on your evening dresses and go to dinner." In her characteristically outspoken, no-nonsense way, Bethune cut the women down cold. The NCNW was not to become another women's "society club." It was to have solid roots, a broad vision, and give extensive service. Bethune wanted to get women of all classes and occupations together. She strongly believed that class or occupation should not separate women and the NCNW should always be an inclusive organization.[22] Future conferences included working-class representatives from the rural South and the inner cities.

21. NCNW, Series 5, Box 16, Folder 262.
22. Banks interview, 181; Hilda Orr Fortune interview, November 17, 1976, Tape Recording, NCNW.

The classist behavior exhibited by those attending the meeting was one of the problems Bethune had to confront in redefining a black women's community. A more serious problem was Bethune's struggle within herself. Bethune also held a fair degree of bourgeois tastes; even her closest friends described her as quite "vain."[23] She regularly indulged in having her hair "rolled," and in getting facials and pedicures and dressing in the finest clothes. In effect, Bethune was at war with a part of herself in her efforts to beat back classism within the membership. However, perhaps her attitude also stemmed from her resentment of these "society ladies." Bethune had worked hard to transform herself from a poor country girl to a respected, sophisticated black leader, yet the social elite had never fully accepted her into their ranks. There always seemed to be an invisible barrier that she was unable to cross. Now that she had complete control of the council, she could decide what was considered appropriate behavior and determine how the organization would function. Bethune took control immediately and left no question as to her authority.

The first immediate problem the council faced was how to improve the declining quality of life for African Americans during the depression. This was obviously too large a problem for any one organization to handle alone, so the NCNW joined with the YWCA, the Brotherhood of Sleeping Car Porters and Maids, the National Negro Congress, the NAACP, and various other groups to address the issue. Bethune used her position as director of Minority Affairs in the NYA to supply members of the NCNW Employment Committee as well as the representatives of other agencies statistics on black participation in the workforce, on Federal Work projects, in the CCC, and in the NYA. Other committees took on issues in educational and recreational opportunities, health and housing conditions, and security and legal circumstances. The analysis resulting from these efforts became a part of the National Conference on the Problems of the Negro and Negro Youth held in January 1937, originally proposed by John P. Davis and A. Philip Randolph of the National Negro Congress. Although this mobilization against discrimination was hard-hitting and quite impressive, it resulted in only a meager redistribution of work-relief jobs for black men and gave even fewer opportunities to black women. It also did little to force the government to incorporate African Americans in government-sponsored job training classes. Not being able to force substantive change led Bethune to redouble her efforts to unite African American leaders at least on the major issues. Nevertheless,

23. Jeanetta Welch Brown, Interview by Susan McElrath, July 10, 1992, Tape recording, NCNW.

opportunities for blacks remained limited until the onset of World War II gave them added advantages.

Bethune also learned an important lesson about the role of women in working with men in conferences. Although she became the general chairperson and organized the meeting, working with male-led groups undermined her agenda for incorporating women into leadership positions. Men headed all four committees at the conference. No woman served on the Employment Committee, and a limited number of women occupied lesser positions on the panels of the Education and Recreation Committee, the Health and Housing Committee, and the Security and Legal Committee.[24] If African American women were to become visible political actors, they would have to use the NCNW to create and manage effective programs on their own. This was the "practical separatist" aspect of Bethune's vision of community.

Bethune insisted the NCNW focus on including black women in the political process and advancing educated black women by securing opportunities for them as administrators in federal programs. Once the council accomplished this, these women administrators would ensure that African Americans were receiving their fair share of government benefits. According to historian Susan Ware, many black and white women still believed that women were society's "moral force." These "social feminists" argued that because women were less focused on gaining individual power and measured success by how much they helped others, they were the logical choice to head New Deal programs that focused on humanitarian and social issues.[25] Since social welfare programs addressed issues directly related to family welfare—women's special province—women were most qualified to run these programs.

When Bethune arrived in Washington in 1935, a white women's network was already in place. Since 1933, Molly (Mary W.) Dewson had worked with Eleanor Roosevelt to mobilize white women and enlarge their influence in New Deal programs. Dewson recruited women for prominent government positions, demanded and received a greater number of patronage positions for women, and fostered an awareness of women as a special interest group among top-ranking government officials. Bethune immediately saw that "doors are not closed on white women"[26] in Washington, but they were closed to African

24. "The National Conference on the Problems of the Negro and Negro Youth," President's Personal File, FDR; "Recommendations of the National Conference on the Problems of the Negro and Negro Youth," President's Personal File, FDR.

25. Ware, *Beyond Suffrage*, 14.

26. Ware, *Beyond Suffrage*, 43–67; Mary McLeod Bethune, "Refining Our Structure," NCNW, Series 2, Box 2, Folder 21.

American women. Dewson's network did not cross racial lines, and patronage positions did not go to black women. Bethune's focal point, then, was to create a black women's network: a nonpartisan coalition of politically active and astute black women who would use the NCNW as a base of operations.

To achieve this goal, Bethune began a long-term program to promote political inclusion for black women through citizenship training. She argued that women could no longer afford to believe they had "no interest in the political life of my community." As the NCNW Committee on Citizenship Training Manual pointed out, politics was not merely campaigning to hold office or voting; "Politics translated into everyday needs, politics means food at prices you can afford to pay; housing at prices you can afford to rent or buy; adequate educational facilities and equal educational opportunities for your children; equal protection under the law; equal participation at the polls; the right to petition and be heard; and many other citizenship rights which should be enjoyed alike by all Americans."[27] Women were political because politics affected the personal decisions women made on a daily basis.

Through its Citizenship Training Manual, the NCNW Committee on Citizenship instructed Metropolitan Councils to spearhead programs of aggressive community action by organizing community workshops designed to instruct local women in their responsibilities as members of a democracy in areas where local communities had not yet organized. Metropolitan Councils were to help local women launch investigations of basic community problems, establish discussion groups to analyze local and regional political campaigns and party platforms, and clarify problems and issues that threatened the well-being of the community. Council women were to set up Town Meeting forums to discuss important issues and develop programs for community action. Lugenia Burns Hope, chair of the Committee on Citizenship, reported that by 1940 the program had reached sixty-three thousand women in twenty-six states.[28]

Foreshadowing the voter registration drives and citizenship schools of the 1960s civil rights movement, local activists associated with the NCNW organized voter registration drives by studying state constitutions and voting laws and then mobilizing all qualified women voters. Local council members taught women how to use a voting machine or mark a ballot. They encouraged

27. "Women Must Lead the Way," Community Workshop for Citizenship Training Manual, NCNW, Series 13, Box 7, Folder 80.
28. "Women Must Lead the Way"; Records of the NCNW, *Aframerican Women's Journal* 1, no. 4 (1941), NCNW, Series 13.

women to take part in local political organizations, to study and publicize the voting records of local, state, and national officials, and to draw up petitions to meet community needs and present those petitions at public hearings to their local governments. Women learned how to uncover the positions of the candidates on important issues before they cast their ballot and how to hold the candidates to their promises.[29] Metropolitan councils designed community citizenship workshops to show women that political power began with the power of the vote.

On the national level, the citizenship program stressed women's responsibility to be intelligent and competent members of the electorate. It was time for women to build political strength and solidarity, support only qualified candidates, and be willing and prepared to accept political office. The first step in this process was to have black women appointed on policy-making committees and boards so racial problems received adequate attention and consideration. In April 1938, Bethune arranged for sixty-five NCNW members and government officials to meet at the Department of the Interior under the direction of Forrester B. Washington, director of the Atlanta School for Social Work. White women administrators including Margaret Anderson (Women's Bureau), Katherine Lenroot (Children's Bureau), and Molly Dewson (Social Security Board) gave an overview of their government departments and related their experiences in private agencies. A few days after the conference, Eleanor Roosevelt called the members of the NCNW committee and several government officials to the East Room of the White House for further discussion. Bethune called on the officials present to appoint "qualified Negro women" who "are in closer touch with the problems of their own group" to administrative positions in the Children's Bureau, Bureau of Public Health, Women's Bureau of the U.S. Department of Labor, Bureau of Education, Federal Housing Administration, and the Social Security Board.[30]

Bethune knew that the NCNW would not get all of the appointments, and certainly not without additional pressure on the administration, but she succeeded in opening a door for black women that previously had been closed. She brought the NCNW citizenship program to the attention of the administration and put the administration on notice that the NCNW was serious about developing the political power of African American women. The

29. "Women Must Lead the Way."

30. *Aframerican Women's Journal* 1, no. 1 (spring 1940), and (summer/fall 1941), NCNW, Series 13; "Negro Women in Federal Welfare Programs," Conference Report, NCNW, Series 4, Box 1, Folder 3; Executive Secretary Report, 1938, NCNW, Series 2, Box 1, Folder 4; "Women Seek More Federal Positions," n.d., BFC I.

NCNW would continue to pressure government administrators until they afforded African American women their rightful place in government administration. Bethune also met a larger goal through the conference. She made the administration aware that there were "a myriad of prepared Negro women" who were trained and ready to work, and the policy of the NCNW was "to try to get in as many as possible and get as many informed concerning our abilities as we possibly can."[31]

The NCNW chipped away at segregation through conferences, petitions, and reform initiatives, but this was a long-term process that yielded few immediate results. In a speech given at the thirty-second annual meeting of the Association for the Study of Negro Life and History in Oklahoma City in 1947, Bethune could finally speak of increasing numbers of African American women taking their place in all phases of American public life. Among this group were active members of the NCNW. They included Fannie Williams, Margaret Bowen, Sadie Daniel, Arenia Mallory, Artemesia Bowden, and Charlotte Hawkins Brown in education; Sadie M. Alexander, Edith Sampson Clayton, and Eunice Hunter Carter in law; Jeanetta Welch Brown in politics; Dorothy Ferebee in medicine; Mabel Staupers and Estelle Riddle in nursing; Mme. C. J. Walker and Cecil Spaulding in business; Marian Anderson and Carol Brice in art and music; Jane Hunter, Dorothy Height, Eartha M. M. White, and Pauline Redmond Coggs in social work; Olive Diggs, Venice Spragg, and Rebecca Stiles Taylor in journalism; and Constance Daniel, Frances Williams, Vivian Carter Mason, Crystal Bird Fauset, Venita Lewis, and Ora Brown Stokes in government.[32]

In addition to the effort to involve African American women in politics, the NCNW also established a program that encouraged and trained women to apply for civil service and public administration positions. Through the NCNW quarterly journal, *Aframerican Woman,* and the monthly newsletter, *Telefact,* the council kept women informed of upcoming openings in civil service jobs and exam dates. The council also began a résumé project. Any woman interested in job opportunities could send her résumé to the NCNW, where it would be kept on file. The employment committee regularly reviewed the résumés and matched qualified applicants with job openings when they became available. In conjunction with the résumé project, the NCNW em-

---

31. Executive Secretary Report, 1938, NCNW.

32. Mary McLeod Bethune, "Recent Achievements of Negro Women," October 26, 1947, Address given at the thirty-second annual meeting of the Association for the Study of Negro Life and History, Oklahoma City, OK, BFC I.

phasized job training for women even if no jobs currently existed in a particular field. Bethune believed women should be prepared to take advantage of new opportunities as they arose. Her philosophy was that it was better to "stand on the streets begging and not even have a job—but TRAINED to do a job when a job comes along." Bethune did not advocate special consideration for blacks simply because of the color of their skin. She firmly believed African Americans must "understand that they are not going to receive simply because they are Negroes, but they must be prepared like other people if they hope to get their places."[33]

While Bethune strongly advocated training and preparation for the job market, she was certainly aware of the effects of racism on job opportunities for blacks. For that reason, the NCNW was also involved in fighting for civil service reform measures. After a conference held in February 1939 under the auspices of the NYA, the council joined with other black organizations to recommend changes in the procedures for the Civil Service Commission. As a result of the conference, Aubrey Williams, administrator of the NYA, sent a letter to Harry B. Mitchell, head of the U.S. Civil Service Commission, outlining the recommendations of the conferees. While Mitchell agreed that the "wider extension of the civil service in government employment and appointments based on competitive examinations" was desirable, he wavered on the elimination of the photograph as a means of identification in connection with examinations. Mitchell asserted that photographs were used only as a means of eliminating illegal activity among applicants. Although the use of fingerprinting had been considered, Mitchell argued photographs were necessary because "the Commission examines hundreds of thousands of persons each year. These applications are received from all parts of the country. The fingerprinting of these applicants, together with comparing such fingerprints with those taken at the time of appointment, would result in a greatly increased expense to the government."[34]

The conference also recommended that selection for appointments be made strictly by rank of eligibility, doing away with the discretionary power of the appointing office. Mitchell contended that he had no power to change this practice as the attorney general had ruled "Congress cannot, by act, restrict the choice of a head of a department to the point where he would have no choice." The suggestion that all civil service lists be made public was also

33. *Afraamerican Women's Journal* 3, no. 3 (1943), NCNW, Series 13; Roane interview, 215; Executive Secretary report, 1938, NCNW.
34. Harry B. Mitchell to Aubrey Williams, April 11, 1939, BFC I, 1.

rejected based on the bureaucratic red tape involved in compiling these lists. Mitchell maintained that even the commission did not have a list for its own use. In reality, there was not one list, there were "at present about fifteen hundred individual registers" being "worked over constantly by our specially trained register clerks." Mitchell explained, "Limitations of the Commission's authority and the dictates of practicality do not permit the Commission to alter circumstances with respect to a number of points raised in the conference report." In short, these were legislative issues. Nevertheless, the council continued to press for changes, working for the appointment of an African American to the Board of Appeals of the Civil Service Commission and calling on the Council on Personnel Administration authorized by Roosevelt to overhaul the entire personnel system of the government to appoint at least one black member.[35] Despite Bethune's personal efforts and those of the NCNW, procedures remained unchanged until President Harry Truman changed the operation of the Civil Service Commission.

American entry into World War II enriched and expanded the NCNW program. With the advent of the war, Bethune redefined her concept of "community." The black community was no longer merely a local, state, regional, or even national entity: it was a global community. She increased her efforts to make black Americans recognize their connection to people of color worldwide. Bethune believed African Americans needed to realize that the political and economic problems faced by blacks in the United States were in fact worldwide problems for peoples of color. She told African American women they must be aware of their "special problems" and try to find solutions for them, but they also needed to recognize that their "problems are the problems of the weak and oppressed everywhere," and their "rights like the rights of all people are rooted in the common humanity of all men." Bethune saw the war as a means to teach "lessons of interdependence and cooperation." America entered the war to fight "against those misguided doctrines of a master race that would subjugate mankind." Bethune believed black women were uniquely qualified to join in this struggle because "We Negroes—we Negro women—know the full meaning of such a struggle, for we have been engaged in it, not for four years, or for ten years, but for generations."[36]

35. Harry B. Mitchell to Aubrey Williams, April 11, 1939, BFC I, 3; Memorandum from Mary McLeod Bethune to President Franklin D. Roosevelt, n.d., BFC I.

36. Mary McLeod Bethune, "President's Address to the 15th Biennial Convention of the National Association of Colored Women," MMB, 20; Mary McLeod Bethune, "Annual Report," October 15, 1943, NCNW, Series 2, Box 1, Folder 18; Mary McLeod Bethune, "President's Address," October 1943, NCNW, Series 2, Box 1, Folder 19.

As America went to war, the council concentrated on encouraging volunteerism and patriotism. It instituted a series of regional conferences in conjunction with the Women's Interest Section of the War Department to inform black women about the war effort. The NCNW distributed materials and information designed to stimulate morale, interest, and participation in the activities of various war agencies. NCNW members cooperated with the Office of Price Administration in consumer education programs, local Civil Defense Councils in salvage campaigns and air raid duties, and worked with the United Service Organization (USO).[37]

Bethune was always patriotic, resolutely championing American democracy, and the NCNW "I Am an American" program reflected her loyalty to the government. Still, she was not a blind patriot unaware of American democracy's shortcomings. She was not afraid to state publicly, "Democracy has a *long way* to go *yet*." As she saw it, "The problem of democracy *is interpretation as much as enactment*, and that is our *major* concern at this time."[38] Although Bethune was aware of and critical about America's democratic practices, she never encouraged disloyalty to the United States. Throughout the war years she warned women to beware of "subversive" influences. America was their home and they must defend it: "despite our grievances over prejudice, discrimination, and segregation, both within our government and without, we are determined as American women to do all in our power to serve our country in keeping with our transition of loyalty and patriotism and to preserve democracy for ourselves and our children."[39]

Bethune encouraged women to get involved in voluntary programs on the home front by publicizing her status as general of the Women's Army for National Defense (WANDs). Lovonia H. Brown organized the WANDs as a black women's voluntary war service organization. Through local chapters the WANDs sold war bonds and stamps, became hostesses at USO centers, made bandages, served breakfast to inductees, wrote letters, furnished transportation, sent personal items to soldiers, and visited camps.[40] The WANDs and the NCNW cooperated with the War Bond Sales section of the Treasury De-

37. "Negro Women in Civilian Defense Work," *Aframerican Women's Journal* (1943), NCNW, Series 13.

38. Mary McLeod Bethune, Radio interview with Jean Beckwith on WOOK, n.d., Tape Recording, NCNW.

39. *Aframerican Women's Journal* 2, no. 3 (winter 1941–1942), NCNW, 8.

40. "Women's Army for National Defense" pamphlet, NCNW, Series 18, Box 8, Folder 13.

partment and succeeded in selling $1 million in war bonds through the "Buy Bonds and Be Free" campaign that allowed the council to sponsor and launch the Liberty ship S.S. *Harriet Tubman*. Black women also cooperated with the Children's Bureau by conducting surveys on the need for day care for children of working mothers and served with the American Women's Voluntary Services (AWVS), as well as on special committees for the American Red Cross. Because of the segregation of the armed forces, African American women established home hospitality centers for black soldiers. The NCNW publicized black women's support for the war effort through "We Serve America" weeks.[41]

One of the most active NCNW programs during the war years was a reflection of Bethune's concern with women's economic independence. By early 1942, the council instituted a "Hold Your Job" program and sponsored a series of Wartime Employment Clinics funded by a six-thousand-dollar grant from the Julius Rosenwald Fund. The campaign focused on protecting the jobs of hundreds of thousands of black women who entered the industrial sector for the first time during the war. Early on, the NCNW recognized that industrial cutbacks, returning veterans, and reconversion would mean that black women workers would be the first fired in the postwar period. The NCNW Department of Employment designed the wartime employment clinics to help women empower themselves to retain better-paying industrial jobs.[42] The clinics were intended to promote black women's industrial employment through collective planning, organization, and action while simultaneously changing employer's attitudes about black women workers.

The clinics were an attempt to help women adjust to the industrial sector by emphasizing issues of worker health, attendance, personal appearance, attitude, efficiency, behavior on the job, and union participation. Workers learned to practice good work habits such as arriving at work on time, being "particular about their dress, behavior and attitude on the job and in public places," consciously trying to improve their job performance, and how to get along with other people even in an "unpleasant" situation. The NCNW also recognized that to secure wartime employment gains, black workers would have to embrace unionism. To that end, the "Hold Your Job" program steadfastly

41. "Negro Women in Civilian Defense Work," *Aframerican Women's Journal* (1943), NCNW, Series 13; Mary McLeod Bethune, "Activities in the War Effort," BFC I.

42. "Hold Your Job" Manual for the Organization and Operation of Wartime Employment Clinics, NCNW, Series 5, Box 11, Folder 196.

endorsed union membership and supported organized labor in free collective bargaining.[43]

The NCNW also sought to increase and strengthen African American women's position in national defense industries by pushing employers to include women in apprenticeship programs. Clinic organizers arranged meetings with employers to discuss workers' problems and resolve them by appealing to concerns for profit. Organizers stressed that an adjusted worker meant a smooth-running shop, less absenteeism, a lower rate of turnover, and increased production. Clinics for employers tried to convince foremen and supervisors to accept black women workers and facilitate their adjustment to the job.[44] The "Hold Your Job" program and its Wartime Employment Clinics did not attempt to reorder the industrial system. Rather, the NCNW promoted the integration of black working-class women into the industrial workforce and tried to secure their economic independence.

The NCNW advised its metropolitan councils to target certain strategic economic sectors and encourage the full participation of all community organizations in working for job security for black women. Clinic participants discussed issues relating to the status of black women workers in the community, the problems presented by their employment, and possible solutions for these problems. Subcommittees dealt with each specific problem identified. Once the groundwork was set, workers were encouraged to attend the clinics through a publicity campaign that mirrored the government campaign which encouraged women to join the labor force. Clinic organizers placed announcements in local newspapers and radio stations and posted notices in the factories; churches publicized the meetings and distributed handbills. Local clubs also made individual and group contacts. Clinics used panel discussions and forums, movies, question-and-answer formats, speakers, short plays and skits, and block dances to reach large numbers of workers.[45]

The job campaign raised the consciousness of women workers, although it ultimately failed to secure their place in the industrial sector. African American women returned to domestic service in 1946, but the lessons they learned through the employment clinic were also put to use. Many black domestic

43. Jeanetta Welch Brown and Mary McLeod Bethune to Anna Rosenberg (War Manpower Commission), May 14, 1943, NCNW, Series 5, Box 29, Folder 434; *Telefact* 1, no. 2, NCNW, Series 13; *Aframerican Women's Journal* (summer/fall 1941) and 3, no. 3 (1943), NCNW, Series 13; "The Negro Woman in National Defense" conference, June 28–30, 1941.
44. "Hold Your Job" Manual for the Organization and Operation of Wartime Employment Clinics; *Telefact* 1, no. 2, NCNW, Series 13.
45. "Hold Your Job."

workers now demanded contracts from their employers guaranteeing minimum pay, standard working hours, and paid vacations. In New York, domestic workers formed their own union and fought for standardized work conditions and benefits. The NCNW "Hold Your Job" campaign empowered participants to protect their interests through collective organization and action.

Another wartime change for women came when Secretary of War Henry L. Stimson authorized the organization of a Women's Army Auxiliary Corps (WACS) under the direction of Oveta Culp Hobby, former head of the Women's Interest Section of the War Department. The purpose of the WACS was to enlist women volunteers for army service to replace and release enlisted men for combat service. WAC units served in foreign as well as domestic zones of operation, but only in noncombat duties. Up to 150,000 women could join the corps after army commanders trained 450 officers and noncommissioned officers at the First Officer Training School in Des Moines, Iowa.[46] Bethune immediately saw the establishment of the WACS as another way that African American women could publicly demonstrate their loyalty to the government as well as their leadership and administrative abilities. President Roosevelt appointed Bethune as a special assistant to the secretary of war in the selection of the first officer candidates. She was determined to ensure that African American women received their fair share of appointments to the corps, successfully persuading Stimson to set aside 10 percent of the WAC officer corps positions for African American women.

Bethune attended the opening of the Des Moines WACS training facility and participated in the opening exercises.[47] She took an active interest in recruitment and training, yet despite her influence, military leaders at the Des Moines center immediately instituted segregation in living and dining accommodations, USO centers, and recreational facilities. Camp commanders assigned the thirty-one black officer candidates to one platoon and housed them at the east end of the line of barracks. They also assigned black women to special tables in the dining hall by military order. Administrators set up a specified swimming time for black candidates at the post pool. There was one "whites only" and one "blacks only" service club, but army personnel served black women at the post canteen without discrimination. Classroom training was integrated, as were drills and physical training. According to Colonel Don Faith, commandant of the school, it was army policy to segregate housing,

46. "Details of Women's Army Auxiliary Corps," Press release, May 16, 1942, War Department, Bureau of Public Relations, BFC I.

47. "Mary McLeod Bethune (Activities in the War Effort)," n.d, BFC I.

recreation, and dining facilities. However, inspectors found that there was no specific federal law that required segregation in the army, and furthermore, Iowa state laws specifically prohibited the segregation of African Americans. The report concluded that the army could not adequately justify violations of state laws at the Des Moines training center.[48]

Bethune went into action immediately. She contacted Eleanor Roosevelt and arranged a meeting to discuss the issue. She mobilized the NCNW. Groups of women traveled to Des Moines to inspect the camp and meet with black women trainees to discuss complaints. The NCNW spearheaded a campaign to bring charges by civilian and military personnel pertaining to conditions at the camp. Metropolitan Councils brought the issue before the public by organizing special events honoring black WACS and reporting on their activities. Still, in November 1942, Walter White, secretary of the NAACP, advised Bethune that black women officers no longer taught mixed classes. The commanders at Des Moines were extending segregation.[49] Despite meetings with Eleanor Roosevelt, investigations, reports, NCNW activities, lobbying, and public conferences addressing race discrimination in the war effort, the NCNW was defeated in its attempt to desegregate the WACS facility.

All was not lost, however. While African American WACS were segregated at the training facility, they were not automatically assigned to segregated units once they left Des Moines. After a tour of six military hospitals from Massachusetts to Pennsylvania, Bethune found that "The democratic spirit of integration and service to all patients and to nurses and WAC Technicians spelled out for me democracy in action." Black nurses were included in the general nurses program; there were integrated officer's club rooms, dining rooms, and recreational facilities. Despite these signs of acceptance, Bethune reported that there were no black doctors at any of the hospitals she visited. She "came away with a great question mark in my mind as to why," but hoped that this situation would be speedily remedied, as "We are more and more wanting to work *with* others than have others work *for* us."[50]

48. "Handling of Negro Officer Candidates," report to Mary McLeod Bethune from Charles P. Howard, August 26, 1942, BFC I.

49. "The National Council of Negro Women 1935–1949," NCNW; Walter White to Mary McLeod Bethune, November 4, 1942, BFC I.

50. "Report of observations made by Mary McLeod Bethune, a member of the National Civilian Advisory Committee of the Women's Army Corps from a tour of general hospitals in the eastern area where WACS are located," Press release, n.d., BFC I, 4.

Bethune was on an emotional roller coaster in late 1942 and early 1943. She was dejected about having to accept the failure of the NCNW's efforts at Des Moines, then encouraged in finding black nurses and WACS integrated into the work at eastern-area hospitals, but her spirits were dashed again when she realized there were no black physicians at any of the six facilities. Unfortunately, Bethune soon encountered another emotional setback as her loyalty to America came under scrutiny by Representative Martin Dies of the House Un-American Activities Committee (HUAC). In early 1943, Dies publicly accused Bethune of being a communist, although his reasons for doing so are unclear.

The House of Representatives established HUAC in the late 1930s to combat subversive right- and left-wing movements. From its inception, HUAC was inclined to see communists everywhere in American society, even announcing that communists had infiltrated the Boy Scouts. At first, Bethune refused to justify the accusation with a reply, but false accusations were not something she could ignore. In a public statement, Bethune maintained that Dies's accusation was a "malicious misstatement of the truth" and that he had named her a communist because of her "outspoken belief in a true democracy," and her "incessant efforts in seeking for all Americans the constitutionally guaranteed rights of full citizenship regardless of race, creed or color, my endeavors to enlist the full cooperative strength of America in our victory efforts." She then tried to turn the tables against Dies by asserting that his accusations against loyal Americans would help America's enemies win the war.[51]

Bethune also fought to defend herself with affidavits and letters of reference from prominent people worldwide. Everyone acquainted with Bethune knew, of course, the accusation was "utterly fantastic and vicious," and came to her defense. Charles Houston, legal counsel for the NAACP, believed that Dies had attacked Bethune because she was "a black women holding an important government position with influence in high governmental places, and for a black person to have such a position and such influence is to be ipso facto 'red' with Mr. Dies." Walter White and Houston coordinated a letter-writing campaign asking sixty-six prominent black Americans to write letters affirming Bethune's loyalty to the government to John H. Kerr, chairman of the investigating subcommittee. Houston represented Bethune before HUAC in

---

51. "Statement of Mary McLeod Bethune Re: Dies Accusation of Being a Communist," 1943, NCNW, Series 5, Box 10, Folder 184.

April 1943, and the committee quickly exonerated Bethune.[52] However, she was not one to quickly forgive and forget. In January 1944, Bethune launched an NCNW campaign against Dies's efforts to obtain an additional seventy-five thousand dollars in funding for his investigation of the Civil Service Commission. Despite her efforts, HUAC continued to function and actually picked up the pace of its investigations throughout the 1940s.

On the surface, Bethune's reaction to the HUAC allegations was calm and gracious. She told her NCNW staff and colleagues that obviously "someone with professional jealousy or [a] racist" was trying to undermine her political influence, and asserted, "You really haven't achieved anything unless you've been attacked." Yet, the accusation had deep-rooted repercussions. HUAC accusations destroyed lives, careers, and organizations. Bethune undoubtedly feared the allegations would destroy not only her reputation but also Bethune-Cookman and the NCNW. She was unwilling to take this chance. Continuing HUAC investigations caused Bethune to distance herself from associates if she believed their personal actions could link her to communist activity in any way. In 1946, Bethune abruptly distanced herself from Vivian Carter Mason, first vice-president of the NCNW from 1943 to 1945. The dispute stemmed from two separate incidents, yet clearly Mason's affiliation with the Women's International Federation in Europe and her visit to Moscow in October 1946 pushed Bethune to cut off her connection. The Women's International Federation was an international coalition of women from forty-three countries concerned with human rights and committed to a program of political action. The American branch of the federation, the American Congress of Women, was named as a "communist dominated" organization. Bethune telegraphed Mason to "cease immediately using National Councils name in any activities or speeches." Bethune's severing of her relationship with Mason was the fall-out of the HUAC investigations, but it turned out to be a short-term rupture. Within two years, Mason became active in the NCNW again and served as its third president from 1953 to 1957.[53]

The repercussions were not over, however, and even affected the internal operations of the NCNW, extending to the question of union representation for NCNW clerical workers. In 1946, four members of the staff—Marian

52. Walter White to Martin Dies, September 25, 1942, NAACP; Charles Houston to Walter White, March 20, 1943, NAACP; NCNW, Series 5, Box 14, Folder 213.

53. Fortune interview; Vivian Carter Mason to Mary McLeod Bethune, November 1, 1946, NCNW, Series 5, Box 2, Folder 27; Vivian Carter Mason to Mary McLeod Bethune, October 6, 1946, NCNW, Series 5, Box 2, Folder 27; NCNW, Series 6, Box 2.

Williams, research secretary, Katherine Shryver, public relations secretary, Gladys Thomas, business secretary, and Ellen Randolph, office secretary—decided to unionize through the United Office and Professional Workers of America (UOPWA). This incident between the clerical employees and the NCNW is a curious one. The Personnel Committee held meetings to discuss the issue, but the chair impounded the minutes and the proposed union contract. Since Shryver was the public relations secretary, the council by-passed the Public Relations Committee and issued its own press release about the incident. According to one remaining record, the Executive Committee held a "vigorous discussion" about the provisions of the proposed union contract and the "general attitude" of the staff involved. Members reviewed personnel practices, commenting on the council's willingness to provide paid vacations, personal leave time, over-time pay, sick pay, and competitive salaries to clerical workers. The Executive Committee concluded that the council had been more than generous with the women as far as working conditions and benefits were concerned. The general consensus was that there were deeper undercurrents of dissatisfaction at work among the employees and that they had engaged in "acts of disloyalty" by taking their grievances outside the council.[54]

Publicity over the council's resistance to union recognition put the NCNW and Bethune in an awkward position. Bethune was a strong supporter of the industrial labor movement. She actively stressed the importance of the labor movement to black women workers, yet the NCNW was a nonprofit organization not subsidized by any foundation. Since the council was dependent on funding from voluntary contributions and membership dues, the Executive Committee argued it was in no financial position to enter into any binding agreement. At the time of this incident, the council had less than five hundred dollars in its treasury and slightly more than twenty-five hundred dollars in unpaid bills. Moreover, the council had no immediate resources it could depend on to correct their financial situation. The bank had refused to give the NCNW a loan because they had no collateral, and no one on the committee would agree to take a mortgage on the council house. Bethune was forced to "volunteer" to loan the council approximately two thousand dollars to avoid default. The Executive Committee unanimously decided that the only recourse was to admit the precariousness of the council's financial condition, make no further obligations, pay the outstanding debts, and proceed on a limited program. This "limited program" would also include keeping a

54. Executive Committee Report 1946–1947, NCNW, Series 3, Box 1, Folder 26.

limited staff—only the executive director and housekeeper would remain as paid employees. The committee then prepared and released a carefully worded statement to council members, the UOPWA union representative, staff, and press alleging that the "present financial status of the Council—which may be substantiated by an audit of the books—places it in a position of not being able to enter into any contractual agreement at this time."[55] Mary McLeod Bethune signed the statement.

The financial crisis and subsequent firing of the four staff members seeking union representation led to negative press coverage and caused internal upheaval. In a letter written two days after the NCNW released its statement, the dismissed employees charged that the NCNW released them because of union activity. They claimed they were fired because they "sought to discuss working relations" for "the purpose of discussing and negotiating an agreement" with the Executive Committee. The women claimed they had held an informal meeting with Bethune in December to discuss the union and "received Mrs. Bethune's assurance of interest and support." They quoted Bethune as saying, "All my life I have fought for labor. The NCNW has grown up. To have a union here is just common sense." The UOPWA also issued a flyer about the incident asking for supporters to come to a meeting at the Phyllis Wheatly YWCA on the evening of January 28, 1947. Those who could not attend were asked to write in protest to Executive Committee members Edith Sampson, Mame Higgins, Eunice Carter, or to Bethune directly. Williams, Shryver, Thomas, and Randolph also contended that there was no official proposal before the Executive Committee and no demand for higher wages despite the fact that the UOPWA did submit a standard agreement to the Executive Committee. Although technically there was no demand in the agreement for an immediate wage increase, there was a provision for "annual increases" to be agreed upon for professional and clerical workers. Further fallout included the resignation of Mame Mason Higgins as executive director on March 15, 1947. Higgins cited the "smear campaign" undertaken by the released employees, which she saw as "intended to undermine the leadership at the core of the organization itself." Higgins hoped that her resignation would end "these cheap and superficial attacks."[56]

55. Executive Committee Report 1946–1947, NCNW, Series 3, Box 1, Folder 26; Press release, January 27, 1947, BFC I.

56. Press release from United Office and Professional Workers, Local 27, CIO, January 28, 1947, BFC I; Flyer from United Office and Professional Workers, Local 27, CIO, January 28, 1947, BFC I; Marian Smith Williams, Katherine Shryver, Gladys G. R. Tomas, and Ellen

Higgins's resignation did not end the controversy. On April 26, 1947, the New York Metropolitan Council sent a memorandum to Bethune and the Executive Committee about the dismissed employees. Although pledging their allegiance to the NCNW and its leadership, the New York Council made specific recommendations. First, the NCNW should secure a new executive director who would make fund-raising her first priority. Next, the NCNW should *immediately* set up a committee "composed of Regional Directors of the Councils, representation from each Metropolitan Council, and selected individuals from the general membership" that would be charged with redefining the NCNW's role as a "coordinator of the activities of Negro women," outline a new administrative policy, and implement "the technical routines attendant to operation." In a separate letter sent directly to Bethune, the New York Metropolitan Council called for the immediate reinstatement of the fired employees and for the council to establish "the necessary machinery . . . to bargain collectively" with the employees. President Gertrude A. Robinson then requested a personal meeting with Bethune so that she could "see that the instructions of the body are fulfilled."[57]

Even that was not the end of the matter. More fallout came from Constance Daniel, editor of the *Aframerican Woman* and one of Bethune's most ardent supporters. First, Daniel resigned as editor of the journal because of "the dismissal by your executive committee, without opportunity for conference, of the four employees in your office who sought a modicum of security through union recognition." Daniel went on to point out Bethune's message in the winter edition of the journal that said, "Leadership in 1947 will need to be informed as never before but power must walk hand in hand with humility. Intellect must have a soul." Daniel wrote, "I know you meant just what you wrote; but it seems that the control of the Council actions is now in the hands of women who believe otherwise. They have made themselves the spokesmen for the Council's thousands. I cannot, through the Journal, represent their thinking, for that thinking has subjected the Council to national censure as an organization insincere in its profession of liberalism."[58]

Randolph, January 30, 1947, BFC I; "Agreement between United Office and Professional Workers of America, Local C.I.O. and The National Council of Negro Women, Inc.," BFC I; Report of Executive Director to the Executive Committee, March 15, 1947, NCNW, Series 3, Box 3, Folder 64.

57. Memorandum from the New York Metropolitan Council to Mrs. Mary McLeod Bethune, et al., April 26, 1947, BFC I; Gertrude A. Robinson to Mary McLeod Bethune, February 25, 1947, BFC I.

58. Constance Daniel to Mary McLeod Bethune, February 6, 1947, BFC I.

In a long, handwritten letter, Daniel told Bethune that the incident had caused the people most interested in progressive movements to doubt her commitment to progressive causes. Their attitude was now, "Well, we'll just have to count her [Bethune] out, if that's the way she wants it." According to Daniel, "They are readying themselves to go ahead without you." By refusing to meet with progressive leaders after the incident, Bethune allowed speculation as to her intentions. Some surmised that "someone had controls" on her, others decided she was "not a free agent," and still others believed Bethune was told to "keep still" and those who had "dragged her into the situation" were still holding her there. Then Daniel got to the heart of the situation, and the explanation that makes sense in light of the Dies accusations. She raises the possibility that Bethune agreed to dismiss the employees because the UOPWA was rumored to be a communist-dominated labor union. Daniel wrote, "The 'hush-hush' talk about 'there were Communists involved' stinks pretty bad, and adds fuel to the fires of resentment. The charges that UOPWA or any other union is dominated by any group, has no bearing on the issue. It is always possible to reject individuals. Also, anyone on the inside of the labor picture knows who is wasting time red-baiting in CIO's upper chamber. . . . A Communist in your office is funny! Who is likely to be contaminated?"[59]

Daniel's one note of optimism was that Bethune's *"real* friends" believed that she had been "maneuvered into a destructive situation" and that they had rejected the statement issued by the Executive Committee. These same friends would "throw their arms around you . . . and welcome your return to the ranks of liberal leadership" if Bethune would just say, "I have been misinformed, and therefore confused." Negative publicity after this incident labeled Bethune as a "union baiter" despite her years of support for labor organization.[60] Uncharacteristically, there is no record of any reaction from Bethune to any of the letters and articles.

Although Bethune continued to carefully avoid "guilt by association," the council did not curtail its activities to expand women's roles in international affairs, nor did Bethune temper her critical assessments of the government. In 1945, Bethune was the only African American woman consultant at the World Security Conference in San Francisco that established the United Nations, and the NCNW maintained an official observer at the United Nations. NCNW conferences in the late 1940s promoted international relations, and the council began sponsoring annual "International Nights," hosting teas for

59. Constance Daniel to Mary McLeod Bethune, March 6, 1947, BFC I, 10–11.
60. James L. Hicks, *Ohio State News* article, February 8, 1947, NAACP.

international dignitaries, and promoting United Nations Day. The council also began sending representatives and observers to meetings in Europe, the West Indies, and Cuba.[61] It participated in every major event dealing with the affairs of women and attended conferences in Trinidad and the British West Indies.

At the end of World War II, the NCNW worked to improve postwar conditions for blacks in America and broadened its program to include African American women in planning the postwar society. The NCNW addressed issues concerning public housing, disfranchisement, abolition of the poll tax, education, price control, public health, inflation, expansion of social security, full employment, and the minimum wage bill, and it opposed Senator Bilbo's appointment to the Civil Rights Committee. Bethune challenged Americans to overcome racism and end racial violence, arguing that America could not save the world unless it first saved its own soul. America could not "find and bring to down-trodden nations the Holy Grail of peace and international accord while our hands are soiled with the lyncher's rope and the bull whip." Blacks had "made some well defined gains in many areas" but were "still, to a large extent, a subject people—men and women with little more than colonial status in a democracy." Bethune called on African Americans to battle against racism and discrimination not with guns, but with the ballot, and called on black women to "supply the driving force and inspiration" on the uphill road to peace.[62] World War II clearly established that the world was an interconnected global community, and African American women had to be informed and active participants in that community.

The postwar period also allowed Bethune to use the NCNW to turn the anticommunist rhetoric of the Cold War into a weapon for racial justice in America. America could triumph over communism and encourage democratic forms of government among the colored peoples of Asia, Africa, the West Indies, and elsewhere only if Americans repudiated racial segregation and discrimination. How could America preach the superiority of its governmental system when that system routinely discriminated against people of color at home? The federal government must take an active role in repudiating segregation in all of its forms and bringing an end to racial violence and

61. NCNW, Series 5, Box 8, Folder 142; Brown interview, NCNW; NCNW, Series 5, Box 9, Folder 168.

62. "Which Way America?" Radio interview, BFC I; Opening statement of Mary McLeod Bethune at National Conference of Negro Leaders, June 23, 1945, NCNW, Series 5, Box 23, Folder 340.

discrimination in the United States. Accomplishing this required presidential action in appointing qualified African Americans to policy-making levels of government, integrating blacks into new agencies, and appointing African Americans to foreign and diplomatic service.[63]

More important, postwar America presented opportunities for American women to take the lead in strengthening democracy at home and ensuring national security. Bethune told *all* American women that they had to decide beyond question whether they were aligned based on skin color or ideology. Ideology, she contended, should be the primary factor in determining whether another woman was friend or foe. Totalitarianism had to be fought just as hard whether it was found "clothed in a white skin, or in a yellow, or brown or black skin." By expanding its working relationship with interracial groups such as the National Council of Catholic Women, National Council of Jewish Women, National Council of Women of the U.S., National YWCA, and the National Women's Trade Union League, the NCNW put theory into practice. Participating in interracial conferences allowed women of all colors, creeds, and religions to explore the "methods of joint social action in areas of education, economic security, health, housing, and citizenship."[64] This interracial work had implications for the future. It was the foundation of the interfaith and interracial committees organized by the NCNW in the 1960s to advance civil rights activism.

During its first fourteen years under Bethune's leadership, the NCNW pursued an ambitious agenda, instituted many programs, and addressed every major social, economic, and political issue. African American women gained increasing political representation, became active, astute political citizens, and acquired access to a wider variety of government jobs through the NCNW. The council's wartime programs empowered working women to plan, organize, and act on their own behalf. Even though there were setbacks—the failure to desegregate the Des Moines WAC training center, for example—the NCNW efforts made segregation a visible political issue. Bethune believed in women, gave selflessly to build the NCNW, and used her entrée to the top tiers of government to make sure that all African American women had access to government's highest levels. However, building an organization that brought together women of diverse political beliefs, opinions, and leadership

63. "Statement to President Truman at the White House," February 28, 1951, BFC I.

64. Mary McLeod Bethune, "Women in Crisis," July 29, 1950, BFC I; Committee for Building Better Race Relations, NCNW, Series 5, Box 9, Folder 116–167.

styles was not an easy task. Bethune found the road strewn with obstacles—organizational problems, disagreements, and disunity. Bethune's personality exacerbated many of these problems.

Bethune's tendencies to sometimes be domineering, outspoken, and controlling could be divisive. Some of her followers admired her strong will, seeing it as the means to accomplish difficult goals. Others resented what they saw as her unwillingness to share authority. Factions developed based on whether one was able to work with Bethune, support her leadership, and endorse her agenda. Like all organizations that try to unite people with wide-ranging points of view, conflict within the NCNW was common. Despite all efforts to stem the tide, internal "politicking," petty concerns, and jealousies constantly threatened to undermine the council and tear it apart. Jeanetta Welch Brown represented one faction. She was one of Bethune's most devoted admirers. Brown saw Bethune as an inspiration, someone who was "intensive and creative," giving "selflessly to people." Brown recalled that if "she [Bethune] believed in you, she trusted you. If she believed that *you* thought you could do it, no matter what anybody else said, she believed that you could do it. She let people be themselves, create on their own and develop self-respect." More important, Brown respected Bethune because "she never went anywhere alone, she always carried another Negro along with her."[65] Brown called Bethune "Rose Petal" because she saw her as fragile and delicate with an inner beauty and power.

Hilda Orr Fortune was another of Bethune's admirers. Fortune described Bethune as "perceptive." According to Fortune, Bethune knew "Power was important and she [Bethune] knew power came with numbers, and she knew that it would be necessary to organize women. To make an impact on the power structure . . . women had to be organized, that they had to have a voice. Women must have a 'common spokesman' . . . a 'channel.'" Fortune saw Bethune as being at the forefront of the black woman's movement. Bethune's greatest contribution was in bringing other organizations into the NCNW. Bethune motivated Fortune to "get all people to move together," undivided by class or occupation. Fortune learned the meaning of *inclusion* from Bethune.[66]

Brown, Fortune, and women like them protected Bethune from any opposition. At an early council meeting a group of women led by Vivian Mason Carter decided they were going to unseat Bethune on the pretext that

65. Brown interview.
66. Fortune interview.

they were concerned about her health and that she was "too old" to run the NCNW. They planned to offer an alternative slate of candidates once the nominating committee opened presidential nominations. Brown made sure Bethune knew of the plan well in advance. When the conference began, Bethune stood facing the group, hands on her hips, and said, "Girls, as the slate goes out I understand some people want to run for president of the national council. I want to tell you that you need not bother about bringing in a slate because *I* am the next president of the National Council of Negro Women."[67]

Bethune believed the NCNW program could "only be executed through a head office and an officer with vision, who can understand, who has the entrée, and who will know how to present it when it comes."[68] As far as she was concerned, she was the only person in the NCNW at the time with the vision, access, and know-how to present that vision to others. Bethune was adamant about this. She and she alone, among NCNW members, had access to President Roosevelt, Eleanor Roosevelt, and other high-ranking government officials. When she wanted something done, she commanded an audience and went to the top. Despite what some women in the organization thought of her leadership style or ability, if Bethune believed any constitutional right had been violated she went to the president with the attitude that this was a right, "you have the power [to correct the problem], NOW exercise it."[69]

Of course, Bethune was an astute politician. She knew there "were times when one must stand still instead of giving back" and at times, it was "wiser for me to say nothing rather than speak." Yet, whenever Bethune decided it was time to stand still, her opposition attacked. Dorothy Height, a social worker with the New York YWCA and active NCNW volunteer, remembered those times, "And it used to bother me that the women would say all kinds of nasty things about Mrs. Bethune, and were ready to murder her and say that she was an Uncle Tom, and she was this and she was that. Some of those women weren't nearly so active in social action as she was, but that would be what they would do." According to Height, Bethune's reaction was to put those women into action. Bethune pressed her critics. Her attitude was "this woman needs

67. Brown interview; Fortune interview.
68. Executive Secretary report, 1938, NCNW.
69. Vivian Mason Carter interview by Barbara Grant Blackwell, July 1977, Transcript, Barbara Grant Blackwell, "The Advocacies and Ideological Commitments of a Black Educator," 195–96.

to know that this is a time for her to be something greater than she's acting like she is." Height did not merely admire Bethune, she respected her because she saw Bethune as a woman "with whom you became involved and you got involved." Bethune had tremendous energy, a capacity to see something in women, and a talent for making women move.[70]

Bethune faced the challenges to her leadership, and despite declarations to the contrary, she encouraged internal debate and discussion. The one thing she could not abide from council members was a public show of disunity. A constant theme for Bethune was that the women were to keep their disagreements "inside." Airing "dirty laundry" weakened the entire organization in the eyes of outsiders. The NCNW was supposed to be the authoritative voice of African American women. If the members publicly disagreed, how could Bethune approach those in power and claim to be speaking with one voice for eight hundred thousand African American women? Bethune experienced a significant letdown in 1942 when her friend Charlotte Hawkins Brown publicly criticized the NCNW in an interview published in the *Pittsburgh Courier.*

Brown criticized the NCNW for failing to achieve any "real organized effort and worthwhile result" through their programs. She accused the council of being an "air castle" and a "myth" to the average African American woman. Brown maintained that the principal problem with the council was Bethune's leadership style. Bethune had not clearly defined the aims and purposes of the NCNW; therefore, the average black woman was unable to relate to the NCNW in any tangible way. Brown went on implicitly criticizing Bethune's leadership, saying, "I think fear dominates the thinking of some of the women, even those of strong minds. They are afraid to disagree with the leader who, I know, is far too broad to wish to guide the thinking of this intelligent group of followers—but they do practically nothing after they leave the meeting. We do not have a definite program of action."[71] It took Bethune seven months to recover from what she saw as Brown's vicious attack. In a private reply Bethune said,

> When I read it [the news article] I must confess to you that I was simply floored. It has been a struggle for the past ten years to get the Council over to the women what I was thinking. That stand, coming from you,

70. Mary McLeod Bethune to Daisy S. George, September 18, 1947, NCNW; Height interview, 28, 29–30.
71. Statement of Charlotte Hawkins Brown, *Pittsburgh Courier,* October 1942, NCNW, Series 5, Box 4, Folder 67.

was to me a "Pearl Harbor Stab." It was "below the belt," Charlotte. I
felt it then and I feel it this morning. I think you ought to know that it
so completely floored me that I can never feel, or be, in relationship to
you, the Mary McLeod Bethune of all the years. It took something out
of me that only a friend could take out. Whatever your intentions were,
I must confess that the stroke was too severe for me at that time.[72]

There is no record of Brown's response to Bethune's letter. Brown's criticism hurt Bethune deeply, but it also forced her to look realistically at the
NCNW. What she saw shocked her. With the exception of a relatively few
committed supporters, there was "no soul interest and understanding" of what
the NCNW was trying to accomplish. The relationship between the council
and its affiliates needed clarification, redefinition, and reinterpretation. The
NCNW had to make its member organizations understand that the national
program was an extension of their work. The council had to analyze and explain their contribution to member organizations, "select some unique service
to meet people's needs," translate statements into action, and supplement local
programs by conducting some meaningful program at the national level. As
far as the national organization was concerned, the membership had to decide
what scope of activity the council should pursue and what direction it should
take. Bethune had done her best to open opportunities for black women, had
brought them to important conferences and showed them what unified efforts
could do. Still, the NCNW did not have the full cooperation of its member
organizations. Bethune castigated the members for their petty jealousies. She
reminded them that it did not make any difference what they did individually
because African American women "will be sized up as a group."[73]

The council was also coming under scrutiny by organizations that contem-
plated joining the NCNW. The Ladies' Auxiliary to the International Brotherhood of Sleeping Car Porters raised questions of class and gender ideology when they considered joining. Halena Wilson, president of the auxiliary,
wrote to Jeanetta Welch Brown, executive secretary of the NCNW, about her
hesitation in recommending affiliation with the council. According to Wilson, the auxiliary was "interested in the unskilled and unorganized men and

72. Mary McLeod Bethune to Charlotte Hawkins Brown, May 5, 1943, NCNW, Series
5, Box 4, Folder 77.
73. Commission to Study Finance and Structure of the NCNW, September 14, 1947,
NCNW, Series 5, Box 7, Folder 132; Refining Our Structure Panel, October 14, 1944,
NCNW, Series 2, Box 2, Folder 21.

women of the race who are badly in need of the advantages and the protection which accrue from labor organizations." Although Wilson had "very high regard" for Bethune personally, she wanted assurances that the NCNW intended to include the "so-called common man and woman in its plans." Both Bethune and Brown tried to reassure Wilson that the NCNW represented all women regardless of class. In correspondence with Wilson, Bethune portrayed herself as "simply a common woman working for the masses of my race and the world."[74]

Beyond the rhetoric, Bethune was active in dealing with various working-class issues. The NCNW pursued extensive lobbying in Washington that addressed the economic disadvantages of the black working class, particularly related to expanding public housing, social security benefits, and social welfare programs. On a personal level, Bethune received numerous letters from men and women asking for her help in securing positions or dealing with specific problems they encountered in their jobs. While she could not solve every problem, she made considerable efforts to direct those who sought her help to more appropriate agencies.[75] She advocated labor unionization as the only possible way to achieve better industrial working conditions, increased wages, and promotions.

Brown also corresponded with Wilson at length on the issue of unionization. Brown made it clear that the only way to ensure that the NCNW represented working-class women was for working-class organizations to join the council. Brown wrote to Wilson, "The Council cannot represent a group of people if they refuse to cooperate with the Council . . . if your organization represents a certain group of people, that group of people will be kept out of plans as long as you, yourself, keep them out, for it is only by participation and representation of any group on a committee will they be so represented . . . it is as much your responsibility to make this organization what you would have it, as it is for us to make it the kind of organization you want." Brown assured Wilson that the council was conscious of the advantages and protections labor organizations brought to their members and reinforced the fact that the NCNW was working closely with both the AFL and the CIO. Brown also emphasized her personal ties to unionization. Brown was one of a very few

74. Halena Wilson to Jeanetta Welch Brown, September 29, 1943, NCNW, Series 18, Box 1, Folder 12; Mary McLeod Bethune to Halena Wilson, October 4, 1943, NCNW, Series 18, Box 1, Folder 12.
75. NCNW, Series 5.

black women who actively worked to help organize the United Auto Workers in the Ford Motor Company in Detroit.[76]

Bethune, Brown, and Wilson outwardly addressed class-related issues in their correspondence, but differing views about the role of women complicated the discussions. According to historian Melinda Chateauvert, Wilson saw the male-led International Brotherhood of Sleeping Car Porters as "the boss." Her fraternal association with Eastern Star, a Masonic auxiliary, reinforced the idea of complementary roles for men's and women's organizations. Apparently, Bethune had been trying to convince the Ladies' Auxiliary to join the NCNW since 1938. Bethune spoke at the founding convention of the Ladies' Auxiliary and invited the newly formed organization to join the NCNW as a representative of women's economic interests. A. Philip Randolph, president of the male-led International Association of Sleeping Car Porters, advised the Ladies' Auxiliary to refuse Bethune's invitation. Wilson followed Randolph's advice because it fit comfortably with her notions of women's proper roles. As historian Deborah Gray White has argued, auxiliary leaders held "traditional" views of gender roles. Men were the primary breadwinners and women supported them by exercising power as informed consumers and community organizers, and by encouraging their husbands, sons, and brothers to join and support the union. The auxiliary believed women should work for racial advancement behind the scenes at the grassroots level and in the context of their roles as wives and mothers. Men should hold public roles.[77]

Bethune had already rejected the legitimacy of widely held notions of women's *proper* roles. She concluded that commonly accepted boundaries were too confining and that there were no limits to what women *could* do if gender ideologies that limited women to home, kitchen, and children were eradicated. Women, as well as men, should be free to develop all of their talents and use those talents to improve the quality of life for the entire race. Moreover, the NCNW was an independent women's organization unaffiliated with any

---

76. Jeanetta Welch Brown to Halena Wilson, October 16, 1943, NCNW, Series 18, Box 1, Folder 12; Brown to Wilson, October 4, 1943, NCNW.

77. Melinda Chateauvert, *Marching Together: The Women of the Brotherhood of Sleeping Car Porters,* 72, 92; Bethune to Wilson, October 4, 1943, NCNW; "Brotherhood of Sleeping Car Porters Await Speech Sept. 25," *Atlanta Daily World,* September 18, 1938, BFC I; Deborah Gray White, "The Slippery Slope of Class in Black America: The National Council of Negro Women and the International Ladies' Auxiliary to the Brotherhood of Sleeping Car Porters, A Case Study."

male-led association. It promoted women's independent actions, albeit based on traditional views of women as the moral fiber of civilization. The NCNW always followed a strategy of placing black women in positions of influence that would affect policy-making and political agendas and lead to racial advancement. In the NCNW, it was perfectly acceptable for black women to work for racial advancement independently of black men. This was not so in the auxiliary. According to Chateauvert, the Ladies' Auxiliary joined the NCNW in 1943, but withdrew one year later after the council raised dues and Wilson and Randolph decided the NCNW did not sufficiently address economic issues. Gender ideologies between women's groups were not easily reconciled.

Bethune was a realist. She was seventy-five years old, and the asthma that plagued her throughout her life was becoming worse. Long hospital stays were becoming common, and the NCNW staff had to cover for her so that "outsiders" would not know of her illnesses. Between 1935 and 1943, Bethune wore three organizational hats: director of Minority Affairs in the NYA; president of Bethune-Cookman College; and founder and president of the NCNW. In 1949, poor health convinced Bethune it was time for her to step down and give younger women the opportunity to make the NCNW work as she envisioned it. She looked at the council and knew that "much of her dream and vision had been expressed, but very little of it had been realized."[78]

Bethune's handpicked successor was Dorothy Height. As a teenager, Height was active in church and community organizations. After receiving her B.A. and M.A. degrees from New York University, she worked with the YWCA and a variety of youth groups. In the fall of 1937, Height was working at the Harlem branch of the YWCA in Harlem where Bethune was holding a NCNW meeting. Height was assigned the task of bringing Eleanor Roosevelt into the meeting to make a speech. She remained at the meeting for the First Lady's speech, and as Height was about to leave to take Mrs. Roosevelt out to her car, Bethune tugged on her skirt. Bethune asked Height her name, then asked what she did. Bethune then said, "Well, come back, we need you." Height returned to the meeting after seeing Mrs. Roosevelt to her car and before she knew it, Bethune had put her on the resolutions committee. She recalled that Bethune "put her hand on me." Height became one of many young people Bethune brought into the NCNW. According to Height,

78. Height interview, 38.

Bethune surrounded herself with young women in the NCNW because she wanted "people in the forefront of the day to update what she was thinking, what she was saying."[79]

Bethune tried to get Height to come and work full-time for the council because she saw herself and Height as "on the same kind of wavelength." Bethune went so far as to try to get Height released from the YWCA. She came to New York and told Mrs. Ingraham,[80] "I think if Dorothy could work with me, I think she and I, we're two different generations, but I think we could produce something." Height did not leave the YWCA, but she continued to work with Bethune in the NCNW. She credits Bethune for teaching her one important thing: "I think Mrs. Bethune helped me understand the way in which you just can't leave a generation gap, that there has to be some way in which each generation has to be free to move in its own direction. But if it does this without roots or without hooking onto something, pretty soon it becomes disillusioned, it becomes deradicalized, it becomes more conservative . . . I think Mrs. Bethune . . . [was] always examining, looking on, standing outside. In it, but looking at it; in it but examining it."[81]

Bethune's mentoring intensely affected Height. Moreover, Bethune's vision of the council and its work had resonance for Height, who was "interested in organizations dealing with struggle, not just activities."[82] Women's organizations such as the NCNW kept critical issues before the public and gave direction to social action. After serving for twenty years in a number of appointive positions within the NCNW, Height became the council's fourth president in 1957, a position she held until 1998. Dorothy Height's goal was to make the council the organization Bethune had in mind. Bethune had given the NCNW a blueprint to follow. It was a pattern that was imperfect in detail, yet had a well-defined outline. Under Height's direction, the pattern began to take on a sharper image. Many of the member organizations moved forward as Bethune had foreseen—through their immediate problems into broader and more general concerns. They began working together to unite women of various occupations, races, colors, religions, and nationalities for democratic action and peace.

Bethune retired as president of the NCNW in 1949, but she did not retire from her active public life. She returned to Florida and immersed her-

79. Ibid., 67, 68.

80. Ingraham was president of the YWCA branch where Height was then employed. Height interview, 73.

81. Ibid.

82. Ibid., 83.

self in Daytona Beach's political life by studying and commenting on local political races. She expanded her interest in human rights by becoming an active member in the international Moral Re-Armament movement that promoted worldwide unity and human rights. She traveled to Haiti, Canada, and Switzerland. In January 1952, she fulfilled her girlhood dream by traveling to Africa as a U.S. delegate to the inauguration of President William Tubman of Liberia. Bethune continued to speak to diverse groups nationwide.

In April 1952 anticommunist hysteria again touched Bethune. Under the influence of the McCarthy hysteria, the Englewood, New Jersey, Board of Education canceled a speech Bethune was to give because the local anticommunist league publicly charged that Bethune was affiliated with twenty-two subversive organizations. Strong negative interracial reaction to the incident forced the board to reschedule the speech. At her second appearance, Bethune called upon all Americans to work together to strengthen American democracy by ending the subversive hysteria that was sweeping the country and destroying American freedom.[83]

Bethune had dedicated her life to ending racism, discrimination, and prejudice. She did not live to see African Americans organize and come together to fight for civil rights, but she did witness the 1954 *Brown v. Board of Education* decision. While she applauded the Supreme Court decision, she also sounded a note of caution in her speeches and weekly column in the *Chicago Defender*. She cautioned African Americans not to initiate any violence in trying to integrate America's schools, and not to be intimidated by "any selfish group." Bethune wrote that with the *Brown* decision, desegregation became a "constitutional duty." She urged blacks not to be reluctant or complacent; they must recognize the larger meanings of integration. She wrote: "There are those speaking for us who say we do not want equality and did not want integration. . . . It is not history repeating itself; it is the same history. The law of the land has freed us and guarantees us the right to vote, to earn our living, and now to go to school without distinction or discrimination. Let no man, black or white, say for the rest of us that we do not want to be full citizens. History still speaks. It speaks for the rights of all citizens. And it will not be quiet."[84] Bethune fought for freedom and equality for African Americans until her death from a heart attack at her home on May 18, 1955.

83. "Dr. Bethune Gets Warm Welcome in Her Second Appearance Here," *Bergen Evening Record*, June 17, 1952, BFC I.

84. NAACP Papers; "Program Today for Transfer of Home to Foundation," *Daytona Beach News*, May 10, 1953; "The Mary McLeod Bethune Foundation Has Been Born to Inspire Posterity," *Chicago Defender*, n.d.; "Methodists Declare Dr. Bethune Loyal, Sincere American,"

❧

Establishing the NCNW was an important step forward for African American women. Bethune's political skills opened doors for black women in Washington that otherwise would have remained closed. Yet, her need to wield power and control limited the scope of achievements. Organizational leaders who found Bethune too domineering or who did not want to give up autonomy refused to join the council. The absence of working-class associations and labor organizations inherently made the NCNW less representative than it could have been during Bethune's tenure as president. Nevertheless, the council tried to reach a wider audience by working with and supporting the programs of the Union for Democratic Action, NAACP, Southern Conference for Human Welfare, YWCA, American Jewish Congress, General Federation of Women's Clubs, National Council of Jewish Women, the National Women's Trade Union League, and the Congress of Industrial Organizations.[85]

Bethune understood the importance of power and recognized quite early that if black women *would* unite they *could* effect social, economic, and political change. In founding the NCNW, she asked other black women's groups to give up some of their individual autonomy to attain a greater measure of group power. She guided the NCNW through its perilous beginnings and helped African American women move from their marginal place as informal political activists into mainstream political activity. Despite her domineering personality, she succeeded in aligning twenty-two black women's organizations with the NCNW and bringing in a diverse array of individually talented women. She used their skills and personal resources to make the NCNW an advocate for African American women worldwide.

The council informed its membership of important issues and problems through its official publications, the *Aframerican Woman* and *Telefact*. It cooperated with federal agencies and nonprofit organizations in sponsoring conferences and advocated for the appointment of qualified black women to

Daytona Beach News, April 27, 1952; "What Is Subversive?" *The Sunday News-Journal,* April 27, 1952; "Dr. Bethune Gets Warm Welcome"; Mary McLeod Bethune, "Full Integration— America's Newest Challenge," June 11, 1954; "Supreme Court's Desegregation Ruling Will Work, But We Must Have Patience About It," *Chicago Defender,* January 22, 1955; "U.S. Will Make 'The Grade' In Integrating All Its Schools," *Chicago Defender,* June 4, 1955, BFC I; Mary McLeod Bethune, "Warns Against Violence or Hesitation at Integration," *Chicago Defender,* October 2, 1954; Mary McLeod Bethune, "A Great People Hears Its Conscience Speak; Realizes Segregation Not Decent," *Chicago Defender,* October 16, 1954.

85. NCNW, Series 5, Box 13, Folder 228.

high-level government positions. It implemented basic civil rights programs through political education and voter registration campaigns. The council lobbied for legislation to end lynching and the poll tax, and to promote equal education, public health, and equal employment opportunities. By creating a constituency of politically active women independent from partisan political control, the National Council of Negro Women allowed African American women of all political persuasions to enter the decision-making process and shape America's local, state, and national political agenda.

Conclusion

Mary McLeod Bethune was one of the best politicians of her day. Through her work in education, women's organizations, and as a government appointee, Bethune trained future generations of black female political activists and significantly contributed to the development of American political culture. Bethune's effectiveness as a leader allowed African American women to create both informal and formal political networks, develop new concepts of female leadership, and promote political activism designed specifically to influence the direction of public policy. She nurtured women's political activism by organizing and teaching them to lobby the government for programs and training for African Americans on a scale large enough to make a difference. Bethune realized earlier than many black leaders that the focal point of black protest should not be to change individual attitudes and behaviors, but rather to reform the social, economic, and political institutions that were important in influencing public opinion. Her goal was to fashion a women's political coalition that would work to alter these basic American institutions. She encouraged young black women to organize and lead a liberal force, composed of educators, professionals, and social and religious activists with common political objectives. She worked with women to transform community institutions into black political power bases. Bethune knew that to effectively combat racial inequality in America, local leaders had to transform community-oriented social programs into a unified national political movement. In effect, Bethune sought to unite African American women to bring about a complete remodeling of the American political economy and create a liberal, multilayered, and multifaceted black political power base.

Measured by any standards, Bethune's life was extraordinary. She began life as the fifteenth child born to Samuel and Patsy McLeod, illiterate former slaves who struggled to survive as sharecroppers in a community that offered few opportunities to African Americans. Yet, she went on to establish and preside over one of the first fully accredited four-year colleges for African Americans in Florida, advised four presidents on child welfare, education, and civil rights, served two terms as president of the National Association of Colored Women, held the highest government post created for a black woman in the New Deal, and founded the National Council of Negro Women in addition to receiving numerous awards and honorary degrees. In and of itself, her life story is truly amazing, quite fascinating, and worthy of our interest. However, Bethune's life offers more than simply the narrative of a unique individual. It highlights the evolution of a generation of black women activists and allows insight into the institutions that worked to politicize African American women.

Bethune was not born into a leadership position. She achieved it through a powerful socialization process and a particular understanding of the duties of educated womanhood. Socially responsible individualism shaped Bethune's perception of herself as a vehicle for racial advancement. Parents, teachers, and mentors instilled and reinforced the belief that because of their preparation, educated women had the ability and a duty to uplift the race and change American society. Socially responsible individualism offered an alternative to the highly individualistic success ethic of white society. It prepared many women of Bethune's generation to work both individually and collectively to create institutions that served the needs of the black community. From the beginning, Bethune's family, teachers, and mentors groomed her for leadership. She more than adequately fulfilled that role and then went on to establish Bethune-Cookman College and the National Council of Negro Women, institutions that worked to socialize future generations of African American women to fight for economic, social, and political inclusion. Bethune is important because she created educational and political institutions that assured the continuation of African American women's political power.

Bethune came to recognize the interconnection between illiteracy, racial inequality, and powerlessness through her personal experiences. She witnessed whites denying blacks property rights and literally holding the power of life or death over them. These incidents led to her deeply ingrained lifelong belief in the transformative power of education. African Americans were powerless because the dominant society denied them an education—education was empowering. She dedicated most of the first part of her life to educating herself and others in Mayesville, Augusta, Savannah, Palatka, and Daytona Beach. Bethune founded the Daytona Educational and Industrial School for Negro Girls specifically to educate girls who she believed were "hampered by lack of educational opportunity" yet needed a "distinctive education" because of their "responsibilities in the world." Bethune taught academic subjects as well as marketable domestic arts, reflecting her belief that black women needed to be economically self-sufficient despite discriminatory racial practices and limited access to jobs.[1]

Bethune also socialized "her girls" to be community activists. She organized and carried out community outreach programs that offered her students working examples of effective informal political activity. She involved them in the programs and taught them to approach county officials for funding. Through weekly chapel talks and Sunday community programs, she reminded students that black women had an obligation to share their education with others through community improvement projects. Bethune involved her students in community improvement programs designed to teach a new generation of women activists how to "uplift" the race, develop their communities, gain a more equitable place for blacks in mainstream society, and create important leadership positions for themselves. Bethune saw black women as agents of change in the community. The extent of Bethune's effect reached far beyond her school, and her influence lived on after her death. The informal political activities Bethune engaged in (and those of many of her contemporaries) are an important reason historically black colleges became centers of political activism during the civil rights movement of the 1960s.

In the early twentieth century, segregation and anti-black violence continued to gain momentum, and conditions for African Americans continued to decline despite clear indications of racial progress. At the same time, Bethune's experiences in the suffrage campaign, the women's club movement, and social reform movements gave her formal experience in organizing women for political action. In the 1920s, Bethune focused on mobilizing women to use the ballot as a political weapon to force systemic changes aimed at improving the status and conditions of the race. She also became more vocal in her criticisms of American democracy. For the first time, she outwardly accused the federal government of ignoring its obligations to African Americans. She began to use her position in the black women's club movement to raise the political consciousness of black women and looked for ways to use black women's clubs to promote African American women for decision-making positions in government. She encouraged block voting whenever pos-

---

1. Bethune, "Faith That Moved a Dump Heap," 34; see also Peare, *Mary McLeod Bethune;* Poole, *Mary McLeod Bethune, Educator;* Sterne, *Mary McLeod Bethune;* Holt, *Mary McLeod Bethune.*

sible, and pushed the NACW to take a more active role in the legislative process and become a clearinghouse for studying and advocating black women's political concerns. She wanted the NACW to act as a bulwark for black women's participation in the formal political sphere. When NACW members rejected her ideas, Bethune began developing a framework for a new women's group that would act as a voluntary nonpartisan political association to advance black women.

As director of the Office of Minority Affairs of the National Youth Administration, Bethune used her federal position to force the NYA to become one of the few New Deal programs that gave African Americans their fair share of government benefits. She had the opportunity to work with both blacks and whites with a seemingly endless array of viewpoints and managed to gain their approval and secure a following. As the driving force behind the Black Cabinet, she learned to connect with people, shape their worldviews, and inspire them to follow her lead. In her position as director of Minority Affairs, she learned the inner workings of American government and politics and honed her political skills. Bethune's federal post gave her access to those at the highest levels of government, and she became an adept political negotiator.

However, as a government appointee who served at the pleasure of the New Deal administration, Bethune walked a fine line. Roosevelt expected loyalty from his administrators and public support for his programs. Bethune was well aware that many New Deal programs, especially those aimed at economic recovery, were not fully benefiting African Americans. During her years in the NYA, she found herself constantly confronted with these two conflicting realities. Her deeply ingrained sense of loyalty to the race dictated that she must do something to make sure program benefits reached the black community, yet she must have realized that harsh public criticism of the administration would mean her removal from office. She compromised. Inside the government bureaucracy, Bethune privately voiced her criticisms and concerns to both Roosevelt and Aubrey Williams. She used both the threat of the loss of black political support and her power of persuasion to convince the administration to place African Americans in meaningful positions that advanced black interests. She concentrated her efforts on the redistribution of NYA benefits through the placement of black state administrative assistants. She subtly reoriented the program so that black local and state administrators reported directly to her, thereby giving a federal agency at least limited control over state distribution of funds. Finally, she kept her protest activities separate from her official activities through her association with various independent groups. She organized an independent Black Cabinet and used it to disseminate information on various government programs, plans, and agencies to independent black protest organizations. In this way, she helped shape black protest during the 1930s and 1940s.

Despite the shortcomings of New Deal programs, Bethune saw the development of the social welfare state under Roosevelt as the perfect vehicle for advancing black women into high positions in policy-making agencies. Yet in an era when interest-group politics was paramount, Washington bureaucrats did not recognize black women as an important interest group. To make any impact, black women needed strong, unified representation. Women of all political persuasions and opinions had to come together to form a nonpartisan political power base. African American women could not hope to shape public policy unless they pooled their experiences, expanded their programs, and united to advance large and important issues. Bethune's NYA experience drove home the importance of unity. African American women could only effect social, economic, and political change on a national level if all black women's groups could work as one. She believed women could only make a difference if they entered formal politics grounded in strong networks.

Bethune organized the NCNW specifically to advance African American women, agitate for equal opportunity, and secure full citizenship rights. Through the NCNW, the federal government began to formally recognize African American women as political activists and lobbyists who advocated for equal opportunity for women of color worldwide. The council kept its members informed on all important political issues, sponsored conferences, and fought to have qualified black women appointed to the highest levels of government. The NCNW united a wide variety of women's groups in education, business, religion, and fraternal organizations and directed their energies to relevant issues at the national level. It attempted to combine the talents and skills of all women, act as a catalyst for change, encourage all women to recognize that they had important contributions to make, and develop women's leadership abilities. The council promoted legislation against lynching, to abolish the poll tax, and to promote equal education, public health, and equal employment opportunities. It laid the foundations for the modern civil rights movement through its citizenship training and voter registration program. Through the NCNW, Bethune helped African American women enter the decision-making process, gave them representation in national affairs, raised the status of black women on the national level, and made them an educated, eloquent, and effective force in American politics. Bethune's life clearly demonstrates that African American women's political activism did not sprout in infertile soil. Bethune, and others like her, sowed the seeds by establishing both informal and formal institutions that sustained a tradition of political protest even in a hostile racial and political climate.

The organization of the NCNW also illustrates how the changing realities of the twentieth century affected Bethune's commitment to socially responsible individualism. The socialization process Bethune and her contemporaries underwent took place at a time when educational opportunities for black women were limited and the majority of blacks were poor, rural, agricultural workers with little or no political representation. Increasing access to basic education, the growing industrial base, and demographic change forced more formally educated women to redefine their relationship to their communities. Local activists organized community self-help programs independently, and their growing political power forced local and state politicians to recognize their concerns. Highly educated black women "diplomats" were no longer necessary. Bethune encouraged African Americans to mount campaigns against systematic oppression. Her organization of the NCNW reflects these new realities. Bethune designed the NCNW to unite women and secure social justice for all African Americans. She designed its structure to promote cooperative efforts between local, regional, and national women's groups in their efforts to achieve social justice. Not coincidentally, the NCNW also created new roles for highly educated black women as policy-makers at the national level. These women worked to undermine the systematic nature of race and gender inequality. Bethune believed that NCNW should follow a multilayered approach to racial and gender advancement and work to *empower* others to do the same.

Bethune's major shortcomings in leading the NCNW were her inability to garner the support of all black women's organizations and to gain the unconditional support of many NCNW member organizations. Bethune realized that women must unite to effect social, economic, and political change. They could not effectively change the national political agenda as individuals or separate organizations. Affiliating with the NCNW meant member associations had to give up power. Some leaders of women's organizations interpreted this as a threat to their personal political power bases and either refused to join the council or chose not to fully cooperate with its program. Moreover, Bethune's strong-willed, dominant personality coupled with high-handed tactics often exacerbated internal conflict. Even though her tremendous personal power engendered respect for the NCNW concept, she nevertheless failed to create the administrative and financial base necessary for such an undertaking during her tenure as president.

Mary McLeod Bethune's legacy lives on in Bethune-Cookman College and the National Council of Negro Women. Today, Bethune-Cookman is a career-oriented, coeducational liberal arts college and the fourth-largest of the thirty-nine United Negro College Fund colleges. Bethune's focus on "head-heart-hand" remains a fundamental tenet of the educational program, and her motto, "Enter to learn; depart to serve," continues to have relevance. Bethune-Cookman offers the Bachelor of Arts and Bachelor of Science degree in thirty-nine major areas in business, education, humanities, nursing, science/mathematics, and social sciences. The school's thirty-five buildings include eight residence halls and cover sixty acres of land. More than twenty-five hundred students from the United States, the Caribbean, and thirty-five other foreign countries attend, and the college operates eight extension sites in Florida.[2]

The NCNW has become an organization that works at all levels and in a variety of ways in its quest to "leave no one behind" and improve the quality of life for women. The NCNW continues to unite national organizations and has recently begun developing strategies to mobilize grassroots movements. The NCNW now consists of "38 affiliated national organizations, 250 community-based Sections chartered in 42 states, 20 college-based Sections and 60,000 individual members." Overall, the NCNW reaches more than four million women.[3] The National Centers for African American Women sponsors five separate programs to foster community empowerment. The Bethune Program Development Center carries on Bethune's work of education and advocacy at the local level. It "provides technical assistance and training; public information and advocacy; and strategies for the development of partnerships and collaborations to community-based programs" that work on issues relating to health, education, and community life. The Economic and Entrepreneurial Development Center offers women technical assistance in establishing and maintaining businesses. Continuing Bethune's emphasis on women's economic autonomy, the EEDC encourages economic development as a method of overcoming women's poverty. The International Development Center establishes "social, cultural, academic and economic partnerships with women's organizations in Africa." The Dorothy I. Height Leadership Institute works with established and newly emerging African American women leaders to teach strategies for community mobilization. Perhaps the Research,

---

2. Bethune-Cookman College, http://www.bethune.cookman.edu/, October 8, 2001.
3. "About NCNW," http://www.ncnw.com/about/aboutbody.html, November 16, 1999.

Public Policy and Information Center has most closely followed and expanded upon Bethune's political vision for the NCNW. The RPPIC gathers and disseminates "information to empower African American women and stimulate advocacy to improve the quality of life for themselves, their families and communities."[4] Even though Bethune did not live to see the NCNW reach its full potential, she gave African American women the tools they needed to make her dream a reality. She would be proud of the work her successors have accomplished. The pattern has taken shape. African American women hammered at the portals of government and succeeded in improving African American life and American democracy. This is Bethune's legacy.

4. "Centers for African American Women," http://www.ncnw.com/centers/centersbody. html, November 16, 1999.

Bibliography

Archival and Manuscript Sources

Mary McLeod Bethune Papers. New Orleans: Amistad Research Center Microfilms.

Mary McLeod Bethune Papers—Bethune-Cookman College Collection. Bethesda, Md.: University Publications of America, 1996.

Mary McLeod Bethune Papers: Bethune Foundation Collection. Part I. Edited by Elaine M. Smith. Bethesda, Md.: University Publications of America, 1996.

Mary McLeod Bethune Papers: Bethune Foundation Collection. Part II. Edited by Elaine M. Smith. Bethesda, Md.: University Publications of America, 1996.

Nannie Helen Burroughs Papers. Library of Congress, Washington, D.C.

National Association for the Advancement of Colored People Papers. Part 18, Series B, Library of Congress, Washington, D.C.

Papers of the National Association of Colored Women's Clubs, 1895–1992: Part I. Edited by Lillian Serece Williams. Bethesda, Md.: University Publications of America, 1993.

Records of the National Council of Negro Women. Bethune Museum and Archives, Washington, D.C.

National Urban League Papers—Southern Regional Office. Library of Congress, Washington, D.C.

National Youth Administration Papers—Office of Negro Affairs, Records of the Director, Record Group 119, National Archives, Washington, D.C.

Ratner Center for the Study of Conservative Judaism, Jewish Theological Seminary. Joseph and Miriam Ratner Center for the Study of Conservative Judaism, New York.

Eleanor Roosevelt Papers. Franklin D. Roosevelt Library, Hyde Park, New York.

Franklin D. Roosevelt Papers. Franklin D. Roosevelt Library, Hyde Park, New York.

Mary Church Terrell Papers. Library of Congress, Washington, D.C.

Aubrey Williams Papers. Franklin D. Roosevelt Library, Hyde Park, New York.

Secondary Sources

"About NCNW." URL: <http://www.ncnw.com/about/aboutbody.html> November 16, 1999.

Ackelsberg, Martha, and Irene Diamond. "Gender and Political Life." In *Analyzing Gender: A Handbook of Social Science Research,* edited by Beth B. Hess and Myra Marx Ferree. Newbury Park, Calif.: Sage Publications, 1987.

American Child Health Association Papers. "Scope and Content." *Herbert Hoover Papers.* URL: <http://hoover.nara.gov/research/hooverpapers/hoover/commerce/acha5.htm> August 8, 2001.

Anderson, James D. *The Education of Blacks in the South, 1860–1935.* Chapel Hill: University of North Carolina Press, 1988.

———. "Historical Development of Black Vocational Education." In Harvey Kantor and David B. Tyack, eds., *Work, Youth and Schooling: Historical Perspectives on Vocationalism in American Education.* Stanford, Calif.: Stanford University Press, 1982.

Aptheker, Herbert, ed. *A Documentary History of the Negro People in the United States.* 4 vols. New York: Carol Publishing Group, 1992.

Arnez, Nancy L. "Selected Black Female Superintendents of Public School Systems." *Journal of Negro Education* 51, no. 3 (summer 1982): 309–17.

Banks, Henrine Ward. Interview by Barbara Grant Blackwell, July 7, 1977. Transcript in Barbara Grant Blackwell, "The Advocacies and Ideological Commitments of a Black Educator." Ph.D. diss., University of Connecticut, 1979.

———. "The Purpose of the National Council of Negro Women." In Barbara Grant Blackwell, "The Advocacies and Ideological Commitments of a Black Educator." Ph.D. diss., University of Connecticut, 1979.

Barnett, Bernice McNair. "Black Women's Collectivist Movement Organizations: Their Struggles during the 'Doldrums.'" In *Analyzing Gender:*

A Handbook of Social Science Research, edited by Beth B. Hess and Myra Marx Ferree. Newbury Park, Calif.: Sage Publications, 1987.

Bassard, Katherine Clay. "Black Women's Autobiography and the Ideology of Literacy." *African-American Review* 26, no. 1 (spring 1992): 119–29.

Beckwith, Karen. *American Women and Political Participation: The Impacts of Work, Generation, and Feminism.* Westport, Conn.: Greenwood Press, 1986.

Bell, Howard Holman. *A Survey of the Negro Convention Movement, 1830–1861.* New York: Arno Press, 1969.

Bernhardt, Virginia, Betty Brandon, Elizabeth Fox-Genovese, Theda Perdue, and Elizabeth Haynes Turner, eds. *Hidden Histories of Women in the New South.* Columbia: University of Missouri Press, 1994.

Berry, Mary Frances. "Twentieth-Century Black Women in Education." *Journal of Negro Education* 51, no. 3 (summer 1982): 288–300.

"Bess Truman's Greetings Are Very, Very Brief." *Pittsburgh Courier,* November 23, 1946.

Bethune, Albert, Jr. Interview by Barbara Grant Blackwell on July 8, 1977, in Barbara Grant Blackwell, "The Advocacies and Ideological Commitments of a Black Educator." Ph.D. diss., University of Connecticut, 1979.

Bethune, Albert, Sr. Interview by Barbara Grant Blackwell, July 8, 1977. Transcript in Barbara Grant Blackwell, "The Advocacies and Ideological Commitments of a Black Educator." Ph.D. diss., University of Connecticut, 1979.

Bethune, Mary McLeod. "The Adaptation of the History of the Negro to the Capacity of the Child." *Journal of Negro History* 24, no. 1 (January 1939): 9–13.

———"Army Erases Blot on the Escutcheon of Our Democracy." *Chicago Defender,* February 12, 1949.

———"The Association for the Study of Negro Life and History: Its Contribution to Our Modern Life." *Journal of Negro History* 20, no. 4 (October 1935): 406–10.

———. "Certain Unalienable Rights." In Rayford W. Logan, ed., *What the Negro Wants.* New York: Agathan Press, Inc., 1969.

———"Clarifying Our Vision with the Facts." *Journal of Negro History* 23, no. 1 (January 1938): 10–15.

———"Desegregation Is Both a Human and National Problem." *Chicago Defender,* May 14, 1955.

———"Fair-Skinned, Blue Eyed, Blond Haired Walter White, Worker for Equal Justice." *Chicago Defender,* April 9, 1955.

————"A Great People Hears Its Conscience Speak: Realizes Segregation Not Decent." *Chicago Defender,* October 16, 1954.

————"Ignorance, Root of Prejudice, Is Serious Foe of Democratic Living." *Chicago Defender,* March 19, 1955.

————"Its Founder Takes Objective View of Women's National Council." *Chicago Defender,* January 7, 1950.

————"Leader Recalls Pioneer Days When Organizing U.S. Women." *Chicago Defender,* January 15, 1955.

————"My Last Will and Testament." *Ebony* 18 (September 1963): 150–56.

————"Negro Needs the Equality of the Unrestricted Ballot." *Chicago Defender,* April 23, 1955.

————"The Negro in Retrospect and Prospect." *Journal of Negro History* 35, no. 1 (January 1950): 9–19.

————"No Barrier Should Impede Progress of American People." *Chicago Defender,* February 19, 1955.

————"The Privileges of a Democracy Are Not without Common Sense." *Chicago Defender,* April 22, 1950.

————"Says Question of What Negroes Want Is too Obvious for Answer." *Chicago Defender,* March 5, 1955.

————"Sees White South Resigning Itself to Integrated Life." *Chicago Defender,* April 2, 1955.

————"Supreme Court's Desegregation Ruling Will Work, But We Must Have Patience about It." *Chicago Defender,* January 22, 1955.

————"The Torch Is Ours." *Journal of Negro History* 36, no. 1 (January 1951): 9–11.

————"U.S. Will Make 'The Grade' in Integrating All Its Schools." *Chicago Defender,* June 4, 1955.

————"Warns against Violence or Hesitation at Integration." *Chicago Defender,* October 2, 1954.

————. "What Are We Fighting For?" Jefferson Award Address, 1942.

"Bethune Brown Feuding." *Pittsburgh Courier,* November 19, 1949.

Bethune-Cookman College. URL: <http://www.bethune.cookman.edu> October 8, 2001.

Blackwell, Barbara Grant. "The Advocacies and Ideological Commitments of a Black Educator: Mary McLeod Bethune, 1875–1955." Ph.D. diss., University of Connecticut, 1979.

Bookman, Ann, and Sandra Morgan, eds. *Women and the Politics of Empowerment.* Philadelphia: Temple University Press, 1988.

"Boom Mrs. Bethune as Administrative Aide to President." *Palmetto Leader,* April 14, 1945.

Bond, James A. "Bethune-Cookman College: Community Service Station." *Crisis* 48 (March 1941): 81–94.

Brawley, Benjamin G. *Negro Builders and Heroes.* Chapel Hill: University of North Carolina Press, 1937.

Breckenridge, Sophonisba. *Women in the Twentieth Century: A Study of their Political, Social and Economic Activities.* New York, 1933.

Breen, William J. "Black Women and the Great War: Mobilization and Reform in the South." *Journal of Southern History* 44, no. 3 (August 1978): 421–40.

Brooks, Evelyn. "The Feminist Theology of the Black Baptist Church, 1880–1920." In Amy Swerdlow and Hannah Lessinger, eds., *Class, Race, and Sex: The Dynamics of Control.* Barnard College Center, 1983.

———"Religion, Politics, and Gender: The Leadership of Nannie Helen Burroughs." *Journal of Religious Thought* 44 (winter–spring 1988): 7–22.

Brooks Barnett, Evelyn. "Nannie Burroughs and the Education of Black Women." In Sharon Harley and Rosalyn Terborg-Penn, eds., *The Afro-American Woman: Struggles and Images.* Port Washington, N.Y.: National University Press, 1978.

"Brotherhood of Sleeping Car Porters Await Speech Sept. 25." *Atlanta Daily World,* September 18, 1938.

Brown, Elsa Barkley. "African-American Women's Quilting: A Framework for Conceptualizing and Teaching African-American Women's History." *Signs* 14, no. 4 (summer 1989): 921–29.

———. "Negotiating and Transforming the Public Sphere: African American Political Life in the Transition from Slavery to Freedom." In Cathy J. Cohen, Kathleen B. Jones, and Joan C. Tronto, eds., *Women Transforming Politics: An Alternative Reader.* New York: New York University Press, 1997.

———. "What Has Happened Here: The Politics of Difference in Women's History and Feminist Politics." *Feminist Studies* 18, no. 2 (summer 1992): 295–312.

———."Womanist Consciousness: Maggie Lena Walker and the Independent Order of Saint Luke." *Signs* 14 (spring 1989): 610–63.

Brown, Jeanetta Welch. Interview by Susan McElrath, July 10, 1992. Tape recording, Bethune Museum and Archives, Washington, D.C.

Brownlee, Fred L. "Educational Programs for the Improvement of Race Relations: Philanthropic Foundations." *Journal of Negro Education* 13, no. 3 (summer 1944): 329–39.

Bunche, Ralph J. "A Critique of New Deal Social Planning as it Affects Negroes." *Journal of Negro Education* 5, no. 1 (January 1936): 59–65.

———. *The Political Status of the Negro in the Age of FDR.* Chicago: University of Chicago Press, 1973.

Burroughs, Nannie Helen. "Not Color but Character." *The Voice of the Negro,* 277–79.

Butchart, Ronald E. *Northern Schools, Southern Blacks, and Reconstruction: Freedmen's Education, 1862–1875.* Westport, Conn.: Greenwood Press, 1980.

Cantarow, Ellen. *Moving the Mountain: Women Working for Social Change.* Old Westbury, N.Y.: Feminist Press. Reprt., New York: McGraw Hill, 1980.

Calton-LaNey, Iris. "Elizabeth Ross Haynes: An African American Reformer of Womanist Consciousness, 1908–1940." *Social Work* 42, no. 6 (November 1997): 573–84.

Carlson, Shirley J. "Black Ideals of Womanhood in the Late Victorian Era." *Journal of Negro History* 77, no. 2 (spring 1992): 61–73.

"Carol Brice Offers Aid to NCNW for Civil Rights." *Atlanta World,* November 23, 1948.

Carroll, Charles. "The Negro a Beast"; or, "In the image of God; The Reasoner of the Age, the Revelator of the Century! The Bible as It Is! The Negro and His Relation to the Human Family! . . . The Negro Not the Son of Ham . . ." Savannah, Ga.: The Thunderbolt, Inc., 1968.

Carter, Vivian Mason. Interview by Barbara Grant Blackwell. Transcript in Barbara Grant Blackwell, "The Advocacies and Ideological Commitments of a Black Educator." Ph.D. diss., University of Connecticut, 1979.

"Centers for African American Women." URL: <http://www.ncnw.com/centers/centersbody.html> November 16, 1999.

Chateauvert, Melinda. *Marching Together: The Women of the Brotherhood of Sleeping Car Porters.* Urbana: University of Illinois Press, 1998.

Christianson-Ruffman, Linda. "Women's Conceptions of the Political: Theoretical Contributions to a Study of Women's Organizations." In Beth B. Hess and Myra Marx Ferree, eds., *Analyzing Gender: A Handbook of Social Science Research.* Newbury Park, Calif.: Sage Publications, 1987.

"Citizens Query Mrs. Bethune on Firing Staff." *California Eagle,* August 27, 1947.

"Clubwomen Seeking 500,000 New Members." *Atlanta World,* January 25, 1949.

Cooper, Arnold. *Between Struggle and Hope: Four Black Educators in the South.* Ames: Iowa State University Press, 1989.

Cott, Nancy F. "Feminist Politics in the 1920s: The National Women's Party." *Journal of American History* 71, no. 1 (June 1984): 43–68.

———"What's in a Name?: The Limits of 'Social Feminism' or, the Expanding Vocabulary of Women's History." *Journal of American History* 76, no. 3 (December 1989): 809–29.

Cowan, E. P. "Haines Normal and Industrial School." *The Church Home and Abroad* (September 1987).

Daniel, Walter G., and Carroll L. Miller. "The Participation of the Negro in the National Youth Administration Program." *Journal of Negro Education* 7, no. 3 (July 1938): 357–65.

Daniels, Lee, and Lewis Jones. "Bethune Admirers Recall Greatness." *Washington Post,* July 10, 1974.

Daniels, Sadie Iola. *Women Builders.* Washington, D.C.: Associated Publishers, 1931.

Davidson, Liliane R. "Bethune-Cookman College Gears to New War Production Program." Reprinted from the *Daytona Beach News-Journal,* November 29, 1942.

———. "Mary McLeod Bethune, World Famed Educator, Dies of Heart Attack." *Daytona Beach Morning Journal,* May 19, 1955.

Davis, Almena. "It's Better to Hear, My Dear." *Radio Week,* May 17, 1949.

Davis, John P. "A Survey of the Problems of the Negro under the New Deal." *Journal of Negro Education* 5, no. 1 (January 1936): 3–12.

"Dr. Bethune Blasts Lynching and Poll Tax at Conference." *Black Dispatch,* December 14, 1947.

"Dr. Bethune Calls Meeting to Consider Candidates." *Daytona Beach Evening News,* October 26, 1952.

"Dr. Bethune Dedicates Home." *Daytona Beach Morning Journal,* May 11, 1953.

"Dr. Mary McLeod Bethune Receives Thomas Jefferson Award." *Opportunity* 20 (June 1942): 185.

Doriani, Beth Maclay. "Black Womanhood in Nineteenth Century America: Subversions and Self-Construction in Two Women's Autobiographies." *American Quarterly* 43, no. 2 (June 1991): 199–222.

Drago, Edmund L. *Initiative, Paternalism, and Race Relations: Charleston's Avery Normal Institute.* Athens: University of Georgia Press, 1990.

Du Bois, W. E. B. *The Autobiography of W. E. B. Du Bois.* Edited by Herbert Aptheker. New York: International Publishers, 1968.

———. *Dusk of Dawn: An Essay toward an Autobiography of the Race.* New York: Schocken Books, 1968.

———. *Economic Co-Operation among Negro Americans: Report of a Social Study Made by Atlanta University, under the Patronage of the Carnegie Institution of Washington, D.C., Together with the Proceedings of the 12th Conference for the Study of Negro Problems, held at Atlanta University, May 28, 1907.* Atlanta: Atlanta University Press, 1907.

———. "The Evolution of Negro Leadership." *The Dial* (July 16, 1901): 53–55.

———. *The Souls of Black Folk.* New York: New American Library, 1969.

———. "The Talented Tenth." In *The Negro Problem: A Series of Articles by Representative American Negroes Today.* New York: J. Pott and Co., 1903.

———. *Writings.* Edited by Nathan Huggins. New York: Viking Press, 1986.

Dunnigan, Alice A. "Bill Would Permit Bethune Memorial." *Pittsburgh Courier,* September 5, 1959.

Elshtain, Jean Bethke. *Public Man, Private Woman: Women in Social and Political Thought.* Princeton, N.J.: Princeton University Press, 1981.

Enck, Henry S. "Black Self-Help in the Progressive Era: The 'Northern Campaigns' of Smaller Southern Black Industrial Schools, 1900–1915." *Journal of Negro History* 61, no. 1 (January 1976): 73–87.

———. "Tuskegee Institute and Northern White Philanthropy: A Case Study in Fund Raising, 1900–1915." *Journal of Negro History* 65, no. 4 (autumn 1980): 336–48.

Estes-Hicks, Onita. "The Way We Were: Precious Memories of the Black Segregated South." *African-American Review* 27, no. 1 (spring 1993): 9–18.

Fairclough, Adam. "'Being in the Field of Education and Also Being a Negro . . . Seems . . . Tragic': Black Teachers in the Jim Crow South." *Journal of American History* 87, no. 1 (June 2000): 65–91.

Findley, James. "'Moody,' 'Gapmen,' and the Gospel: The Early Days of Moody Bible Institute." *Church History* 21 (1962): 322–25.

"55,000 Aided by the NYA Program, Says Dr. Bethune." *Washington Tribune,* April 23, 1938.

Fishel, Leslie H., Jr. "A Case Study: The Negro in the New Deal." In Alonzo L. Hamby, ed., *The New Deal: Analysis and Interpretation.* New York: Weybright and Talley, 1969.

Fleming, Shelia Y. *The Answered Prayer to a Dream: Bethune-Cookman College, 1904–1994.* Virginia Beach, Va.: Donning Co./Publishers, 1995.

Foner, Eric. *A Short History of Reconstruction.* New York: Harper and Row, 1990.

Franklin, John Hope. *Racial Equality in America.* Columbia: University of Missouri Press, 1976.

———, and Alfred A. Moss. *From Slavery to Freedom.* 6th ed. New York: Alfred A. Knopf, 1987.

Franklin, V. P. *Black Self-Determination: A Cultural History of African-American Resistance.* Chicago: Lawrence Hill Books, 1992.

———, and Bettye Collier-Thomas. "Biography, Race Vindication, and African-American Intellectuals: Introductory Essay." *Journal of Negro History* 81, nos. 1–4 (winter–autumn 1996): 1–16.

Fraser, Walter, R. Frank Saunders, Jr., and John Wakelyn, eds. *The Web of Southern Social Relations: Women, Family, and Education.* Athens: University of Georgia Press, 1985.

Frazier, Steve, and Gary Gerstelle, eds. *The Rise and Fall of the New Deal Order, 1930–1980.* Princeton, N.J.: Princeton University Press, 1989.

Freedman, Estelle. "Separatism as Strategy: Female Institution Building and American Feminism, 1870–1930." *Feminist Studies* 5, no. 3 (fall 1979): 512–29.

Gaines, Kevin. *Uplifting the Race: Black Leadership, Politics, and Culture in the Twentieth Century.* Chapel Hill: University of North Carolina Press, 1996.

Gatewood, Willard B. *Aristocrats of Color: The Black Elite, 1880–1920.* Bloomington: Indiana University Press, 1990.

Giddings, Paula. *When and Where I Enter: The Impact of Black Women on Race and Sex in America.* New York: Bantam Books, 1984.

Gilkes, Cheryl Townsend. "Building in Many Places: Multiple Commitments and Ideologies in Black Women's Community Work." In Ann Bookman and Sandra Morgan, eds., *Women and the Politics of Empowerment.* Philadelphia: Temple University Press, 1988.

———. "Holding Back the Ocean with a Broom: Black Women and Community Work." In LaFrances Rodgers-Rose, ed., *The Black Woman.* Beverly Hills, Calif.: Sage Publications, 1980.

———. "W. E. B. Du Bois, Nannie Helen Burroughs and 'The Intellectual Leadership of the Race': Toward a Theory of African-American Women and Social Change." Lecture given at the University of Connecticut, October 13, 1992.

Gilmore, Glenda Elizabeth. *Gender and Jim Crow: Women and the Politics of*

White Supremacy in North Carolina, 1896–1920. Chapel Hill: University of North Carolina Press, 1996.

———. "Southeastern Association of Colored Women's Clubs." In Darlene Clark Hine, Elsa Barkley Brown, and Rosalyn Terborg-Penn, eds., *Black Women in America: An Historical Encyclopedia,* vol. 2. Bloomington: University of Indiana Press, 1993.

Gordon, Anne D., with Bettye Collier-Thomas, eds. *African-American Women and the Vote, 1837–1965.* Amherst, Mass.: University of Massachusetts Press, 1997.

Gordon, Linda. "Black and White Visions of Welfare: Women's Welfare Activism, 1890–1945." In Vicki L. Ruiz and Ellen Carol DuBois, eds., *Unequal Sisters: A Multicultural Reader in United States Women's History.* New York: Routledge, 1994.

———. *Pitied but Not Entitled: Single Mothers and the History of Welfare, 1890–1935.* New York: Free Press, 1994.

Grant, Madison. *The Passing of the Great Race.* New York: C. Scribner, 1916.

Grantham, Dewey W. "The Contours of Southern Progessivism." *American Historical Review* 86, no. 5 (December 1981): 1035–59.

Griggs, A. C. "Lucy Craft Laney." *Journal of Negro History* (January 1934).

Guy-Sheftall, Beverly. "Black Women and Higher Education: Spelman and Bennett Colleges Revisited." *Journal of Negro Education* 51, no. 3 (summer 1982): 254–65.

———. "Daughters of Sorrow: Attitudes toward Black Women, 1880–1920." In Darlene Clark Hine, ed., *Black Women In United States History,* vol. 11. New York: Carlson Publishing Co., 1990.

Hamby, Alonzo M. *The New Deal: Analysis and Interpretation.* New York: Weybright and Tolley, 1969.

Hamilton, Dona Cooper. "The National Urban League and New Deal Programs." *Social Service Review* (June 1984): 227–43.

———, and Charles Hamilton. "The Dual Agenda of African American Organizations since the New Deal: Social Welfare Policies and Civil Rights." *Political Science Quarterly* 107, no. 3 (autumn 1992): 435–52.

Harlan, Louis R. *Booker T. Washington: The Making of a Black Leader, 1856–1901.* New York: Oxford University Press, 1972.

———. *Separate and Unequal: Public School Campaigns and Racism in the Southern Seaboard States, 1901–1915.* Chapel Hill: University of North Carolina Press, 1958.

———. *The Wizard of Tuskegee, 1901–1915.* New York: Oxford University Press, 1983.

Harley, Sharon. "Beyond the Classroom: The Organizational Life of Black Female Educators in the District of Columbia, 1890–1930." *Journal of Negro Education* 51, no. 3 (summer 1982): 254–65.

———. "The Middle Class." In Darlene Clark Hine, Elsa Barkley Brown, and Rosalyn Terborg-Penn, eds., *Black Women in American History: An Historical Encyclopedia*, vol. 2. Bloomington: University of Indiana Press, 1993.

———. "Nannie Helen Burroughs: The Black Goddess of Liberty." *Journal of Negro History* 84, nos. 1–4 (winter–autumn 1996): 62–71.

———, and Rosalyn Terborg-Penn, eds. *The Afro-American Woman: Struggles and Images*. Port Washington, N.Y.: National University Press, 1978.

Harrell, James A. "Negro Leadership in the Election Year 1936." *Journal of Southern History* 34, no. 4 (November 1968): 546–64.

Hartmann, Susan M. *From Margin to Mainstream: American Women and Politics since 1960*. Philadelphia: Temple University Press, 1989.

Hartshorne, William Newton, ed. *An Era of Progress and Promise*. Boston: Princella Publishing Co., 1910.

Height, Dorothy Irene. Interview by Polly Cowan, April 10, 1974. Transcript in Ruth Edmonds Hill, ed., *Black Women Oral History Project*. Westport, Conn.: Meckler, 1991.

Herrick, Genevieve Forbes. "Loved, Feared and Followed." *Bethune-Cookman Advocate* 1 (November 1950).

———. "Queen Mary: Champion of Negro Women." *Negro Digest* 9 (December 1950): 32–39.

Hewitt, Nancy A., and Suzanne Lebsock, eds. *Visible Women: New Essays on American Activism*. Chicago: University of Illinois Press, 1993.

Hicks, Florence Johnson, ed. *Mary McLeod Bethune: Her Own Words of Inspiration*. Washington, D.C.: Nuclassics and Science Publishing Co., 1975.

Higginbotham, Evelyn Brooks. "African-American Women's History and the Metalanguage of Race." *Signs* 17, no. 2 (winter 1992): 251–74.

———. "Clubwomen and Electoral Politics." In Anne D. Gordon with Bettye Collier-Thomas, eds., *African-American Women and the Vote, 1837–1965*. Amherst: University of Massachusetts Press, 1997.

———. "In Politics to Stay: Black Women Leaders and Party Politics in the 1920s." In Louise A. Tilley and Patricia Gurin, eds., *Women, Politics and Change*. New York: Russell Sage Foundation, 1990.

———. *Righteous Discontent: The Women's Movement in the Black Baptist Church, 1880–1920*. Cambridge, Mass.: Harvard University Press, 1993.

Hine, Darlene Clark. "Housewives' League of Detroit." In Darlene Clark

Hine, Elsa Barkley Brown, and Rosalyn Terborg-Penn, eds., *Black Women in America: An Historical Encyclopedia*, vol. 1. Bloomington: University of Indiana Press, 1993.

———. "Lifting the Veil, Shattering the Silence: Black Women's History in Slavery and Freedom." In *Black Women in United States History*, vol. 9. New York: Carlson Publishing Co., 1990.

———. *Speak Truth to Power.* New York: Carlson Publishing, 1996.

———, Elsa Barkley Brown, and Rosalyn Terborg-Penn, eds. *Black Women in America: An Historical Encyclopedia*, vols. 1 and 2. Bloomington: University of Indiana Press, 1993.

Holt, Rackham. *Mary McLeod Bethune.* Garden City, N.Y.: Doubleday, 1964.

Hull, Gloria T. *Color, Sex, & Poetry.* Bloomington: Indiana University Press, 1988.

———. *Give Us Each Day: The Diary of Alice Dunbar Nelson.* New York: W. W. Norton and Co., 1984.

Hunter, Tera. "The Correct Thing: Charlotte Hawkins Brown and the Palmer Institute." *Southern Exposure* (September/October 1983): 37–43.

———. "Domination and Resistance: The Politics of Wage and Household Labor." In Sharon Harley, Elsa Barkley Brown, and Rosalyn Terborg-Penn, eds., *The Afro-American Woman: Struggles and Images.* Port Washington, N.Y.: National University Publications, 1978.

Ihle, Elizabeth L., ed. *Black Women in Higher Education: An Anthology of Essays, Studies, and Documents.* New York: Garland Press, 1992.

Johnson, Guion Griffis. "Southern Paternalism toward Negroes after Emancipation." *Journal of Southern History* 23, no. 4 (November 1957): 483–509.

Johnson, James Weldon. *Negro Americans, What Now?* New York: Viking, 1934.

Johnson, Kay. "Council Members Take Tea at White House." *Pittsburgh Courier,* October 23, 1948.

Johnson, Palmer O., and Oswald L. Harvey. *The National Youth Administration, Staff Study Number 13.* Prepared for the Advisory Committee on Education. Washington, D.C.: Government Printing Office, 1938.

Jones, Adrienne Lash. "Jane Edna Hunter: A Case Study of Black Leadership, 1910–1950." In Darlene Clark Hine, ed., *Black Women in United States History*, vol. 12. New York: Carlson Publishing Co., 1990.

Jones, Beverly W. "Mary Church Terrell and the National Association of Colored Women's Clubs, 1896–1901." *Journal of Negro History* 67, no. 1 (spring 1982): 20–33.

———. "Quest for Equality: The Life and Writings of Mary Eliza Church Terrell, 1863–1954." In Darlene Clark Hine, ed., *Black Women in United States History*, vol. 13. New York: Carlson Publishing, Inc., 1990.

Jones, Jacqueline. *Labor of Love, Labor of Sorrow: Black Women, Work, and the Family from Slavery to the Present.* New York: Vintage Books, 1986.

———. *Soldiers of Light and Love: Northern Teachers and Georgia Blacks, 1865–1873.* Chapel Hill: University of North Carolina Press, 1980.

Jordan, Winthrop. *White Man's Burden: Historical Origins of Racism in the United States.* New York: Oxford University Press, 1974.

Kelley, Robin D. G. *Hammer and Hoe: Alabama Communists during the Great Depression.* Chapel Hill: University of North Carolina Press, 1990.

Kellogg, Charles Flint. *A History of the National Association for the Advancement of Colored People.* Vol. 1, 1909–1920. Baltimore, Md.: Johns Hopkins Press, 1967.

Knupfer, Anne Meis. " 'If You Can't Push, Pull, If You Can't Pull, Please Get Out of the Way': The Phyllis Wheatley Club and Home in Chicago, 1896–1920." *Journal of Negro History* 82, no. 2 (spring 1997): 221–31.

Laney, Lucy C. Hampton Negro Conference Number III, "The Burden of the Educated Colored Woman," July 1899. In Bert James Lowenberg and Ruth Bogin, eds., *Black Women in Nineteenth-Century American Life.* University Park: Penn State Press, 1976.

Lasch-Quinn, Elisabeth. *Black Neighbors: Race and the Limits of Reform in the American Settlement House Movement, 1890–1945.* Chapel Hill: University of North Carolina Press, 1993.

Leffall, Delores C., and Janet L. Sims. "Mary McLeod Bethune—The Educator; also Including a Selected Annotated Bibliography." *Journal of Negro Education* 45, no. 3 (summer 1976): 342–59.

Leloudis, James L, II. "School Reform in the New South: The Women's Association for the Betterment of Public Schoolhouses in North Carolina, 1902–1919." *Journal of American History* 69, no. 4 (March 1983): 886–909.

Lemons, Stanley J. *The Woman Citizen: Social Feminism in the 1920s.* Urbana: University of Illinois Press, 1973.

Lempel, Leonard. "African American Settlements in the Daytona Beach Area, 1866." Proceedings of the Florida Conference of Historians, Annual Meeting, March 11–13, 1993, Orange Park, Fla., n.p., 1993.

Lerner, Gerda, ed. *Black Women in White America: A Documentary History.* New York: Vintage Books, 1973.

————. "Early Community Work of Black Club Women." *Journal of Negro History* 59, no. 2 (December 1972): 158–67.

————. *The Majority Finds Its Past: Placing Women in History.* New York: Oxford University Press, 1979.

Leuchtenburg, William E. *Franklin D. Roosevelt and the New Deal.* New York: Harper and Row, 1963.

Lewis, David Levering. *W. E. B. Du Bois: Biography of a Race, 1868–1919.* New York: Henry Holt and Co., 1993.

Lindley, Betty, and Ernest K. Lindley. *A New Deal for Youth: The Story of the National Youth Administration.* New York: Viking Press, 1938.

Litwack, Leon. *Trouble in Mind: Black Southerners in the Age of Jim Crow.* New York: Alfred A. Knopf, 1998.

Lowenberg, Bert James, and Ruth Bogin, eds. *Black Women in Nineteenth-Century American Life.* University Park: Penn State Press, 1976.

Lowitt, Richard, and Maurine Beasley, eds. *One Third of a Nation: Lorena Hickok Reports on the Great Depression.* Chicago: University of Illinois Press, 1981.

Ludlow, Helen T. "The Bethune School." *Southern Workman* 41 (March 1912): 144–54.

Luker, Ralph E. "Missions, Institutional Churches, and Settlements: The Black Experience, 1885–1910." *Journal of Negro History* 69, nos. 3–4 (summer–autumn 1984): 101–13.

————. *The Social Gospel in Black and White: American Racial Reform, 1885–1912.* Chapel Hill: University of North Carolina Press, 1991.

McAfee, Ward M. "Reconstruction Revisited: The Republican Public Education Crusade of the 1870s." *Civil War History* 62, no. 2 (spring 1996): 133–53.

————. *Religion, Race, and Reconstruction: The Public School System in the Politics of the 1870s.* Albany, N.Y.: State University of New York Press, 1998.

McClusky, Audrey T. "Mary McLeod Bethune and the Education of Black Girls." *Sex Roles* 21, nos. 1–2 (1989).

————. "Multiple Consciousness in the Leadership of Mary McLeod Bethune." *NWSA Journal* 6, no. 1 (spring 1994): 69–81.

McGern, Michael. "Political Style and Women's Power, 1830–1930." *Journal of American History* 77, no. 3 (December 1990): 864–85.

McGinty, Doris E. "Gifted Minds and Pure Hearts: Mary L. Europe and Estelle Pickney Webster." *Journal of Negro Education* 51, no. 3 (summer 1982): 266–77.

McPherson, James M. "White Liberals and Black Power in Negro Education, 1865–1915." *American Historical Review* 75, no. 5 (June 1970): 1357–86.

"Mary Bethune Files $150,000 Suit in Florida." *Pittsburgh Courier*, April 16, 1955.

Mason, Mary G. "Travel as a Metaphor and Reality in Afro-American Women's Autobiography, 1850–1972." *Black American Literary Forum* 24, no. 2 (summer 1990): 337–56.

Mason, Vivian Carter. Interview by Barbara Grant Blackwell, July 1977. Transcript in Barbara Grant Blackwell, "The Advocacies and Ideological Commitments of a Black Educator." Ph.D. diss., University of Connecticut, 1979.

Matthews, Glenna. *The Rise and Fall of Public Woman: Women's Power and Place in the United States, 1630–1970.* New York: Oxford University Press, 1992.

"Matriarch." *Time*, July 22, 1946, 55.

Meier, August. *Negro Thought in America, 1880–1915.* Ann Arbor: University of Michigan Press, 1988.

Meier, August, and John H. Bracey, Jr. "The NAACP as a Reform Movement, 1909–1965: 'To Reach the Conscience of America.'" *Journal of Southern History* 59, no. 1 (February 1993): 3–30.

Mintz, Steven, and Randy Roberts. *Hollywood's America: United States History through Its Films.* St. James, N.Y.: Brandywine Press, 1993.

"Mrs. Bethune Invited to White House Again." *Savannah Tribune*, November 19, 1931.

"Mrs. Bethune Says NYA Has Challenging Program." *Baltimore Afro-American*, August 8, 1936.

"Mrs. Bethune Tells of Many Accomplishments of NYA." *The Black Dispatch*, February 26, 1938.

"Mrs. M. M. Bethune Speaks at Tuskegee." *Daytona Beach News-Journal*, October 31, 1931.

"Mrs. Fauset Not to NYA." *Baltimore Afro-American*, August 19, 1939.

"Mrs. Roosevelt Guest at Merner Home, Hillsborough." *The Times and Daily News Leader*, October 3, 1942.

"Mrs. Roosevelt's Talk Before Second Youth Conference." *The Informer*, February 25, 1939.

Mitchell, Lucy Miller. Interview by Cheryl Townsend Gilkes, June 17, 24, July 1, 6, 25, 1977. Transcript in Ruth Edmonds Hill, ed., *Black Women Oral History Project.* Westport, Conn.: Meckler, 1991.

Moody, William R. *The Life of Dwight L. Moody.* New York: Fleming B. Revell Company, 1900.

Moore, Jesse Thomas, Jr. *A Search for Equality, The National Urban League, 1910–1960.* University Park: Pennsylvania State University Press, 1981.

Morris, Milton D. *The Politics of Black America.* New York: Harper and Row, 1975.

Moss, Barbara A. "African-American Women's Legacy: Ambiguity, Autonomy, and Empowerment." In Kim Marie Vaz, ed., *Black Women in America.* Thousand Oaks, Calif.: Sage Publications, 1975.

Moton, Robert R. *Finding a Way Out.* New York: Doubleday, Page and Company, 1920.

"NCNW Barred From DAR Hall." *Louisville Defender,* November 27, 1948.

"NCNW to Launch $500,000 "Rights" Drive With "Protest" Concert." *Black Dispatch,* January 1, 1949.

"NCNW Supports Housing Plan." *Pittsburgh Courier,* May 10, 1941.

"Negro Angel: Mary McLeod Bethune, College Founder, Sees Bright Future for Her Race." *Literary Digest,* March 6, 1937.

"Negro Leader Indorses Stevenson." *Chicago Sun-Times,* October 15, 1952.

Neverdon-Morton, Cynthia. *Afro-American Women of the South and the Advancement of the Race, 1895–1925.* Knoxville: University of Tennessee Press, 1989.

———. "The Black Woman's Struggle for Equality in the South, 1895–1925." In Sharon Harley and Rosalyn Terborg-Penn, eds., *The Afro-American Woman: Struggles and Images.* Port Washington, N.Y.: National University Publishers, 1978.

———. "Self-Help Programs as Educative Activities of Black Women in the South, 1895–1925: Focus on Four Key Areas." *Journal of Negro Education* 51, no. 3 (summer 1982): 207–21.

"New Opportunities for Negro Youth." *The Star of Zion,* May 26, 1938.

Ngan-Chow, Esther, Doris Wilkerson, and Maxine Baca Zinn, eds. *Race, Class, and Gender: Common Bonds, Different Voices.* Newbury Park, Calif.: Sage Publishers, 1996.

"The NYA to Continue Aid to Race Students." *Tampa Bulletin,* September 4, 1937.

"NYA Girls Training Camp, St. Augustine." *Tampa Bulletin,* March 20, 1937.

"NYA Student Aid Program Allotted $21,750,000 for Current Fiscal Year 1938–39, Announces Aubrey William, Executive Director." *Tampa Bulletin,* August 20, 1938.

"NYA Trains Negro Farm Youth." *Tampa Bulletin,* September 11, 1937.

Ogunyemi, C. "Womanism: The Dynamics of the Contemporary Black Novel in English." *Signs* 11 (1985): 63–80.

O'Leary, J. A. "Full Civil Rights Plan, D.C. Suffrage Urged By Negro Women." *Washington Star,* December 20, 1949.

Ovington, Mary White. *Portraits in Color.* New York: Viking Press, 1927.

Painter, Nell Irvin. *Sojourner Truth, a Life, a Symbol.* New York: W. W. Norton and Co., 1996.

———. "Sojourner Truth in Life and Memory: Writing the Biography of an American Exotic." *Gender and History* 2, no. 1 (September 1990): 3–16.

Palmer, Phyllis M. "White Women/Black Women: The Dualism of Female Identity and Experience in the United States." *Feminist Studies* 9 (1983): 151–70.

Patton, June O. "Lucy Craft Laney." In Darlene Clark Hine, Elsa Barkley Brown, and Rosalyn Terborg-Penn, eds., *Black Women in American History: An Historical Encyclopedia,* vol. 2. Bloomington: University of Indiana Press, 1993.

Paulson, Morton. "Dr. Mary Bethune Left Own Epitaph." *Daytona Beach Evening News,* July 18, 1955.

Peare, Catherine Owen. *Mary McLeod Bethune.* New York: Vanguard Press, 1951.

Peebles-Wilkins, Wilma. "Janie Porter Barrett and the Virginia Industrial School for Colored Girls: Community Response to the Needs of African American Children." *Child Welfare* 74, no. 1 (January/February 1995): 143–54.

Perkins, Carol O. "The Pragmatic Idealism of Mary McLeod Bethune." *Sage* (fall 1988): 30–35.

Perkins, Linda M. "Heed Life's Demands: The Educational Philosophy of Fanny Jackson Coppin." *Journal of Negro Education* 51, no. 3 (summer 1982): 181–90.

———. "Lucy Diggs Slowe: Champion of the Self-Determination of African-American Women in Higher Education." *Journal of Negro History* 84, nos. 1–4 (winter–autumn 1996): 89–104.

Perkins, Lolita C. "Nannie Helen Burroughs: A Progressive Example for Modern Times." *Affila: Journal of Women and Social Work* 12, no. 2 (summer 1997): 229–40.

Pinderhughes, Dianne M. "Black Women and National Education Policy." *Journal of Negro Education* 51, no. 3 (summer 1982): 301–8.

Poole, Bernice Anderson. *Mary McLeod Bethune, Educator.* Los Angeles: Melrose Square Publishers, 1994.

"President Bethune to White House." *Daytona Beach News-Journal,* November 17, 1931.

"Problems of Race before President." *Crisis* (February 1937): 46, 62.

Randall, Vicki. *Women and Politics.* New York: St. Martin's Press, 1982.

"Reaches F.D. without His Secretary's Aid." *Baltimore Afro-American,* February 20, 1937.

Reed, Linda. *Simple Decency and Common Sense: The Southern Conference Movement, 1938–1963.* Bloomington: University of Indiana Press, 1991.

Richardson, Joe M. *Christian Reconstruction: The American Missionary Association and Southern Blacks, 1861–1890.* Athens: University of Georgia Press, 1986.

Roane, Dr. Florence Lovell. Interview by Barbara Grant Blackwell, July 7 and 8, 1977. Transcript in Barbara Grant Blackwell, "The Advocacies and Ideological Commitments of a Black Educator." Ph.D. diss., University of Connecticut, 1979.

"Roosevelt Tells Aid to Expand NYA Program." *Washington Post,* January 22, 1939.

Ross, B. Joyce. "Mary McLeod Bethune and the National Youth Administration: A Case Study of Power Relationships in the Black Cabinet of FDR." *Journal of Negro History* 60, no. 1 (January 1975): 1–28.

Rothenberg, Paula S., ed. *Racism and Sexism: An Integrated Study.* New York: St. Martin's Press, 1988.

Rouse, Jacqueline Anne. "The Legacy of Community Organizing: Lugenia Burns Hope and the Neighborhood Union." *Journal of Negro History* 69, nos. 3–4 (summer–autumn 1984): 114–33.

———. *Lugenia Burns Hope: Black Southern Reformer.* Athens: University of Georgia Press, 1989.

———. "Out of the Shadow of Tuskegee: Margaret Murray Washington, Social Activism, and Race Vindication." *Journal of Negro History* 84, nos. 1–4 (winter–autumn 1996): 31–46.

Rupp, Leila J. "Reflections on Twentieth-Century American Women's History." *Reviews in American History* 9, no. 2 (June 1981): 275–84.

Rustin, Bayard. "From Protest to Politics." In William H. Chafe and Harvard Sitkoff, eds., *A History of Our Time: Readings on Postwar America.* New York: Oxford University Press, 1995.

Salem, Dorothy. "To Better Our World: Black Women in Organized Reform, 1890–1920." In Darlene Clark Hine, ed., *Black Women In United States History,* vol. 14. New York: Carlson Publishing Co., 1990.

———. "The National Association of Colored Women." In Darlene Clark

Hine, Elsa Barkley Brown, and Rosalyn Terborg-Penn, eds., *Black Women in America: An Historical Encyclopedia,* vol. 2. Bloomington: University of Indiana Press, 1993.

———. "World War I." In Darlene Clark Hine, Elsa Barkley Brown, and Rosalyn Terborg-Penn, eds., *Black Women in America: An Historical Encyclopedia,* vol. 2. Bloomington: University of Indiana Press, 1993.

"Says Money Was Not Cause of Firings." *Cleveland Call and Past,* April 8, 1947.

Scharf, Lois, and Joan M. Jensen, eds. *Decades of Discontent: The Woman's Movement, 1920–1940.* Westport, Conn.: Greenwood Press, 1983.

Scott, Anne Frior. "After Suffrage: Southern Women in the Twenties." *Journal of Southern History* 30, no. 3 (August 1964): 298–318.

———. "Most Invisible of All: Black Women's Voluntary Associations." *Journal of Southern History* 56, no. 1 (February 1990): 3–22.

———. *Natural Allies: Women's Associations in American History.* Chicago: University of Chicago Press, 1993.

———. "On Seeing and Not Seeing: A Case of Historical Invisibility." *Journal of American History* 71, no. 1 (June 1984): 7–21.

———. "A Progressive Wind from the South, 1906–1913." *Journal of Southern History* 29, no. 1 (February 1963): 53–70.

Scott, James C. *Domination and the Arts of Resistance: Hidden Transcripts.* New Haven, Conn.: Yale University Press, 1990.

———. *Weapons of the Weak: Everyday Forms of Peasant Resistance.* New Haven, Conn.: Yale University Press, 1985.

Shaw, Stephanie J. "Black Club Women and the Creation of the National Association of Colored Women." In Darlene Clark Hine, Wilma King, and Linda Reed, eds., *We Specialize in the Wholly Impossible.* New York: Carlson Publishing, Inc., 1995.

———. *What a Woman Ought to Be and to Do: Professional Women Workers during the Jim Crow Era.* Chicago: University of Chicago Press, 1996.

Sherer, Robert G. *Subordination or Liberation? The Development of Conflicting Theories of Black Education in Nineteenth Century Alabama.* Alabama: University of Alabama Press, 1977.

Shufeldt, Robert W. *The Negro: A Menace to American Civilization.* Boston: Badger Press, 1907.

Sitkoff, Harvard. *A New Deal for Blacks: The Emergence of Civil Rights as a National Issue. The Depression Decade.* New York: Oxford University Press, 1978.

Smith, Elaine M. "Mary McLeod Bethune." In Darlene Clark Hine, Elsa

Barkley Brown, Rosalyn Terborg-Penn, eds., *Black Women in American History: An Historical Encyclopedia*, vol. 2. Bloomington: University of Indiana Press, 1993.

———. "Mary McLeod Bethune and the National Youth Administration." In Darlene Clark Hine, ed., *Black Women in American History—The Twentieth Century*, vol. 4. New York: Carlson Publishers, 1990.

———. "Mary McLeod Bethune's 'Last Will and Testament': A Legacy for Race Vindication." *Journal of Negro History* 84, nos. 1–4 (winter–autumn 1996): 105–22.

———. "Scotia Seminary." In Darlene Clark Hine, Elsa Barkley Brown, and Rosalyn Terborg-Penn, eds., *Black Women in American History: An Historical Encyclopedia*, vol. 2. Bloomington: University of Indiana Press, 1993.

Smith, Sandra N., and Earle H. West. "Charlotte Hawkins Brown." *Journal of Negro Education* 51, no. 3 (summer 1982): 191–206.

Spivey, Donald. *Schooling for the New Slavery: Black Industrial Education, 1868–1915*. Westport, Conn.: Greenwood Press, 1978.

Staupers, Mable. Interview, July 11, 1976. Tape recording, Bethune Museum and Archives, Washington, D.C.

Sterling, Dorothy, ed. *We Are Your Sisters: Black Women in the Nineteenth Century*. New York: W. W. Norton and Co., 1984.

Sterne, Emma Gelders. *Mary McLeod Bethune*. New York: Alfred A. Knopf, 1957.

Sternsher, Bernard, ed. *The Negro in Depression and War*. Chicago: Quadrangle Books, 1969.

Sullivan, Patricia. *Days of Hope: Race and Democracy in the New Deal Era*. Chapel Hill: University of North Carolina Press, 1996.

Terborg-Penn, Rosalyn. "Discontented Black Feminists: Prelude and Postscript to the Passage of the Nineteenth Amendment." In Darlene Clark Hine, Wilma King, and Linda Reed, eds., *We Specialize in the Wholly Impossible: A Reader in Black Women's History*. New York: Carlson Publishing, Inc., 1995.

Terrell, Mary Church. *A Colored Woman in a White World*. Salem, N.H.: Ayer Company Publishers, Inc., 1940, 1992.

"'This Is Your Life' Honors Mary Bethune." *Los Angeles Sentinel,* May 17, 1949.

Thomas, Jesse O. "Mrs. Bethune Receives Francis A. Drexel Award." *Journal and Guide,* June 26, 1937.

Tilley, Louise A., and Patricia Gurin, eds. *Women, Politics, and Change*. New York: Russell Sage Foundation, 1990.

Trelease, Allen W. *White Terror: The Ku Klux Klan Conspiracy and Southern Reconstruction*. New York: Harper and Row, 1971.

Trent, W. J., Jr. "The Relative Inadequacy of Sources on Income of Negro Church-Related Colleges." *Journal of Negro Education* 29, no. 3 (summer 1960): 356–67.

"Tribute Paid to Mrs. Mary McLeod Bethune Over NBC's 'This Is Your Life' Program." *California Eagle*, April 17, 1949.

"200 Honor Mrs. Bethune As NCNW Head." *Daily Express*, December 13, 1948.

United States, Department of Commerce, Bureau of the Census. *Ninth Census of the United States, 1870*. Washington, D.C.: Government Printing Office, 1870.

United States, Department of Commerce, Bureau of the Census. *Tenth Census of the United States, 1880*. Washington, D.C.: Government Printing Office, 1880.

United States, Department of Commerce, Bureau of the Census. *Eleventh Census of the United States, 1890*. Washington, D.C.: Government Printing Office, 1890.

United States, Department of Commerce, Bureau of the Census. *Fifteenth Census of the United States, 1930*. Washington, D.C.: Government Printing Office, 1933.

U.S. House. *Reports of the Joint Select Committee to Inquire into the Condition of Affairs in the Late Insurrectionary States*. 42d Cong., 2d sess., 1872, H. Rept. 22.

Wadelington, Charles W., and Richard F. Knapp. *Charlotte Hawkins Brown and Palmer Memorial Institute: What One Young African American Woman Could Do*. Chapel Hill: University of North Carolina Press, 1999.

Walker, Alice. *In Search of Our Mother's Gardens: Womanist Prose*. New York: Harcourt, Brace, 1983.

Walton, Hanes, Jr. *Black Politics: A Theoretical and Structural Analysis*. Philadelphia: Lippencott, 1972.

———. *Invisible Politics: Black Political Behavior*. Albany, N.Y.: State University of New York Press, 1985.

Ware, Susan. *Beyond Suffrage: Women in the New Deal*. Cambridge, Mass.: Harvard University Press, 1981.

Washington, Booker T. *The Booker T. Washington Papers*. 12 vols. Edited by Louis R. Harlan and Raymond Smock. Urbana: University of Illinois Press, 1972.

———. "Chapters from My Experience." *World's Work* 21 (November 1910).

———. "Industrial Education for the Negro." In *The Negro Problem: A Series of Articles by Representative American Negroes Today.* New York: J. Pott and Co., 1903.

Washington, Mary Helen. "Teaching Black-Eyed Susans: An Approach to the Study of Black Women Writers." *Black American Literary Forum* 11, no. 1 (spring 1977): 20–24.

Weiss, Nancy J. *The National Urban League, 1910–1940.* New York: Oxford University Press, 1974.

Welter, Barbara. "The Cult of True Womanhood, 1820–1860." *American Quarterly* 18, no. 2 (summer 1966): 151–74.

Wesley, Charles Harris. *The History of the National Association of Colored Women's Clubs: A Legacy of Service.* Washington, D.C.: National Association of Colored Women's Clubs, 1984.

White, Deborah Gray. *Ar'n't I a Woman?: Female Slaves in the Plantation South.* New York: W. W. Norton and Co., 1985.

———. "The Cost of Club Work, the Price of Feminism." In Nancy A. Hewitt and Suzanne Lebsock, eds., *Visible Women: New Essays on American Activism.* Urbana, Ill.: University of Chicago Press, 1993.

———. "Female Slaves: Sex Roles and Status in the Antebellum Plantation South." In Vicki L. Ruiz and Ellen Carol DuBois, eds., *Unequal Sisters: A Multicultural Reader in United States Women's History.* New York: Routledge, 1994.

———. "The Slippery Slope of Class in Black America: The National Council of Negro Women and the International Ladies' Auxiliary to the Brotherhood of Sleeping Car Porters: A Case Study." In Susan Ware, ed., *New Viewpoints in Women's History: Working Papers from the Schlessinger Library 50th Anniversary Conference,* March 4–5, 1994. Cambridge, Mass.: Arthur and Elizabeth Schlessinger Library on the History of Women in America.

———. *Too Heavy a Load: Black Women in Defense of Themselves, 1894–1994.* New York: W. W. Norton and Co., 1999.

White, Jr., Ronald C. *Liberty and Justice for All: Racial Reform and the Social Gospel.* San Francisco: Harper and Row, 1990.

Williams-Burns, Winona. "Jane Ellen McAllister: Pioneer for Excellence in Teacher Education." *Journal of Negro Education* 51, no. 3 (summer 1982): 342–57.

Williamson, Joel. *The Crucible of Race: Black/White Relations in the South since Emancipation.* New York: Oxford University Press, 1984.

———, ed. *The Origins of Segregation.* Boston: D.C. Heath, 1968.

———. *A Rage for Order: Black/White Relations in the South since Emancipation.* New York: Oxford University Press, 1986.

Woodson, Carter G. *The Mis-education of the Negro.* Washington, D.C.: Associated Publishers, 1969.

Woodward, C. Vann. *The Strange Career of Jim Crow.* New York: Oxford University Press, 1974.

"Women's Council Wages Equality Fight during National Convention." *Pittsburgh Courier,* May 10, 1941.

Yee, Shirley J. *Black Women Abolitionists: A Study in Activism, 1828–1860.* Knoxville: University of Tennessee Press, 1992.

"Yesterday in Negro History—April 20, 1942." *Jet,* April 21, 1960.

Zinn, Howard. *New Deal Thought.* Indianapolis: Bobbs-Merrill Company, Inc., 1966.

Index